Table of Contents

Divining Desire 1

Foreword.. 5

Preface 11

Introduction...17

The Early Years ~ Lost and Alone | Chapter 1 - Early stirrings: pre-puberty (1944-1956)...25

Chapter 2 - A Tortured Teen: (High School, 1958-62) 37

Chapter 3 - Graduating from Guilt (1962-66)...............................65

Chapter 4 - Trying to Fly in the Closet 77

The Middle Years - A Sexual / Spiritual Growth Spurt 103

Chapter 5 - Flying Free! (1972-1979) 105

Chapter 6 - Soaring Higher - (1976-1982 to the present)........................ 137

Chapter 7 (1976) - Unhinged by Michael then major epiphany................. 149

Chapter 8 (1976-79) - Exploring Marriage-like Partnership with Kyle.... 159

Chapter 9 (1979) - Finding "the faeries" 165

Chapter 10 - The 1980s: Continuing Healing the Eros-Spirit Split.......... 177

Shaman Psalm ~ a poem by James Broughton 199

Chapter 11 - The 1990s: Diving deeper into Tantra with all genders 213

The Later Years ~ Ripening into Embodied Wisdom........................ 229

Chapter 12 - The New Millenium: Diving Still Deeper into Tantra 231

Chapter 13 - The 2010s: New Models of Intimacy 251

Chapter 14 - My Young Mentors 261

Chapter 15 - Subtle Eros 293

Chapter 16 - The 2020s: A Time of Change 307

Chapter 17 - Still "Growing Healthier" 311

Chapter 18 - My Final Years 317

Epilogue 321

Appendix: Resources for your own Healing Journey 325

Annotated Table of Contents 359

Acknowledgments 367

"What a life! Sequoia Thom has spent his eight decades on earth as an intrepid adventurer: a seeker of wisdom and experience, of spiritual satisfaction and sexual self-acceptance. His entertaining memoir Divining Desire chronicles his pilgrim's progress from post-World War II Brooklyn to present-day Vancouver, from US Air Force pilot working hard to maintain a façade of butchness to radical faerie to building community around the pleasures of yoga, massage, and erotic playfulness. Along the way he was blessed to encounter a string of high-powered meditation teachers who nurtured his soul, while his romantic nature led him to an abundance of lovers who educated and fed his heart. The journey has never been especially smooth or linear. Sequoia writes honestly about the obstacles he's had to navigate, internally and externally, as a gay man. Yet he has accumulated many tips and tools for creating a good life, and he shares them with a generosity and grace that radiates off the page."

—Don Shewey, therapist, pleasure activist, and author (most recently the memoir *Daddy Lover God: a sacred intimate journey*)

A memoir, to me, should be two things - a story-mirror for the author's soul, and a teaching-mirror for its readers' own different life. In his masterful and engaging book Sequoia Thom does both, with honesty, vulnerability, and passion. Our culture tends to separate spirituality and sexuality, but Sequoia's story is about the dance they do together, from his being a courageous young man exploring gay life to his being a wise teacher and elder. In a time when we're all being called upon to wake-up, own, and act from our inner wisdom - this is the mirror you've been looking for!

Maggid Eli Andrew Ramer, author of *Ever After: the extended lives*

and work of eleven famous writers. andrewramer.com

Divining Desire

~ a queer epiphany ~

Sequoia Thom, M.A.

Tree House Publishing

sequoia.wordpress.com/publishing

coach.sequoia@gmail.com

+1-778-786-3677 [24/7 voice mail only]

"We delight in the beauty of the butterfly,

but rarely admit the changes it has gone through

to achieve that beauty."

~ Maya Angelou

Foreword

Once upon a time I was a 40-year-old gay man seeking to heal the wounds incurred by being born in an era where my natural way of being was not allowed to be. I'd been trying to uncover and address this emotional pain since my teens, but had only managed to touch the surface. I'd been jabbing at this hard-shelled cyst of internalized shame with various lances, some sterilized, some not, but couldn't penetrate it deeply enough emotionally to get all the self-negating gunk out. My body had sealed off the pain so thoroughly that it left me disconnected from myself, isolated from others, and numb to my feelings. Life felt like a fairy tale gone awry.

It would be a couple more years before the film *Brokeback Mountain* pierced open my pustule of poison for good. Jack and Ennis' struggle mirrored my own inner longing and conflict: one demanding his right to a "sweet life" with the man he loved, the other stuck in the closet of his coffin-shaped trailer. Both they and I were haunted by the possibility of a magical, mystical place, high above the comings and goings of society's moral whims, where gay men could exist in a balls-out, open-hearted, spiritually connected way.

At the time, in the fall of 2003, I was living on Vancouver Island, BC, in the backwoods beach town of my birth after many years in Los Angeles. I had returned to care for my father until his death from a brain tumor, and now was caring for my chosen mother who had terminal breast cancer. I was immersed in the energy of death and rebirth transitions, and needed a good threshold guide to help me find my way forward: someone grounded in earthiness, yet unafraid to explore the heavens.

One night, in an online search for some kind of stress-reducing body work that went beyond the rentable rub and tug variety, I discovered a group called **Men In Touch** that offered workshops called ***MMMM—Men's Magical Mystical Massage***, facilitated by a man named Sequoia Thom. The website described these workshops as gatherings where men learned to share nurturing full-bodied touch that was heart-centered and consciously spiritual. I decided that wherever in the world and whenever the next workshop was happening, I would be there. It turned out to be the very next weekend in Vancouver, BC—an easy drive and ferry ride away.

Sequoia had me book a private massage session with him the day before the workshop. I was reassured by this because it fell in line with his stated intention to create a vetted sanctuary for the workshop participants. He explained it would also give me a chance to experience the kind of touch I'd be learning to give. Within moments of entering Sequoia's studio and meeting him face-to-face, I felt I was also meeting him heart-to-heart. And by the time I arose from his massage table, blissfully relaxed and buzzing with well-being, I knew I'd met him grace-to-grace as well. I had a mistrust of men, but with Sequoia it felt safe to be unguarded. In that first workshop, and all the subsequent ones I attended over the next six years, my respect for Sequoia grew. His sincerity was endearing and his knowledge was empowering. I appreciated how in the opening circle of each workshop he would ask us to look around at the faces of all the men and notice any judgments that came up. Some would be attractive, some not. Some you'd want to connect with, some you'd want to avoid. Then, at the end of the workshop, he had us remember those judgments and compare them to how we now saw the other men after three days of sharing physical and emotional nakedness, as well as heart-centered listening and talking, and compassionate touch. With our spirits shining through, we were all uniquely beautiful.

Sequoia was sturdy and majestic in the confident authority of what he had to teach, yet playfully adventurous and airborne in his openness to discovering what more he had to learn. Under his inspiring tutelage, I had extraordinarily healing experiences. One time, in a guided visualization, he suggested we invite our sixteen-year-old selves into the circle. I was shocked at how much

I didn't want my angry younger self to be there, and even more shocked at realizing how much hurt there was beneath his banished rage. He had been a runaway doing what he could to survive on the very same street where the workshop was taking place. I had left him behind to fend for himself for all those years, but now, thanks to Sequoia, I learned I was ready to give that lost adolescent the care he needed to feel found.

Another time I was cradling the weight of an older man's head in my hands, massaging the back of his neck, and it reminded me of holding my father's head as I washed his body in preparation for sending him to the morgue. Suddenly I found myself weeping. Sequoia gently took me aside and I was finally able to grieve for my father and really take in that before he had died, he'd told me how strong I was.

Yet another time, emanating the dignity of his namesake tree, Sequoia was standing tall before us, demonstrating a massage stroke, when in my mind's eye I clearly saw a little boy of three or four clinging to the trunk of his leg. When I told him later, he said I'd seen Tommy, the tender sapling he'd been as a child. The beautiful image of the two of them together touched me because I realized Sequoia was the embodied archetype of the Wounded Healer, having created a way to give to others what he himself needed to heal. He piloted me by example to take responsibility for the reconciliation and well-being of all my own ages and stages.

Sequoia has all the qualities one could wish for in a mentor, and also—as I delightedly discovered—in a friend. I had the chance to spend wonderful times with him in his apartment in Vancouver and at his cabin retreat on Gambier Island, lingering languorously over long, meaningful conversations, hearty meals, and flowing cups of his famous home-brewed chai. I was fascinated to learn about the religious rigidity of his lonely New York childhood, what pre-Stonewall life had been like, his years spent in the US Air Force as a closeted pilot, his service in Vietnam, his stellar career as a flight instructor, his front row seat to the social revolution happening in Berkeley in the 1970's, the horrors of the AIDS crisis in the 1980's, his awakening to authenticity, and the evolution of *Men In Touch*.

I have many snapshots of Sequoia in the memory album of my heart: his eyes shining as he recounted experiencing the original Broadway production of *Hair*, with its glorious songs singing of liberation, letting the sun shine in, and the dawning of the age of Aquarius; gushing and giggling with him over an old black and white photo featuring the gorgeousness of a famous actor's uncircumcised penis; walking through the woods with him and his partner as we spontaneously linked arms and hitch-stepped down the road singing "We're Off To See The Wizard" like three giddy Dorothys on their way to OZ; riding bikes through Stanley Park; sitting in meditation and singing kirtan; and laughing and sharing and catharting about the fumblings and profundities of life.

The apotheosis of my involvement with *Men in Touch* was helping Sequoia host a *MMMM* workshop in my hometown. I had decided to dedicate some time to becoming a public presence as a gay man, creating ways to share with rural gay men the healings I'd been blessed to receive that hadn't been readily available to them. When I told Sequoia about this intention, he said, "When should I be there?" We held the workshop in the house where I'd grown up, and it felt like a graduation.

I love Sequoia and am so thankful to know him. I feel a unique connection to him that transcends time and space and regular in-person visits. There's a poignant thread running through his story that runs through mine as well—an intense longing for the eros of emotional/physical/spiritual peace -—a thread of longing I believe connects us all. His work and friendship contributed to my healing and growth at a crucial time and in no small way helped prepare me to say YES to delving into committed intimacy with my husband, Thomas, and to work on tending to the wounds that went even deeper than the homophobically inflicted ones: the fundamental and trickier-to-reach wounds of childhood emotional neglect, the ones that came from a lack of nurturing sap running through my family tree. Neuroscience is discovering more and more about brain development and self-esteem and the damage caused to our nervous systems and sense of self-worth when deprived of loving touch at crucial developmental stages. Sequoia's work is not just for gay men, it's for all human/sexual/spiritual beings.

How had a Catholic gay boy born at a time when shame was a given, when eros and spirituality were forbidden to mingle, and when living authentically was out of the question, been able to survive such soul-denying bleakness? How did a military-trained Air Force pilot become a fiercely gentle pioneer of nurturing touch, erotic positivity, and fully embodied, lusty spirituality?

You're about to find out, dear reader. Sequoia is a pilot in more ways than one. In *Divining Desire*, his achingly honest and transcendent memoir lifts us into the questing realms between earth and sky where epiphanies dwell—queer and otherwise. Fasten your seat belt for a profoundly human flight.

There may be some dark clouds and sexistential turbulence on the journey, but don't worry: there will also be incredibly clear blue skies, ecstatic views, and horizons wider than you ever dreamed. You're in the safest of sensitive hands. Sequoia Thom has a healer's touch, a poet's vision, the multi-ringed courage of a mighty first-growth tree, and an impeccable record for teaching people how to soar.

David Mielke is a writer, actor, and singer. He has appeared in many regional theatre productions as well as network television shows and his own original stage works. He is the creator of the award-winning *Cozy Grammar* series. He lives with his husband, Thomas Hitoshi Pruiksma, on Vashon Island, WA.

Preface

"Oh God! I'm coming!"

What does sex have to do with God?

What does God have to do with sex?

Have you ever wondered about that connection?

I have: it's been the central conundrum of my entire life.

In my early years, I felt painfully split. That pain has driven me on a life-long quest to fathom the depths of both sex and spirit: to explore their many mysteries and to find where they may be connected.

What follows in this spiritual travelog are the highs and lows, the struggles and insights, and most of all the amazing grace that has guided me on a totally transformational life journey. Many inspiring teachers have gradually guided me to experience sex and love as vehicles to a deep connection with God, which I now understand to be the pure consciousness and love that is who we all are.

If you share even a little of my fascination with the God-sex connection, I invite you to join me on that journey, to share my discoveries, and to make discoveries of your own along the way. Even if you do not identify with my early struggles as a guilt-ridden Catholic gay boy, stick around. I believe you'll agree that many of my discoveries are relevant to all of us, regardless of our gender or sexual orientation.

I want to see a world where people celebrate our sexuality in ways that are affirming of our lust *and* our love. I want us all to live with our genitals, hearts, and souls in happy harmony.

Is that possible? Join me to learn more.

Why I wrote this:

I began journaling around age 20 after being inspired reading Dag Hammerskjold's very personal *"Markings."* What began as an occasional entry of especially momentous events gradually morphed into a daily reflection on my inner reactions to the outer events of my life: a way to fully digest the emotions of each day.

Upon moving into retirement almost sixty years later, in 2021, I had the impulse to do a longer journal as a way to even further digest the many decades of experience life has granted me. In both my daily journal and this memoir *I was writing for myself.*

Then, as I began to see the richness of the teachings I've been given over so many decades, I remembered how much I have been inspired reading others' spiritual biographies. I hope you gain some insights by reading about my own struggles and learnings.

In *Be Here Now*, Ram Dass wrote, "We are all on the journey toward enlightenment and at each stage must share what we have discovered with those who will listen. The sharing is part of the work. The listening is part of the work. We are all on the path[1]."

That is my hope: I offer you my life as an open book. May you find new insights and inspirations as well. May you be blessed to live ever more deeply in your own heart and in the Universal Heart.

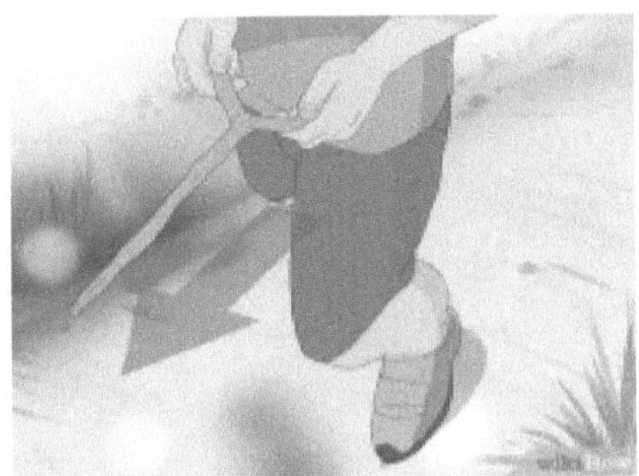

About the title and cover: Divining or dowsing has been used for hundreds of years as a way to search for something: usually a source of water or precious metals, or to tune into subtle energy. The physical tool used is a divining rod.

As I reflected on my experience of sexual desire, which I initially focused on the phallus, I began to imagine the penis as a divining rod: searching for the *divine energy* hidden within sexual energy. I offer a deep bow of gratitude to Parker Green McLean for generously offering his artistic input for the design of the cover layout. He created this striking image of a phallic divining rod

for the book cover.

Then we learned that some retailers do not accept nudity on book covers, so we came up with something more modest for the front cover. The inside cover depicts a Shiva Lingam, which in much of India represents the erotically generative creativity of the universe; (read more in Chapter 12). The image of the yogi with his whole front body exposed and vulnerable, is taken with permission from a cover of the *Yoga Journal*, Jan-Feb, 1978. When I was first teaching *Yoga for Gay Men* in San Francisco in 1980, I received permission to use that image on my flyers and cards from the editor, Deena Brown. The artist is Jad King. I am so grateful for their support.

This volume is in two major parts:

- My personal healing journey is written as a memoir that is roughly chronological, and developmental. The organizing theme is the gradual healing of my early wound: the deep split between eros and spirit. The major questions that guided me: Who/What is "God"? Are God and sex opposed or aligned?

- Appendix: This is a compendium of my most profound learnings, including links to online resources.

- *Cognitive* Resources available for your own journey toward greater wholeness.

- *Experiential* Practices to take your learning below your neck: to fully *embody* every aspect of being human.

Stylistic Notes

Pronouns: Like many of us, in the last decade, I have become much more conscious of moving beyond binary thinking to affirm the full spectrum of gender and sexual expression, and am endeavoring to use more inclusive pronouns. Because this is an historical account, I am continuing to use the binary he/she language of the times I am writing about, as well as using what might now be viewed as sexist language referring to "man", or "men" rather than a more inclusive "person." This is for dramatic effect: to emphasize the culture of the times I was navigating. When writing about more current times, I use more gender-neutral language.

Pseudonyms: To respect the privacy of people who are still living I have given them pseudonyms, unless they have given me express permission to use their real name.

In deference to readers like myself who are dyslexic, I have departed from some style conventions. For example,

- I use numerals instead of spelling out numbers (3 instead of three).

- I use bullet points extensively, because for me as a reader, they make comprehension easier.

- I've included an Annotated Table of Contents at the very end, for those who wish to get a more detailed preview and only read the sections of most interest.

Introduction

Looking back, I see my life thus far in 3 major phases. In the early years before 30, I felt lost and alone. Being attracted to other men felt like a fundamental flaw which alienated me from other people and from God. In the middle years from 30 to around 60, I experienced a steep learning curve and profound healing (becoming whole). Since 60, I've been blessed to share that wholeness with others more and more.

The stereotype of the queer man in the 1950s and 1960s in America was a 98-pound limp-wristed wimp who couldn't throw a ball, was a disappointment to his father, a special son to his mother, extra bright in school, attractive to girls and women but disliked by "regular guys." Yup, that's exactly how my life began. I fit most of those stereotypes, and even the Freudian profile of the doting, smothering mom and the absent father. I had it all!

If we were born before Gay Lib,[2] we were seen by religion as sinners destined for hell, by the shrinks as mentally ill or at best developmentally retarded, and by the media as effeminate and silly. The culture as a whole was either oblivious to our existence, or saw us as sickos, predatory perverts, and even pedophiles. So of course I felt like shit as a kid. I felt deeply flawed, and profoundly lonely - judged by God and humanity as unworthy of love.

In early life I was taught that the body in general, and sexuality in particular (not to mention the unmentionable homo variety), were obstacles on the spiritual path. Saint Paul wrote of a "sting of the flesh," which some speculate was his homo-desires. After several years of utter failure as a teen to curb my carnal cravings, I concluded that any God worth loving must have given us these intensely strong sexual desires intentionally. I longed to find God *through* my sexuality rather than trying to repress, fight, or transcend it. At some deep level I intuited that sex and spirit are one, though I had never heard that expressed anywhere.

In the second phase, from my late 20s into my late 50s, I was on an intense quest to discover the mysteries of human sexuality and how our erotic energies and desires can connect with that almost universal longing to fathom the mysteries of existence itself: Who am I? Why am I here? Those questions guided my search. I was exploring Right Relationship[3] with friends and lovers, and with God, and getting clear that God comes first. I learned that all human love flows out of divine love.

Some mysterious grace led me to encounter the perfect people: exploring friendship with some, a new form of friendly lovership with others, and even trying full-on partnership with a few. That grace led me to several incredibly gifted teachers and powerful teachings, which helped me heal that painful sex-spirit split that was the curse I was born into.

Healing comes from the same roots as whole and holy. My journey has involved healing the deep divide I was experiencing between sex and spirit. That split prevented me from truly loving myself or others, and alienated me from God as I understood "Him[4]" to be in my early years. The often contradictory messages I was hearing about sexuality and spirituality were very confusing. Those two equally compelling parts of me seemed utterly opposed. To heal that split would be to become whole, to be healed.

When I began "coming out" in 1972, after almost 20 years of living a torturously double life in the closet in Catholic schools and the US Air Force, I saw and experienced a lot of below-the-belt sex which was devoid of heart and soul. This satisfied a certain itch and curiosity, while leaving huge parts of me hungry for more. My deeper yearning was for devoted love.

For my personal development, I was intuitively and somewhat mysteriously drawn to explore yoga, meditation, and holistic (sensual, not sexual) massage, finding them wonderfully nourishing yet all *above*-the-belt. The internal split between sex and spirit drilled into me in Catholicism persisted.

In the mid-70s I took my first Tantra workshop in Oakland, California, which was profound. For the first time I got naked with a group of men in a well-lit room. We were guided to breathe with one another while holding eye contact. Then gradually we were led to share slow, meditative touch that included the genitals as part of the whole body. This gave me my first glimpse of healing that rift in my energy body.

From 1976-1982, I dove into (non-sexual) Tantra with an Indian master named Baba Muktananda, who visited California several times. He was able to activate people's "kundalini," which is understood in his tradition to be a normally-dormant aspect of sexual energy. When activated, sexual energy flows *up, rather than out* through ejaculation. This can lead to many other kinds of pleasurable "orgasms," which were wonderfully heart-opening.

Baba taught that ***"God dwells within you. See God in each other."*** This was a radically different view of divinity than I'd been taught; it resonated deeply within me. He experienced and taught that the entire universe is permeated by the same divine pure consciousness, which goes by many names in different traditions. I was like a fish "discovering" water: there is nothing to believe or not believe. Suddenly, I *experienced* that all-pervasive presence as my own deepest essence, and thus, the deepest essence of everyone.

In 1979, I attended the first "Spiritual Gathering of Radical Faeries" in the desert of Arizona with about 200 men from all over North America. We'd all been drawn by Harry Hay's eloquent "call" to come together to connect with one another authentically in body, heart, and soul. This was another hugely transformative experience. It was where, at 35, I took on the name Sequoia. It was magical to romp and play sensually and erotically with men who seemed much more integrated *above and below the belt*. There was a refreshing freedom from shame and guilt: a genuine celebration of men loving men.

By 1980 I was offering *Yoga for Gay Men* in San Francisco, and holistic massage from my home in Berkeley, mostly with fellow faeries. Joe Kramer came to a few of my classes. We discovered that we shared an intense yearning to learn more about the spiritual dimensions of sexual energy. Together we explored some of the Eastern embodiment traditions, especially Taoist energy work with Mantak Chia. Joe was inspired to begin to offer some group touch sessions for men based on those principles, and opened *The Body Electric School* in early 1984. We continued to inspire one another.

In 1981, as part of my *East-West Psychology Masters* program at the *California Institute of Integral Studies*, I led a weekend retreat in Cotati, north of San Francisco, for about 10 faeries, where we shared yoga, meditation, and full-body sensual massage. It turned out to be the prototype for 35 years of **Men In Touch** retreats with essentially the same focus: to demystify Tantra. By combining a few simple yoga movements and intentional breathing, with gentle, full-body "TLC" (tender loving care), men can learn to move sexual energy *up* rather than squirting it out. This helps heal the above/below the belt split between sex and heart/soul that many of us experienced in casual sex.

I was also teaching what I needed to continue learning. Joe's events at *Body Electric* gave me a powerful way to deepen my own all-chakra integration in the company of other erotic explorers. In 1994, on my 50th birthday, I savored a full week of deeper practice at the *Sacred Intimate Training* at Wildwood, a few hours north of SF. That gave me more confidence in working erotically with my massage clients, knowing from my own embodied experience how incredibly powerful such intentional touch can be.

By around 60, that journey was largely complete. I now feel integrated and whole, and profoundly grateful for the grace that has led me to find so many astounding teachers and teachings. My deep well of dark self-image has completely reversed: now my life feels full of deeply loving friendships with people all along the whole gender/sexuality spectrums. I enjoy richly loving erotic relationships. Most importantly, I feel profoundly at one with "God". I marvel at the metamorphosis I've undergone! It feels like nothing but grace.

There! I've used one of the loaded g-words. In fact I've used two: I just wrote "God." God and grace are both misunderstood and maligned in modern culture. Yet I've experienced both in increasing clarity as the decades have progressed.

Okay, what do I mean by "God?" I might as well tackle the toughest question of all right off the top. Lao Tzu begins his mystical *Tao Te Ching* with "Any Tao that can be named is not the true Tao." Many Jews refuse to write or speak any divine name for the same reason: to name the divine would be to limit what is, by definition, limitless and unfathomable by our small, binary computer minds.

Yet the world's religions are replete with countless names. I'm sure you can think of dozens. There are probably hundreds in India alone! Secular spiritual traditions like 12-step programs use their own code words, like "Higher Power." The mystical traditions of the east are more inclined to formless descriptors like "Buddha-nature" or "Pure Consciousness." I like the latter. After 50+ years of meditation it has become increasingly clear to me what the Berkeley bumper sticker said: "Meditation is not what you think." Indeed, I would say "God is not what you think."

Growing up Catholic, I understood God to be a regal patriarch with a white beard sitting on-high passing judgment on all of us sinners. **Now my understanding is very different:**

- "God" is our innermost essence, much deeper than our usual ego-self,

- "God" is the boundless field of consciousness that *underlies all our thoughts.*

- "God" is pure beingness, pure consciousness and pure love.

- Out of That primordial consciousness, thoughts and forms arise. Into That, they/we all return.

● That consciousness is the source of all "stuff." Buddhists call stuff "Form" and pure consciousness "Emptiness." Buddhists also sometimes call our ego Small Mind, and consciousness Big Mind.

● "God" is the Christian mystics' "still, small voice within" that we can only hear when the usual mental chatter gradually subsides during meditation. Some say "the voice of God is silence."

● At the deepest level we are all God. God is all of us and all of this...and beyond all as well.

● In more theological terms, God is both immanent and transcendent.

So I am reclaiming the word God with that understanding.

SEXUALITY IS ONE OF the most complicated and confusing areas of human life. Sex can and should be a source of joy and pleasure. It is way too often a cause of inner conflict and outer aggression or even abuse. In my experience, many people struggle with feeling unattractive or unworthy of love, based on physical appearance or distorted beliefs about themselves. They judge themselves physically (too tall/short, too heavy/thin, too dark/light, too old/young, etc.) or unlovable in other mysterious ways. Many spiritual traditions teach that we are separate from God and unworthy of God's love, so we see ourselves as fundamentally flawed.

However, both sexuality and spirituality are essential to our existence. Each of us came out of the formless and into form through sex. Yet, sadly, many cultures today do not fully integrate sexual energy into their understanding of the sacred. Sex and the sacred are most often at odds. So the pain in my early years is reflective of a deep wound in much of humanity. Repressed and distorted sexual energy may be the root cause of much of the violence and exploitation among humans.

I have come to view Life as a school of love. I am here, and I believe we are all here, to learn first to love ourselves: our own body, mind, heart, sexuality, and soul. Then we are here to learn to love others: family, friends, neighbors, and even strangers. Every great wisdom tradition says that in different ways. Finally, we are here to commune with that ineffable mystery that goes by countless names and is really beyond name and form.

Now as I look back on my nearly 80 year journey, I happily report that it is indeed possible to love God carnally, passionately, in bodily form, and then to take that outer physical passion deeply inward to love the formless God within. This experience, that we are literally made of love, leads me to know in my deepest heart that God dwells in every human heart, no matter how much that inner divine essence may be obscured by the ego.

What follows are the highs and lows, the struggles and insights, and most of all the amazing grace that has guided me to meet inspiring teachers who have gradually transformed my experience of sex and love into a deep inner connection with God: that pure consciousness and love that is who we all are.

If you share even a little of my fascination with the God-sex connection, I hope you'll find this tale of my healing journey informative and inspiring.

The Early Years ~ Lost and Alone
Chapter 1 - Early stirrings: pre-puberty (1944-1956)

I'm three, crying alone in my room: feeling excluded from the drunken party my parents are having with my aunts and uncles. Crying with my Teddy, my eyelids eventually drift shut. Next morning I get up early, open my bedroom door, and am revolted by the stench of cigarette smoke and booze. In the living room, I find overflowing ashtrays and half-finished glasses. Assorted adults are passed out on the sofa, chairs, and floor. My stomach turns and my heart sinks. Revolted, I climb up on a step-stool to reach several half-empty liquor bottles in the kitchen, and empty them down the drain. Later, my parents were not pleased; I had emphatically made my point.

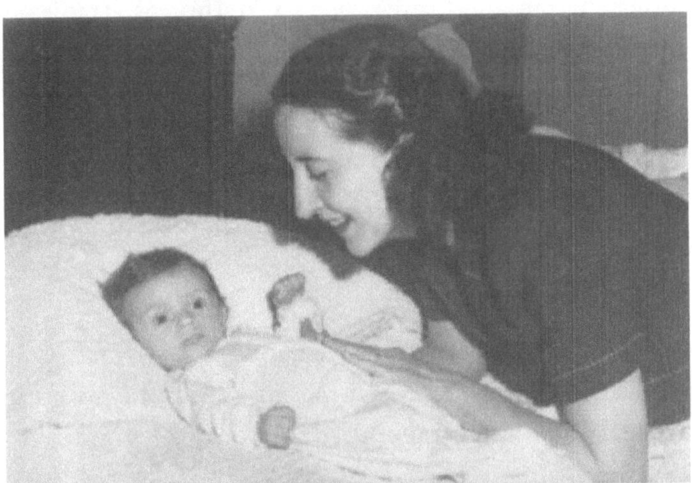

Three years earlier, on a sweltering August 7th in 1944 in Brooklyn, my mother, a former nun, was fraught with anxiety as she birthed her unexpected first and only child, while her husband of 13 years was fighting in the war in Europe[5]. The unintended conception happened days before he went off to the front lines, filling her with dread and fear that she would never see him again. Yet her Catholic faith was strong. She believed in God's grace, the power of prayer, and the guidance of guardian angels.

Mom was the youngest of 6 children born to devout Irish immigrants in Brooklyn. They were determined to have one of their children have a vocation in the priesthood or convent, so they pressured Mom to join the Sisters of Saint Joseph. Although she, too, was quite devout, she quickly realized that the nunnery was not for her. She went to work for the phone company (back when there was only one), and did clerical work till retiring at 65.

I was named Thomas after my father and both grandfathers. In fact the name Thomas was the only name in my father's lineage for the previous 10 generations. Only our immigrant forebear, Richard, had a different name. He was a Quaker who fled religious persecution in Devonshire, England, in 1676 and was an early settler in William Penn's Bucks County, near Philadelphia. My mother's father and brother were also Thomas. Tradition was a powerful force in this family.

My first 10 years were a blur of childhood illnesses. I was anemic even when not overtly sick: the perfect target for bullying boys in my working class Brooklyn neighborhood. Taunted as an unathletic sissy, I felt inferior in any kind of physical activities. *You throw like a girl!* they sneered way too many times.

Indeed Mom encouraged my naturally soft side, welcoming my sissy self. Out in the world I quickly learned it was not welcome, which caused me great confusion and inner turmoil. "How am I supposed to behave?" I wondered.

A lonely only child

By the time my father made it back from the war, when I was 18 months old, my mother and I had an emotionally incestuous bond. Maybe because she did not know whether she would ever see her husband again, she clung to me in a way that made me feel responsible for her happiness. Even at that young age I felt that weighty responsibility. So when my father did come home, I experienced him as an interloper. To make matters worse, he was an alcoholic, and got my mother drinking to keep him company. I hated it. Once they were inebriated, I felt utterly alone.

Despite that, Mom's devotion to my welfare was dependable every day. On school days she always got up first to get breakfast ready. Because I was frail and anemic, she was determined to feed me well. I had red meat for every meal (except of course on Fridays) and she even made me an eggnog everyday after school.

Both my parents were staunch Catholics. Even though I was an accidental addition to their lives, they rose to the occasion and did the best they could to be good parents. They both had solid values around doing one's duty.

Pop was away in the Army several times until I was 8. We always felt awkward around each other whenever he came home, as he would disrupt the easy harmony between Mom and me. My mother described him as a "pillar of the church," as he was often involved in going door-to-door raising funds. He attended Mass every morning except Saturdays.

I never saw my parents touch, except for a perfunctory good-night kiss. Nor were they physically affectionate with me. When I was quite young, Mom let me sleep with her, but she put a stop to that well before grade school. I do remember Pop in those early years taking me on his lap and playing child games like "This Little Piggy." That also stopped when I was quite young. On some level I longed for more physicality with him, though it was never quite conscious. I now know I wanted to feel his love in a bodily way. Instead I went looking for it through sex with strangers.

My sense of being flawed began in kindergarten. At 5, I happened to pee next to a boy my own age, and was intrigued to see another penis for the first time. In fact I was enthralled and very curious because Joseph's penis came to a point, while mine had a knob on the end[6]. I very much liked Joseph's penis and would have loved to have touched it. But my mother had already taught me that it would be deeply dirty, shameful, and sinful. So I stuffed that desire away.

I was also learning to repress any "negative" emotions and even much of my natural childhood exuberance: "Children should be seen and not heard," was my mother's mantra. I also learned from her and others' examples that in Irish Catholic culture, being "nice" is highly valued. "If you can't say something good about someone, don't say anything at all," she admonished and demonstrated. I witnessed and internalized an anesthetized emotional flatness in my family, school, and church. My happy emotions were praised and welcomed while my sadness and especially anger were clearly not welcome. I grieved and seethed in private[7]. Being an only child deprived me of the rough-and-tumble that siblings often share. Being the sissy boy in the neighborhood meant I also could not express any vulnerability... anywhere.

Also in this kindergarten run by nuns, my spiritual yearnings showed up. Here I am playing priest. Throughout my early years, many Catholic relatives and neighbors confided to me, "You're going to be a priest." Part of me felt flattered: they were recognizing that I had a special role in the world. Another part of me felt humiliated: I knew it meant I wasn't destined to be a "real man." Back then the priesthood was the only way people in that tradition knew how to understand boys who were gentle and kind, in short less masculine. Gay was unheard of or, at least, unmentionable.

There were two equally powerful parts of me: a deep yearning to connect with Spirit and to connect with the flesh. I longed to see and touch other boys' and mens' bodies and genitals. Yet spirit and flesh seemed utterly irreconcilable.

In the first grade, the nuns in my Catholic school made it clear we were all besmirched in the eyes of God by "Original Sin." They taught that, for some reason, even though God "created us in His Own image and likeness," He chose to sully us as well. Then "He sent his only-begotten Son to redeem us by his death on the cross." None of that made any sense, yet it instilled deep fear and shame. I felt severely flawed in the eyes of God and others.

They said we had to confess our sins in order to qualify to receive our First Communion: to eat God's body in the form of bread. They made a Really Big Deal of this event. So did my mother, who fussed about getting me dressed up to the max and having a professional photographer document my outfit.

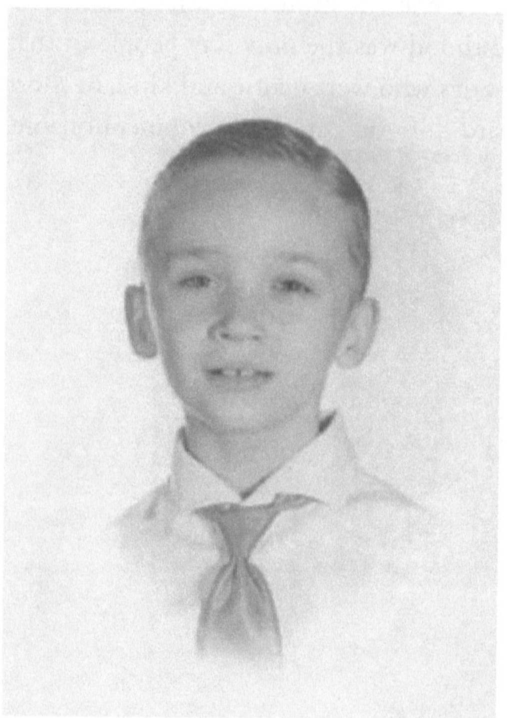

When the Big Day came, I was quite nervous, and didn't really understand what was happening. So it felt like some sort of performance. I somehow got the message that God was watching and I had to Do It Right!

With the stiffly starched collar my mother buttoned around my neck choking me, I felt vaguely ill. Once in church, we all had to line up and go up to the priest and kneel down. When the priest came to me, I put out my tongue to receive the "Body of Christ," and gagged on the dry wafer, barfing it all over the priest. That was a telling early commentary on my later feelings about Holy Mother Church.

Maybe my nervousness was in part because I had already been taught to feel shame about my body. "Your pee is dirty," Mom said. "Always wash your hands thoroughly, and never touch yourself there other than to pee. That would be a sin."

From as early as I can remember, I felt considerable confusion about gender and how I was supposed to behave. I knew I had a penis and was labeled as "boy." Yet I felt softer and gentler than other boys, and not at all competitive. Hearing the nursery rhyme describing little boys and little girls,[8] I identified much more with girls' sweetness.

Mom undoubtedly added to my confusion. She told me several times, "I always wanted a girl." She even enrolled me in a formerly all-girls' primary school run by the same nuns as she had once been. Boys were a recent addition. On the other hand, she squashed my budding interest in cross-dressing. When I was around 8 I took a great interest in an elegant almost-floor-length maroon velvet cape with a rhinestone clasp that she used for formal evening wear that I spied in her closet. I loved playing royalty wearing it, and did not see it as especially feminine. I could have been either a king or queen. Either way, much to my dismay, Mom tossed it out.

At age 8, she coerced me to become an altar boy at our local parish church, which was a grand Gothic affair modeled after Sainte-Chapelle in Paris. For the next 10 years I would serve at Mass every morning for one week each month. The devout part of me loved it. Mom heard glowing reviews from some of the neighborhood ladies about what an inspiring vision I was in my black cassock and white surplice, which Mom religiously starched and ironed

to stiff perfection.

Looking back, I can see that early exposure to religious ritual began to teach me about the power of ritual to create a special mood or state of consciousness that can be a positive antidote to the crass materialism of modern western life. Mass took me outside time in a way, as it referred back to events two thousand years before. It also opened me to the idea of grace, and there being a domain of mystery beyond the ordinary mind's comprehension. These were seeds that bore fruit decades later.

First feeling of sexual lust and love

Also around age 8 some cousins visited from Pennsylvania. Their son was 18. He seemed like a god. Somehow we ended up sitting in their parked family car, a real novelty for me, since my family did not own one. I cannot remember which of us initiated showing our "privates" to one another. I sure remember how good it felt to have such a handsome "grown man" willing to share our secret organs, to admire and touch one another's hidden parts. Feeling no shame, I felt admired and validated by another male—something distinctly lacking in my life up till then. I developed an immediate crush on Paul.

About 30 years later, reading James Broughton's wonderful line, **"The penis is the exposed tip of the heart,"** made me realize that Paul had touched my heart in the most tender and loving way, and I touched his.

A couple of years later, Paul came again for an overnight visit. He was on leave in New York from the Navy and looked even more handsome in his uniform. My excitement and hope that we'd share some more intimate touch led to dismay. Even though he slept in the other bed in my room, he showed no interest in any kind of touch, which made me very sad. Lying in bed awake watching him sleeping in the other bed, longing to crawl in with him and cuddle, I yearned for his warmth and the feel of his flesh, of his manhood. Having fully internalized my shame, and having learned to hide all such feelings, I felt very alone in my sadness. It was my first experience of the heartbreak of letting go of a man I loved erotically. I never saw him again.

This became a pattern in my life: many of the men I fell in love with were either not available at all, or pulled away, or circumstances separated us. Learning to love and let go was always deeply painful, yet ultimately profound in transforming my understanding of love. Gibran wrote in *The Prophet* that *"your pain is the breaking of the shell that encloses your understanding."* Indeed, my heart broke open again and again.

Looking back on that first exciting experience with Paul of mutually touching one another's "exposed tip of the heart," I see that led to decades of seeking to feel *loved* by other men through genital contact. It was *male love* I yearned for, in a form that felt missing in my family and upbringing. Back then, men never touched except for brief handshakes. I wanted so much more.

Chapter 2 - A Tortured Teen: (High School, 1958-62)

Puberty hit me early and hard. Mom's daily menu of red meat, eggs and milk, which were probably loaded with growth hormones, accelerated my pubescent growth spurt. This awkward 11 year old shot up within 2 years to 6 feet and 175 pounds! I was the tallest in 8th grade.

Around age 10 I began organizing the boys in the neighborhood to show our growing cocks to one another, sometimes in 2s and 3s, and sometimes in a group setting. We weren't yet old enough to ejaculate, yet we did feel pride in showing off our growing manhood. Seeing and being seen in that aroused state was a huge turn-on. Because it was forbidden fruit it was all the more enticing.

Wanderlust

BY AGE 11, JUST BEFORE puberty, my parents gave me my first full-sized bike, a one-speed Schwinn cruiser that was styled like 1950s cars with whitewall tires, chrome fenders, and even a shock absorber. For me it was a ticket to freedom. Another boy in our building got the identical bike at the same time and we became biking buddies. I remember long rides to Prospect Park, Sheepshead Bay and even Idlewild Airport (now JFK), a 10-mile (16km) trek.

I was excited to show up for my first job: delivering newspapers in my neighborhood. I rode my big, shiney new bike down a long hill to the depot to fetch my quota of papers. The depot manager was in his 20s with hairy, muscled forearms like Popeye. My eyes popped all right! On the wall was a carefully hand-lettered sign that proclaimed, "Cleanliness is next to godliness."

They gave me a big canvas sack filled with about 30 pounds of papers. I slung the sack over my handle bars, and headed up that same hill, which was suddenly much longer. Wow! My 11 year old legs got quite a workout. Making the rounds every day, **I began noticing men.** Everything about men's bodies suddenly fascinated me: their muscles, their body hair, their "five o'clock shadow" [all men were clean-shaven back then; facial hair was unheard of], and of course that barely perceptible bulge lurking between their legs This was the mid-1950s: men never bared any skin, except forearms, even in warm weather. I longed to see their hairy chests or legs. Sadly, even if their collars were open, they wore t-shirts. Their legs were always covered in long pants. Sometimes I'd stop a man on the street to ask the time, just to get a moment to look more closely, and maybe catch a glimpse of some chest hair peeking up over his t-shirt!

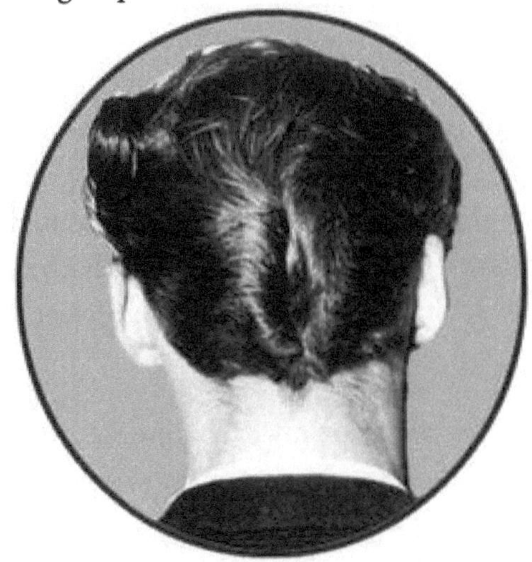

The one exception to the ubiquitous clean-cut look in the 50s and early 60s was Puerto Rican men, who had a swarthy sexiness with longer hair slicked back into a "DA" (short for duck's ass) and mustaches. I lusted for them and envied their freedom to be so overtly sexy. At urinals, glimpsing their intact,[9] dark-skinned members was a huge turn-on.

Every weekday afternoon I'd see that same inscrutable sign, "Cleanliness is next to godliness." It must have had some mysterious power: I began to love showers! At home the bathroom became my refuge to explore my rapidly changing body. I loved looking at myself in the mirror: excited to see the first signs of body and facial hair. The sensuality of showering my body led me to discover the pleasure of soaping my swelling manhood. I polished my knob till it glistened! Afterward I would emerge glowing. Sometimes my mother would comment how clean I looked!

Inside I felt dirty! I had deeply internalized her teaching many years earlier that touching myself was impure and sinful. The nuns in school had taught us any sort of sexuality outside of marriage was a mortal sin. And at 11 I was already too aware of the disgust with which the neighborhood boys called me faggot and queer. I knew it was true, and I felt deep shame: an utter failure as a male.

Facial hair was so rare that any sight of it, or even reference to it, turned me on. I distinctly remember watching a western movie on TV during this period. The scruffy cowboy ambles into the small town barber to get cleaned up for Saturday night at the saloon. In asking for a shave, he tells the barber, "Not too close: the ladies like a little scratch." A voice inside me clearly exclaimed, "Yeah, we do!"

As Pop observed puberty having its obvious effects on my body, one Saturday he sat me down to tell me the Facts of Life. I'm not sure which of us felt more awkward. He was doing his fatherly duty and I was dutifully polite and modest, reassuring him I understood the mechanics of plumbing and babies. Of course I could not allude to my raging hormones and lusty diddling with other guys. The chasm between us felt huge.

He had been a regular guy, and quite an athletic lad, becoming a letterman in high school basketball and baseball. He tried to teach me those skills plus football, and I was hopelessly inept. I felt ashamed sensing his disappointment. He persevered and finally discovered I had a modicum of ability in 10-pin bowling, so that became one of our ways of bonding on many Saturday mornings. He got me involved in a church group for young men, and encouraged me to take leadership. I volunteered to edit and publish a mimeographed newsletter. Then at his suggestion we created a bowling league for those guys. He was doing his best to teach me manly skills.

Just before my 12th birthday, one of the other neighborhood boys had begun jerking off and ejaculating, and he showed me how to do it. He invited me to climb the fence into our neighborhood park after it closed at 5 p.m. when it was getting dark. We found some privacy behind the admin building. He took out his cock and stroked it hard, and I imitated. I was a little shocked to see him shoot: a new experience. I was fascinated and envious and kept stroking but to no avail. Feeling disappointment and failure, I wanted what he was having. So I began stroking myself in the shower, at first to no effect. Then one day, I had my first glorious gush. After that I practiced often, although it was never easy to "get off."

That same summer, still not quite 12, I had an intense sexual attraction to a guy in a shower: so strong it has created a longing for a similar-looking guy all these many decades since. Two of the neighborhood boys I sometimes played with were going to the beach with their mother, Helen, who invited me to join them. Driving in their convertible was the height of luxury to me, as my parents refused to own a car. After an hour's drive across Brooklyn to Jacob Riis Park, Helen sent us into the men's change room to get into our swimsuits. I was enthralled: men were walking around naked under the open sky (there was no roof on this labyrinthine maze of lockers and showers). I was very excited, yet had to hide that and stick with the brothers to rejoin Helen and find a spot on the sand. All I wanted to do was explore the maze. A couple of times, between dips in the ocean, I feigned needing to use the toilet and returned to explore the men. There were many open-air shower rooms, each with about 6 shower heads. It was exciting to peek into each one. My already active gaydar told me at least some of these guys were more interested in each other than in the beach. Many were older. Then I spied one lovely lad a few years older than I: maybe 18. He was tall, slender, and blond, with the classic "swimmers' build." What, uh, stood out for me about him was his beautiful member, which was long and intact. (The lad pictured here, whom I found on Google, reminds me of him. In my memory he was hung like a donkey, though I suspect memory has added mass to his magnificence.)

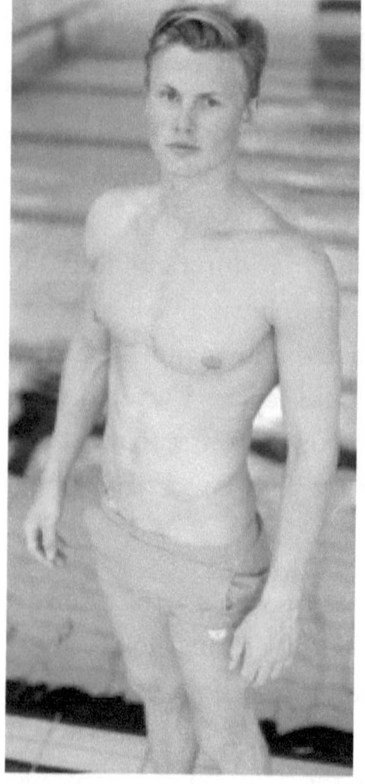

I eagerly joined him, removed my suit, and pretended to be merely showering, while stealing glances his way. My glances aroused him, which got me hard, which got him hard, which got me even harder. I had never felt so excited. It was intoxicating.

We were too far apart to touch and did not dare move closer: we could be seen by anyone passing by. My heart was racing. I was trembling with excitement, and I sensed he was too. Then I heard one of the brothers call my name: "Hurry up. Mom is waiting in the car." I stuffed my erection back into my bathing suit, went to the locker, and quickly changed. I never saw him again. In the car I was so excited I could hardly speak, yet had to pretend nonchalance.

In hindsight I see that having to conceal my excitement and pleasure was intensely isolating. It deepened my sense of loneliness, of being weird, a freak. I knew I'd be shamed if I told anyone. I kept it all bottled up inside.

My Fetish

The image of that statuesque lad, who had my ideal perfect body and cock, has stayed with me ever since. I'm amazed how permanently that brief encounter has hardwired my sexual nervous system. To this day, ultra-lean men like him, especially those with generously proportioned intact endowments, invariably arouse my attention. Indeed it's hard to feel an intense genital charge with anyone with a less magnificent appearance.

Even though in the decades since I've learned many other ways to feel and express my sexuality, my Inner Teenager is still alive and well. He likes to be acknowledged from time to time. I do that online. When I look at porn, I look for someone like him who is showing off his manly member for all the world to see. Happily there are many such lads on the web these days. When I join them virtually for a wank, my erections and ejaculations are often more intense and pleasurable than in my teens. That is because I choose to rarely cum[10], and have learned how to "edge" (to delay my ejaculation until I've built up a good head of steam). Also, now I am free of guilt and can enjoy the journey, the deliciously sensual slow build-up to the splendid spluge.[11]

Back then, this kind of cock play, alone or with others, caused me great guilt: I still believed the Catholic Church's teaching that any sexual conduct outside of marriage was a "mortal sin," meaning if I died before confessing my sins and being given absolution by a priest I would burn in Hell forever...yikes! I was an altar boy at the time and the very model of pious virtue, which on one level was genuine. Yet I had this shameful, hidden side.

Every week I'd confess my sins on Saturday, so I could receive Holy Communion on Sunday with my parents. I was aware I wanted to appear virtuous to them. Alas, within a day or two I'd be wanking again and feeling horrible. Each time after Confession I'd sincerely promise myself never to sin again, inevitably to fail within days. I saw myself as a miserable wretch in the eyes of a judgmental God.

My summer idylls

The school year was always hard: feeling lonely living with my alcoholic parents, and feeling inferior to other boys in my neighborhood and in school. Happily, I got to escape all that every summer by staying with my father's Aunt Marion. I first met her when I was 3. My parents took me on a summer vacation to her island cottage, which was among the Thousand Islands where Lake Ontario flows into the Saint Lawrence River.

It felt heavenly. I urged them to return every year during their 3 weeks of vacation, which they did, despite Mom's fears of water. By the time I was 11, I made the case that I should spend entire summers with Aunt Marion "to help her out:" that she was getting up in years and could use an energetic lad like me to run errands. I would go to the post office each day to fetch mail, to a well on a nearby island to fill bleach bottles with safe and delicious well water, and to the mainland for groceries. Those summers were idyllic: away from the sweltering streets of New York (often 95F/35C with 95% humidity) to the cool fresh air of the Saint Lawrence River. Everyone there was in vacation mode. The boys and girls my age were much more wholesome than the rough boys in my Brooklyn neighborhood.

AROUND THE SAME TIME, I began saving the money I was earning on my paper route with an eye toward buying my own boat. Pop took me to the International Boat Show at the Coliseum to window-shop for an outboard boat I might buy to run around the St. Lawrence. That summer I proudly bought a 12-foot fiberglass runabout and rented a 15 horsepower outboard motor. Suddenly I had the freedom to wander the river at will: to explore for fun as well as to run errands for my aunt. Both my bike and my boat gave me a thrilling sense of freedom and autonomy. They were harbingers of the similar thrill I later felt with my first car at age 20, and learning to fly the following year. Being at the controls of any moving vehicle has been a life-long joy. Now, living in Vancouver, I rarely need to use a car. Biking has become my main way to get around. Even in my late 70s, riding my bike gives me the same thrill I've always had. Now on an ebike, I still feel like a happy boy!

Even though doting in some ways, my parents were remarkably permissive about letting me wander New York on my own at a young age, beginning at puberty. I guess they saw my rapid physical maturing as a sign I was ready for more freedom. All they asked was to be kept informed of my whereabouts, and that I be home in time for dinner. I could take the bus or subway to downtown Brooklyn or even Manhattan to go to movies or browse department stores. The public library was also a permissible destination. That gave me a lot of latitude to go cruising with only a slight bending of the truth.

Around then, the neighborhood boys discovered girls and lost interest in my homo-erotic play. I was both longing for, and afraid of, sharing some kind of sexual touch with grown men. It was then that I discovered toilets. Public toilets back then had no partitions between urinals, so I could appear to be innocently peeing while covertly gazing sideways to see others' members exposed. It was thrilling. Sometimes I'd get hard. Then to my delight I discovered a neighbor getting hard too and we'd stroke ourselves: proudly sharing our erections and ejaculations. Eventually I got more bold and reached over to stroke my neighbor and to let him stroke me. This was intoxicating. It was also furtive and quick. The combination of sexual arousal plus the fear of getting caught was a heady brew of hormones. I quickly got hooked on the combo of arousal and adrenaline.

I guess I had what I later heard described as "gaydar," which led me to a few places where I could find equally fearful, shameful guys to secretly look at and touch. One was a washroom in a big department store, at the urinals or looking/reaching under the partitions between toilets. During high school, instead of engaging in sports or clubs, during the couple of hours between when school ended at 3 and my parents got home around 5:30, I would "go shopping" downtown. Then my guilt was even worse. What could be more shameful? In those years, the worst insult was being called a fag or homo[12]. I knew that's what I was, though I resisted the label. I told myself I was "just fooling around," yet I also knew what I liked and found ever more ways to find it. Ironically, my parents each helped me find naked men.

Showers...public showers! My mom was afraid I'd drown when visiting my favorite aunt's summer cottage on the St. Lawrence River. So she enrolled me in swimming lessons at the local Y. Back then, in the 1950s, there was total gender segregation. The YMCA really was all male, and all nude. The swim class was all boys about my age... naked in the pool and showers. How exciting: homo-heaven! The showers were a voyeur's delight, although only furtively so. We were all curious to see each other's endowments, yet also knew it was shameful to look directly. My peripheral vision became very acute. I secretly loved being seen by other boys in my growing manhood...and ashamed. It was a confusing mix, yet the excitement over-rode the shame.

At home I would wash myself all the more enthusiastically, hoping the sound of the rushing water would muffle my irrepressible moans of sexual pleasure. Then remorse again. Knowing I could not take Holy Communion unless I confessed my sins, I would shamefully confess that I had "touched myself impurely" and sincerely vow to not sin again. I could usually hold out two or three days before succumbing to cumming again. The cycle became a weekly ritual: feverishly pleasuring myself then being plunged into remorse, guilt, shame, then confess, take Communion, and repeat the cycle.

My mother was so pleased at my enthusiasm for swimming at the Y (I had become quite regular, long after the lessons ended) that she introduced me to the Saint George Hotel in the heart of Brooklyn Heights. It had a gorgeous, Olympic swimming pool complete with a waterfall and mosaic tile walls. To my delight, the showers had a steam room and sauna, where guys of all ages admired one another's masculine attributes. Again, it was mostly furtive voyeurism, and I found it wonderfully affirming to have grown men admiring my own growing manhood. "Cleanliness is next to godliness." I spent hours in the showers and steam room pretending to be ignoring others while actually eagerly enjoying eyeing their naked splendor. In the steamy secrecy, sometimes some of us would show off our full erection, though rarely was it private enough to engage in any touch. That would have been scary on many levels! Looking was exciting enough, though once in a while I or another guy would surreptitiously stroke ourselves to full orgasm, stifling any sounds of pleasure so no one else could tell. My mother was so pleased I was such an avid swimmer! Yet now my confessions were even more shameful because they involved other men! Years later I learned that Brooklyn Heights was then and is now *"tres gai!"*... an early enclave of "homosexuals," long before there was anything resembling a gay community. Did Mom know? Was she covertly supporting her sissy son to find his tribe? She seemed such a prude, yet I wonder.

I remember all through my teens, always waking hard, feeling I had to hide my manhood from my parents. We had a morning ritual: Mom would call me to wake and I'd be rock hard with a bursting bladder. I'd try to tuck my wood under the waistband of my PJs and walk awkwardly to the bathroom, where my dad would always be in the shower. I could not pee standing because it was impossible with such a hard erection and I did not want him to see me like that. So I'd sit to pee. If he finished his shower he'd throw the shower curtain open to dry; I longed to look at his cock and did not dare. I felt so much shame about my sexual feelings and desires. I never did see his cock, nor did I let him see mine. How sad.

So of course I went to places where I could be proud of myself as a man, where men were admiring one another. Washrooms and showers were the perfect place to affirm what I was ashamed of at home. My eros would not be repressed. I'm glad I found a way, and also sad it had to be limited to such furtive settings.

My Dad inadvertently led me to the cruisiest toilet in all of New York: Grand Central Station. We took the subway to visit relatives at a nearby hotel. We then had to pass through the station to get to the hotel. Dad felt the urge and took us down into the men's room in the bowels of the station. There were probably 40 urinals along 2 walls facing away from each other. One wall was almost full of guys, and the other was nearly empty. As we arrived, my

Dad steered us to the roomier side. I glimpsed some rapid hand movements and sideways glances happening on the other side. My heart was pounding so hard I could barely breathe, let alone pee. Once again, as at the beach, I felt overwhelming sexual excitement which I had to utterly hide from my dad. I always wondered what, if anything, he noticed of the activity on the opposite wall and what his feelings were about it. I'll never know.

I took note of this location and visited many times in the ensuing years. I quickly discovered that the toilet cubicles allowed viewing one's neighbors' legs. Spread legs were clear body language that genitals were also on display and often erect and being stroked. Sometimes neighbors reached under to caress and/or stroke one another. I began my yoga career practicing deep forward bends to be able to look under those partitions.

Public toilets became my major *modus operandi*: department stores, subway stations, and movie theaters all had toilets that were cruising grounds for quick, anonymous masturbation. Often the partitions between toilets had peep-holes that had been either drilled or created by removing screws from toilet paper holders. These allowed voyeuristic pleasure: seeing others stroking themselves. It was oddly both pleasurable and alienating: the cold partition protected our anonymity but also isolated our humanity from one another: we were mere body parts to one another. It was a kind of living porn.

Movie theaters after school were another source of lonely, horny men. They were fairly empty at that time of day. The men's rooms and the back rows were sometimes good places for a quick hand-job or even a blow job. For this boy who felt so insecure about his masculinity, there was something powerfully affirming about having a grown man down on his knees worshiping my manhood. It was pretty addictive. Again my parents thought I had a passion for movies; I did have a passion for sure.

The Duffield Theater in downtown Brooklyn was cheaper than others because it ran second-run films. It was a bit run down and less busy. My gaydar correctly surmised it might be more cruisy than other theaters nearby. I had a few hot encounters there, and I wondered if the backs of the seats were covered in dried cum, and whether the fellow in the projection booth got off looking down on the action.

During this whole period in high school I continued being devoutly religious, and deeply conflicted. As I mentioned, at my mother's urging I had become an altar boy at age 8. I loved the pomp and ritual, the incense, and the music. The piety was real, as was my growing fascination with men's bodies and genitals. I continued in that role all through high school. By 13, I was 6 feet and 175 pounds with good posture and a poised demeanor.[13] My mother heard glowing reports from other women in church about how inspiring my presence was. Neighbors and relatives often prophesied I was destined to be a priest. Indeed in some ways it appealed. I would not be expected to date or marry women! Yet I felt a wretched sinner as well.

The inner conflict between my sexual desires and my genuine spiritual yearnings was intense. Near the Duffield Theater where I sometimes sinned was a store selling Catholic religious articles: books, statues, crucifixes, and the like. My spiritual side was genuinely drawn there. I liked looking at all that devotional material. One day I saw a crucifix in the window that really drew me. On the plain wooden cross was a hand-carved figure of Jesus in the throes of his passion and pain. His lean body looked so beautiful to me...so, uh, sexy! The crucifix was very expensive: way more than my meager allowance would cover. I went to visit it/Him often, and tried to resist the allure of the back rows or toilets nearby. I prayed to Jesus to save me from my affliction, even as I lusted after his beautifully carved body. As Christmas was coming I told my parents about my desire/devotion to this particular crucifix. They happily indulged me, and I excitedly bought it. He "hung" on my bedroom wall from then on. I had the hots for Jesus,[14] which seemed at the time both genuinely pious and utterly perverse... even more shameful! Yet I was also getting glimmers that His body and hence my body could be sacred. After all, the Church taught that "God created us in His own image and likeness." Could He really be so cruel as to create our bodies capable of such exquisite pleasure, then forbid us to enjoy His creation? The lean figure of Jesus on the cross is still my ideal body type.

Looking back I can see this was the first time I was able to hold sexual desire and spiritual desire in my awareness at the same time, even though I still believed the sexual part was sinful. The Church taught that Jesus was at once fully human and fully God, yet his humanity was portrayed as transcending worldly passions. He came across as asexual. I wondered if it's possible to be both sexual and spiritual. As you will read, in the decades since, I am always much more attracted to men who embody both sexiness and spirituality. In recent decades, I've experienced that erotic passion can be worship of The Beloved, with my partner as an embodiment of God.

I was at an all-male high school run by Christian Brothers. There were about 2,000 "men" attending. I loved that the Brothers always addressed us as "men." Indeed our masculinity was surging. The ambient testosterone level was pungent. I found many of my classmates attractive, and of course they were forbidden fruit; although among all those men, surely others *were* fruits. To show any sign of attraction would mark me as a fag. I kept myself in check, which was torture. The ones I found sexy were the more sexually developed, and often more athletic and outgoing: in short the "jocks." I envied them and knew I'd never be welcome in their circles. We were all required to wear ties and jackets, so our bodies were fully covered below the neck. In class I found it very exciting when a lad at the desk across from mine showed a little bit of furry leg above his socks. Any glimpse of body hair turned me on.

I did find ways to channel some of my attractions into friendliness, and I would hang out with certain fellas during lunch periods. Sadly there was no way to connect after school because most of my fellow students lived a long subway ride away, whereas I lived a short walk from school. Also I feared that hanging out casually outside school would lead to embarrassing questions about girlfriends and sexual exploits. I did not dare to open that kind of conversation. So after school I kept to myself, feeling lonely and like damaged goods. It was fertile ground for compulsive cruising.

The ones I found easiest to hang out with were the more spiritually-oriented. They were gentler, and usually less athletic, which made them less sexy to me and more like kindred spirits. Some seemed nearly asexual. One of the lads I did develop a kind of crush on was Andy, who was sweetly friendly and wholesome. He later went on to become a Brother himself. I never had any sense of him having sexual desires for anyone: just a genuinely sweet and loving soul. We even stayed in touch for a few years after high school until his duties with the Brothers and my own busyness at university caused us to lose touch.

That kind of spirituality was my other side: I genuinely longed for connection with God and to lead a virtuous life. The Brothers set a wonderfully spiritual tone. Each period began with a brief prayer: *"Let us remember that we are in the holy presence of God,"* followed by a few moments of silent prayer or reflection. This kept me in touch with a subtle sense of connection with God that I felt in church. The presence of God was often palpable to me there. I even sometimes sat in the silent church in the afternoon after school instead of going cruising. Looking back, I realize I was practicing a kind of meditation: sitting in silent communion with Spirit. I genuinely longed to deepen that connection even as I felt an irresistible urge to feel the flesh of men. The two seemed utterly incompatible back then. Two sides of me were alienated from one other. I saw no way to connect them.

That painful inner split was accentuated in Senior Year. My high school yearbook committee conducted a survey of all 500 of us in our 4th year, asking us to vote for all the typical categories of "Most..." (Handsome, Athletic, Intelligent, Likely to Succeed, etc.) Months later when the results were announced, I was shocked to learn I had been voted "Most Dignified." I had a flood of conflicted feelings. I found it flattering to be selected for one of only 14 categories, and surprising, as I did not feel all that visible. Yet I also felt deeply embarrassed, even humiliated because I didn't qualify for any of the other categories. "Dignified" felt like a cruel consolation prize. I realized even way back then that they didn't know the real me. I was far from knowing who the "real me" was, yet I knew I was hiding my homo parts for fear of being ostracized. Instead they saw a carefully constructed veneer or facade that they probably found an enigma, so "Dignified" seemed the best descriptor for my mysterious persona. Looking back, I now realize I actually *am dignified.* I have a somewhat regal bearing that feels genuine. They were actually seeing me more deeply than I was able to see myself.

The split between my two sides was excruciatingly enacted nearly every week when I went to Confession. Confessing "touching myself (or another man) impurely" was so embarrassing, I'd go to other churches where no one would recognize my voice or face. Priests always scolded me for such shameful behavior. Never once did I hear any words encouraging self-acceptance. Confessions always concluded by being given a "penance": usually some prayers to say a certain number of times.

For about the thousandth time I confessed my sin of touching myself impurely in bed. The priest had a recommendation sure to stop that filthy habit. He said before bed I should say the rosary, then wrap my wrists in the rosary when I was falling asleep. That would keep me from impure "self-abuse." Wrong! The wrapped wrists force the hands into only one place: right on the genitals! Somehow it added to the charge to stroke myself thus bound! Then I committed the ultimate sin: I besmirched the rosaries with my jizz! Now I knew I'd burn in Hell forever!

It was around then I began to wonder: how could a loving God design humans "in His image and likeness," including giving us genitals that ache to be pleasurably touched, then forbid us from doing so. What kind of perverted God was that?

As I look back now on those years, what stands out is how utterly alone I felt. I did not feel there was anyone I could turn to for guidance or support, nor any role models I could emulate. Nor did I feel there was anyone to tell about my adventures. It was all secret and solitary, and achingly lonely. Sexuality was both mysterious and compelling and, for me, utterly isolating.

The cultural taboo against same-gender affection seemed to force males into channeling their natural affinity for one another into either sports, which permitted a certain kind of intimate contact and camaraderie, or into surreptitious sexuality. Unlike many other cultures (parts of southern Europe and certainly India and Thailand), there was no cultural permission for males to be openly affectionate. I've long suspected that is one of the reasons for so much violence among men in this culture, which is often glorified in sports and films.

I have always ached to see men openly showing affection and care with one another, as they do in some cultures. This ache inspired the workshops I began to offer 25 years later. I am now deeply gratified to see the beginnings of public displays of affection between men in North America, though we still are a long way from other cultures' comfort with men showing love in public.

Flickr: CarbonNYC

My complex, confusing connection with The Feminine

My all-male Catholic high school created an odd period of disconnecting from girls, young women, and from my inner Feminine. Before puberty, I had felt more comfortable with girls and women than with boys and men. I easily got along with the girls in grade school and in the neighborhood and even did a little innocent "playing doctor" with a neighborhood girl I was especially fond of.

The adolescent stirrings of sexual energy in myself and my peers created a sudden shift. Girls' budding eroticism and their erotic attraction to me felt scary. I was attracted to other males in ways that felt compelling. There were mysteries about men I yearned to explore, while I wanted to run from girls'

romantic interest.

The messages about how to be with "the opposite sex" were intensely confusing. The social messages were that guys were supposed to "score" with girls by "getting laid". Yet the Church taught abstinence from sex before marriage. Girls were to be "respected" and treated like the Virgin Mary. I had discovered how easy it was to have quick, functional sex with guys: getting off with them is so uncomplicated. Relating with girls my age was impossibly convoluted. Being in my all-male school made avoiding girls easy and made developing healthy friendships with them very difficult.

Yet there were dances, and I liked to dance. The girls were imported from their own same-gender Catholic schools. Somehow we were expected to negotiate learning to relate intimately on the dance floor. The dances happened in our school cafeteria, which was decorated with a few balloons to add a festive air. Pop tunes played. Clumps of boys stood nervously on one end making small talk and commenting on how the various girls looked. The girls appeared even more awkward as they giggled in clumps on the other end. There was an awkward sexual tension among all of us.

Of course it was expected the boys would initiate a dance by approaching a girl, who almost never refused. It was torture. I tended to choose girls who looked shy, like me: not the ones who looked sexually confident. I covered my shy vulnerability in a facade of pseudo-sophisticated confidence.

We were taught to "leave room for the Holy Ghost" between us: no bumps and grinds. Whew! As each song ended, we boys usually escorted our dance partners back to where we had found them. There was no easy way to hang out and get acquainted: our segregation was so solid that none of us seemed to know what to do with the "opposite sex".

With the third year prom coming up I felt the pressure to find a date, yet lacked the courage to ask any of the girls who attended the dances. I worried aloud to my Mom, who spoke with another neighborhood mom who had a daughter about my age whom I'd never met. The 2 moms arranged our date. My Mom even ordered a corsage of cymbidium orchids! It was an awkward evening for both of us.

The following year when it came time for the fourth year prom, I screwed up the courage to ask one of the girls to be my date. I was expected to be suave and debonair, while she was expected to be shy and demure. Oy! Somehow, we made it through that awkward evening. . Graduation was a few weeks later, and we never saw each other again.

Looking back I can see we were all in the same conundrum. The segregation by gender was damaging in several ways. It institutionalized the binary orientation of those times: one was either female or male and assigned to the appropriate school; there was no in-between. This was the early 1960s when gender-roles were still very rigidly defined and culturally enforced. It made casual friendships between the genders much more logistically complex. There was no easy way to just hang out together and get acquainted. It was necessary to reach out across that huge divide and arrange "dates" with all the inherent charge dating entailed. For me, it made adolescent young women seem like exotic, mysterious creatures: very much "other." It felt way too complex to try to explore their mysteries, when men's mysteries were more compelling and more readily accessible.

Happily I did have opportunities to develop some casual friendships with young women my age during my frequent summer visits with aunt Marion in her summer cottage. Everyone there was in vacation mode. There were a few young people my age I hung out with. It felt way more relaxed: we weren't "dating" but simply being buddies frolicking in summer fun.

There was one family I felt especially drawn to with 2 sisters and a brother, who lived in rural upstate New York and spent their summer in a cottage near my aunt. They were simple, earthy folks I found easy to be with. The girls were not coming on to me. They were just happy to hang out. Their brother, Butch, was my idea of a "dream boat." He was always in a bathing suit revealing his naturally muscular, sun-tanned, farm boy body: a gorgeous hunk with an open heart and friendly manner. I so wished he wasn't straight. I had to content myself with admiring his inner and outer beauty without allowing my intense attraction to show. There was a wholesomeness to our mixed-gender friendships that made the rigid gender segregation in Catholic school seem even more oppressive.

As I reflect and write about summer friendships, I realize I was not avoiding girls at all. I liked girls. It was the weird segregation that made healthy intergender friendship almost impossible at school.

I intuitively knew there was something very wrong with that arrangement. There was so much time, energy, and money put into training our young minds on mostly abstract subjects of the intellect, while no attention was paid to even rudimentary communication skills, either verbal or tactile. We were kept apart except at dances, then thrown into the deep end of the pool and left to thrash around as best we could. To have had meaningful, authentic relationships with "the opposite sex" would have required guidance and instruction that was woefully missing.

I see that my mixed feelings about girls back then was coming from the awareness of that lack. I had also witnessed in my own family how paltry the quality of communication was across genders. I did not want to replicate that, so I took the seemingly easy route of having superficial sex with guys. In the process I cut myself off from half of humanity and from a huge part of my soul.

On another level, I now realize I had deeply internalized the misogynistic messages I had been steeped in my whole life. All media portrayed girls and women as subservient to men: females were seen as weak and docile; they needed to be "protected." In exchange for our manly protection, their job was to serve us by doing the menial domestic chores of cooking and cleaning and raising the kids.

Having been seen as a sissy boy by the rough-hewn boys in the neighborhood, as weaker and less athletic than my peers, I came to believe my soft gentleness was inferior. I did my best to appear strong and "masculine." I disowned my vulnerability, my Inner Feminine. In fact, I was distancing myself from The Feminine in general, especially in "effeminate men," who were almost universally reviled in those years.

Years later, in therapy, I identified another ingredient in my ambivalence about women. Having been accidentally conceived just before my dad went back to Europe and the war, I sensed (maybe even in utero and certainly soon after birth) that Mom was emotionally dependent on me in a way that I found smothering. I of course needed her love, yet it was unhealthy for me that she seemed to so much need my love. I became her "surrogate spouse." I've since heard from many straight men that the fear of being engulfed or smothered by The Feminine is almost universal among males.

Because of that incestuous emotional bond with Mom during my first 18 months, I felt deeply hurt and betrayed when Pop came home: that he took her away from me. I suspect that made me mistrustful of all females. Another betrayal of trust occurred when I was around 8. Being a lonely only child with no close friends, my Teddy was my constant boyhood companion: my playmate and confidant. I distinctly remember telling him about all my troubles. There was no one else I could confide in. He was a very patient listener. One day when I came home from school I could not find Teddy. In dismay I asked Mom. She nonchalantly said, "Oh he was getting so ratty I threw him out." I felt stabbed in the heart. So twice this woman I so depended on for emotional support betrayed me. I remember telling myself, "The only one I can rely on is me." I know that feeling has shaped my entire relationship life.

Still, I always felt way closer to Mom than to Pop. When they would come home from work I would always hang out with Mom in the kitchen. I was not drawn to hang out with Pop as he read the paper or watched TV. I heard comments among aunts and uncles about me being "a momma's boy," which sounded derogatory, and was also true.

They say mothers always know if their son is gay. Back in those days gay life was invisible and unmentionable. Still, once in a while Mom let me know she *liked* men who were "that way." **Liberace**[1] was a regular on TV back then: an uber-flamboyant queen if ever there was one. She never failed to comment "I *like* him!" Also, curiously, more than once she told me "No girl will ever be good enough for you." Hmmm...

---

1. **https://youtu.be/lIqZIKLLvBE?t=33**

Aunt Marion and I were great pals... kindred spirits, despite being 50 years apart in age. By my late teens, she and I spent many happy hours sitting in rocking chairs on the porch watching the river slowly flow by. While we both smoked cigarettes, she regaled me with tales of our family. She was the youngest of 11 siblings, and my father's father (Thomas, of course) was the oldest. So she had lots of stories. Looking back, I realize what drew me to her was her gender fluidity. Her daily outfit was a white tee-shirt and blue denim coveralls. When she went into town, she would nod to convention by putting on a dress, albeit a plain one. Her outfit always included a baseball cap: unheard of for women back then, as was her boyish haircut. She was quite comfortable doing manly chores. She wasn't "butch" in the sense of being overly masculine; she had a wonderful balance of genders. I was not conscious of this at the time. She was the only female I had known who was not subservient to men: she was quite capable. I doubt she was actively lesbian, and I also doubt she was actively hetero. She and uncle Tom (yes: another Tom!) had no children, and seemed utterly asexual. I now know many people of their generation had marriages-of-convenience in order to keep up appearances. She was born in the 1890s. Had she been born when I was, and come of age when feminism or gay lib were blossoming, she may well have been actively queer like me. As it was, we were unspoken queer allies.

It was during those idyllic summers that I began a life-long love of Canada. The international border runs down the middle of the Saint Lawrence River, which is about 7 miles (11km) wide there. About half of the nearly 1800 islands are on the Canadian side. In my teens, I loved to explore the Canadian side, which was way less populated with summer tourists. The Ontario town of Gananoque totally charmed me. The detached houses were quaint, with lovely gardens. It had a real bakery where I could buy bread still warm from the oven; what a contrast from the plastic-wrapped Wonder Bread I was used to back in Brooklyn. They also made a sweet treat called Butter Tarts which delighted me. I'd buy a box full to bring back to the cottage. Many islands were completely uninhabited, which amazed me. It was so different from teeming New York. I loved the spaciousness. I found one uninhabited island especially attractive. Princess Charlotte Island was small: maybe 2 acres. It had a cove protected from the wind which made an easy harbor. There were rocky cliffs of varying heights perfect for diving into crystal clear water[15]. I would hang out there alone and with friends, sometimes building a fire to roast hot dogs and marshmallows. When there alone, I would sometimes masturbate and cum into the river, delighting in being able to connect sexually with nature. I fantasized someday owning the island and building a home there. I loved the idea of living in such isolation and solitude, which is a telling commentary on how I viewed the world.

To sum up, my connection with girls and women was complex and confusing. All I knew for certain is that I did not want to have a conventional heterosexual relationship with them. *What I did want was still quite unclear.*

Back then, genders were completely binary. Only a few people, like Liberace, were brave enough to exhibit gender nonconformity. Most of those who did were shamed or attacked for not fitting this culture's strict binary expectations. I am thrilled that in the last decade, gender fluidity is refusing to be suppressed. How amazing that so many teens are declining to squeeze themselves into an ill-fitting binary box and are insisting on the freedom to be whatever gender(s) they wish.

I now view both gender expression and sexual orientation along spectrums. (See Appendix). I am delighted to see young people leading the way toward the freedom to flow back and forth along both the gender and sexual orientation spectrums.

I wonder what choices I would have made if gender-fluidity was an option when I was young. Decades later, at faerie gatherings, where playing dress-up is the norm, and the feminine is celebrated, I had fun exploring skirts and other flowing things, though I never was drawn to anything very frilly. For me it always felt like a costume, whereas for many it was a liberating expression of their true selves. In the end, I've been quite happy being a cis-guy who prefers guy drag.

Looking back on my obsession with seeing and touching men's bodies and genitals, and my gentle, somewhat feminine spirit, I've sometimes wondered if this is my first incarnation in a male body. Maybe in this lifetime I'm figuring out how to be male. Maybe I was previously a repressed female: attracted to men and unable to fulfill that curiosity and intrigue about them. In this life I've been able to satisfy that deep curiosity. Being in a male body has given me access to men's-only spaces: toilets, locker rooms, and showers, as well as an entry into a different kind of relating than I would have had in a female body. At times I almost felt like an imposter, at least at first. That gradually changed. What *are* men? What are male sex and male love? In some ways I'm more comfortable among women, yet I have hungered for men's bodies and for man-to-man love, which has the potential to be more balanced than the inequality that too often exists between men and women.

Chapter 3 - Graduating from Guilt
(1962-66)

Completing high school and going to university was a wonderful rite of passage for me. It was the end of feeling overly controlled by my too-devoted parents, and the beginning of feeling responsible for my own life. I felt free.

Once again, as in high school, I was in an all-male environment. In 1962, Catholic colleges were not co-ed. Having genders mixing and mingling was seen as too "tempting." Ha! Being in all-male classes was again painfully conflicting for me. My internal homophobia (still deeply feeling/believing that my same-sex attractions were evil and sick) was so entrenched I could not imagine letting my queerness be known by anyone.

One of the most positive aspects of my 4 years at Fordham College was the deep friendship I formed with a fellow student named Paul, who lived in the same dorm. Paul had a gentle strength and deep sincerity I found attractive. He clearly liked me as well. His roommate and my roommate were friends from high school, so the 4 of us often hung out and shared meals. Paul and I began going for walks and sharing more of our lives. He had a high school sweetheart and was thoroughly straight, yet not in the macho way I found so uncomfortable in so many straight men in the 60s. He had a vulnerability and authenticity I found a refreshing role model. Despite that, I was still way too ashamed of being gay to allow any hint of that. So, I was sadly not able to match his authenticity with my own, and that pained me.

When Easter was approaching he invited me to visit his family about an hour west of Boston in Acton, Massachusetts. I jumped at the chance. I felt so grown-up taking the train to Boston, then a commuter rail to Acton. I loved his family immediately. His parents were way more modern and wholesome than my own. They lived in what is now called a "mid-century modern" home in the burbs: all glass and wood on 4 split-levels. They were the embodiment of my ideal family. I wanted them to adopt me. He had three younger sisters. Was I being manipulative in flirting with them? They appeared to enjoy it. Being around girls had become a rarity in my life. My primary school (grade 1-8) was co-ed and I had always enjoyed the company of the girls until puberty began to raise the awkward specter of dating. All through my all-male high school, even though I went to the dances and danced with girls, I could not feel any erotic interest at all. Suddenly, with Paul's sisters, there was the possibility of friendship not fraught with all that awkwardness.

When it came time a couple of years later to find a girl to invite to the Third and Fourth Year Proms, it was just so easy to invite Paul's oldest sister Andrea, who was 2 years younger than us. We were already friends. In between those two dances we began staying in touch by letters. It was sweet to have a girl *friend* who showed no urgency to become lovers. We were, after all, good Catholics, who eschewed sex until marriage, so the topic never even, uh, arose. We were more like pen-pals who got together once or twice a year. I was aware she was giving me cover to pretend to be straight. I suspect I also met a need of hers, as she was too socially awkward to be dating. She was more of a nerdy introvert for whom dating men would be messy.

During my 4th year in high school, when I told my Christian Brothers I was considering Fordham University, a Jesuit school, I was sternly warned "You'll lose your faith." Jesuits are known for intellectual rigor and thinking for oneself. Happily, the Brothers were right. In that environment, at 19, I could look my inner conflict in the eye. My deep spiritual life within the Church was 100% incompatible with my 100% homosexuality and lust. I had tried all through high school to tame my desires for men and had utterly failed. The tension between the two was untenable. By the start of my second year, I left the Church behind. I abandoned going to Mass and taking Communion. It felt right, yet also like a big loss. I was a spiritual orphan with nowhere to find spiritual succor. Yet I never looked back. I trusted I would find my way.

I began cruising with new-found unbridled enthusiasm. It was fall, 1963, and gay life was still way underground. I vaguely knew of Greenwich village, but I was too shy and too busy with a very intense Physics major to spend late nights exploring that world. Besides, I lived in the dorm that fall, and the Jesuits felt they had the responsibility of *in loco parentis*[1] to keep a close eye on their young lads. The campus gates were locked from 11 PM till 7 AM. Also, I shared a dorm with 7 other men (2 to a room), so we were well aware of one another's comings and goings.

My roommate was a brilliant student with a wonderful sense of humor. He was also exceptionally well-hung, and regularly and loudly bemoaned "I'm so hoooorny!" He was expressing the frustration of being a Catholic lad: not free even to masturbate without fear of eternal damnation. I would have loved to jerk off with him; it was totally out of the question. Still I admired his ability to even allude out loud to having sexual feelings. That was very rare on this all-male Catholic campus: a clear sign of how repressed we all were. I was too ashamed of having any sexual feelings to respond to his frequent laments with more than a wan smile. Yet inside my own horniness was raging.

My most regular cruising MO was to take the commuter train that stopped just by the front gate of the campus; it whisked me to Grand Central Station in under 30 minutes. The men's room there rarely failed to titillate. There was something so liberating and affirming about seeing all these men visibly (if furtively) aroused at the long bank of urinals. I knew I was not alone. Other guys were horny for other guys. Yet it was also intensely frustrating: there was almost no possibility of actual physical contact: we were all on guard for fear of being caught *in flagrante dilecto*[16].

One time, an older man in a business suit I'd been standing next to in this row of horny men whispered "follow me" as he zipped up. I was nervously intrigued and did follow. He was maybe in his upper 30s, which seemed so old to me then. Upstairs in the waiting room he said "I have a hotel room near here." I gulped and began walking with him, feeling incredibly

---

1. https://www.ecosia.org/

search?addon=chrome&addonversion=5.1.2&method=newtab&q=in%20loco%20parentis%20meaning

nervous. At that point, the idea of being alone in a room with a stranger felt intensely vulnerable: what would he do to me? He asked my name, and I mumbled "Frank" (my grandfather's name). He was trying to be friendly; I was petrified. After walking about a block, I made up some excuse: "Sorry, I really don't have time" and rushed away. At 19, the world of man-to-man sex was more scary than appealing. I felt so young and inexperienced. Ironically, I felt safer in public bathrooms because in that setting no one could force any unwanted advances on me.

Later that fall of 1963, I met a guy at a movie not far from campus. Julio was a Puerto Rican guy around my age. I already had a long-standing attraction to young Puerto Rican studs. I had noticed throughout my high school years of cruising bathrooms that they were mostly exceptionally well-hung with intact foreskins: such a turn-on for me. Julio was the embodiment of my fantasy. We jerked off together in the washroom and felt very turned on to each other. He gave me his number. I definitely did want to meet again, yet neither of us had a private space. I did not even have a phone number, except the phone in our 8-man dorm, which seemed too risky to share.

I did call him from a public phone a few days later. He said I could come to where he was living: a low-rent tenement walk-up he shared with his grandmother. He told her we were tutoring one another in our respective languages. Back then, Puerto Ricans were definitely an underclass. I was aware I was stepping out of my middle-class university bubble into a different world. I vividly recall sitting with Julio at a tiny gray Formica table tucked in the corner of a small kitchen, where his grandmother was preparing *arroz con pollo* for us. She spoke no English. While she prepared dinner, we pretended to be teaching each other vocabulary. Really all we wanted was to get our hands on each other's cocks. Whenever she left the room we reached under the table to feel each other's throbbing members that were fairly bursting out of our pants. There was nothing more we could do. We knew nowhere else to go. It was exciting and agonizing. We were two horny and very repressed teenage boys. Neither of us expressed any romantic impulses; it was all about the urgency of our hard cocks. I decided to risk giving him my dorm phone number, and casually lied to my dorm-mates about my Hispanic friend with whom I was learning Spanish.

We did manage to get together a couple more times under cover of darkness. The Bronx Botanical Gardens were right behind the campus and were closed at night. I discovered a hole in the fence and told Julio about it. We nervously rendezvoused there a few times, always fearful of being discovered by the security guards. If we weren't so nervous, it might have been romantic to connect erotically in that beautiful setting. As it was, we were too tense to do more than functional, goal-oriented jerking each other off. I do not recall any sort of other touch: no hugs or kisses or affection. We were in a hurry: we'd quickly come then quickly go. I remember this happening 2 or 3 times that fall. In the spring semester I moved off campus with my now-deep friend Paul, and felt I had even less privacy. Julio and I lost contact.

I knew I deeply wanted an erotic friend and lover. I wanted romance with another man like I saw in the movies between men and women. I also knew my life in a Catholic college would not allow being at all visible. I knew I'd have to wait. The newly-released film version of *West Side Story* depicted my longing: "There's a place for us...someday...somehow...somewhere!"

I have another hot memory around then. I was home with my parents in Brooklyn during the summer of 1964. I had been cruising downtown department store bathrooms with no luck. Riding the subway home there was a sexy man around my age standing across from me in the subway car. We each eyed one another up and down and fondled ourselves casually with our hands in our pockets. I was shocked when he got off at my stop. He looked back and I followed him like a puppy...an eager puppy. He was a student at Pratt Institute, famous for art and architecture. I had prowled the Pratt dorms about 8 years earlier, supposedly hawking newspapers. Actually, I was hoping to see some college men shirtless or maybe even more scantily dressed, and even hoped they'd invite me in: alas no such luck! Here finally was a Pratt man clearly hot for me. He lived only 2 blocks from my parents' home. Yikes! He walked up the steps of a classic brownstone and held the door for me to follow. Silently, he led me up another couple of flights of stairs to his room. Were we breathless from the stairs or the impending passion or both? We hurriedly fumbled to open each other's pants and began stroking each other. Then to my surprise he pulled my pants down, got down on his knees, and began eagerly sucking me. It felt astounding. Another big surprise: he gently pushed me back onto his bed, pulled my pants completely off, lifted my legs, and began licking my balls and anus. Ecstatic! The feeling of his tongue probing my butt hole was intensely pleasurable... almost too intense. It also horrified my mind, as my mother had strongly conditioned me about how disease-ridden feces are. So, even as I was writhing in pleasure, my mind was worrying about his health. This was my first taste of (at least partially) surrendering to another's passionate advances; I experienced a potent mixture of fear and delight. Needing to recover some control and return to a more familiar pattern, I stood up and resumed jacking off with him. We both quickly came. Without ever exchanging names or numbers, I hurried off, as I was already late for Mom's dinner. I wonder what I looked like (and smelled like) when I arrived home. I felt totally altered and in disarray. No one seemed to notice. We had a quiet dinner watching TV as usual, while they had their customary "tee many martoonis." We were living in very different realities.

Looking back on that stage of my life I realize that, despite longing for romance with another guy, I could not really imagine it happening. All the romantic images in movies were hetero. I unconsciously assumed romantic love was impossible between two males.

So I settled for functional sex. It was all pure objectification: living porn. I loved to get hard and cum, yet alone I found it difficult to get to orgasm. I needed a lot of stroking, often rubbing my poor penis raw. Seeing other guys hard and stroking themselves really primed my pump. Stroking each other was a huge turn-on. So that was the extent of my erotic life into my mid-20s: objectifying guys to get off.

I was still assuming my love life would be with a woman: maybe Paul's sister. She was so available. It would be easy.

FORDHAM REQUIRED MANY courses in theology and philosophy which did help me explore deeper truths about life. I began to experience "the humanities" including authors who were clearly deeply spiritual without being tied to sectarian dogma.

I was particularly inspired by *Erich Fromm's "Art of Loving,"* which offered the first truly appealing view of love I had encountered. Instead of the Hallmark/Hollywood romantic view, Fromm offered the possibility of love being a skill that can be cultivated and deliberately practiced with many different people as well as with ourselves first. What a concept. I embraced it whole-heartedly and continue to be guided by that perspective.

Reading Viktor Frankl's description of his life in the German concentration camps showed me how Fromm's perspective, that love is more of an intentional practice than fleeting emotion, could apply in even the most extreme situations. Frankl behaved lovingly toward his fellow prisoners and even the guards as a way of maintaining his own sanity in the midst of utter madness. He asserted that we humans always have *freedom of choice* about how we react to life's situations.

My longing for spiritual sustenance outside the Church led me to find Dag Hammarskjold's *"Markings,"* his deeply personal spiritual journal published after his death. The Foreword by W.H. Auden gave me a hint that Dag may have had gay leanings, although I suspect his highly public life[17] prevented him from acting on any desires he may have had toward men. I found his terse entries deeply inspiring. He was clearly struggling to have a direct, mystical relationship with God, one not mediated by any church or dogma. I read his entries as a Christian might read the Bible: one page or so before bed every night. Many of Dag's aphorisms stay with me now, almost 60 years later. He showed me that mysticism is possible in the midst of a very demanding public career.

○ *"In the point of rest at the centre of our being, we encounter a world where all things are at rest in the same way. Then a tree becomes a mystery, a cloud, a revelation, each man a cosmos of whose riches we can only catch glimpses. The life of simplicity is simple, but it opens to us a book in which we never get beyond the first syllable."*

Oddly, one of the most powerfully positive role models for me during university was the movie character, Zorba the Greek. I thoroughly identified with the uptight, middle class Englishman who befriends Zorba, a rough-hewn Greek peasant. Basil and Zorba have many mostly misadventures, during which Basil begins to envy Zorba's free spirit, which is so radically different from his own hemmed-in propriety. Gradually Basil loosens up, and by the end asks Zorba to teach him to dance the ecstatic traditional sirtaki. Basil begins to laugh hysterically as both men enthusiastically dance on the beach. *Basil is liberated.* Zorba has been guiding me ever since. *"You must dance,"* he exhorts Basil. I've taken that to heart both literally and metaphorically. (View this stirring scene on YouTube.)

My search beyond conventional western thinking led me to Kahlil Gibran and his iconic *"The Prophet"*. The ways he spoke of love were much more expansive and inclusive than the narrow, romantic, hetero love language western media was full of. He used "love" in the context of same-sex friends: *"When you part from your friend you grieve not, for that which you love most in him is clearer in his absence, as the mountain to the climber is clearer from the plain."* (Read more quotes here[2].) He greatly deepened and broadened my view of what love can mean and can be.

During my years at Fordham, the Church was undergoing revolutionary changes under Pope John XXIII and Vatican II. Even though I was no longer "a believer" or practicing the faith, I did keep abreast of the liturgical changes, especially the Mass being offered in "the vernacular," i.e. the local spoken language, with the priest actually facing the congregation. A wonderful part of that was the greater freedom of music, especially "folk Masses." It was at one of those that a new song deeply touched my heart. It went beyond all the guilt and shame I had associated with God and the Church. The simple words were, *"God Is Love, and those who abide in Love abide in God, and God in them."* Wow! My entire being cried a resounding YES! Finally I found a religious teaching that I could fully embrace.

---

2. https://www.google.com/

search?q=kahlil+gibran+quotes&rlz=1CATQED_enUS1004US1004&sxsrf=ALiCzsZyvsU0S33CgX

_2BzTfw-EZchY2UA:1667610838096&source=lnms&tbm=isch&sa=X&ved=2ahUKEwiQhYO97p

X7AhUHAjQIHVJuBYwQ_AUoAXoECAEQAw&biw=1396&bih=658&dpr=1.38

WHEN I BEGAN FORDHAM in September, 1962, I had just turned 18, which was a rite of passage for American males back then: the dreaded Draft... an anachronistic holdover from WWII. 1962 was even before there was a lottery, so anyone who had 2 arms, 2 legs, and a penis was required to serve. My family held military service in very high esteem. My dad had been an ordnance officer during the Battle of the Bulge in WWII. It was a foregone conclusion I'd be in the military.

Had I not gone to university right out of high school, I would have been drafted at 18. University qualified me for a 4-year deferment, and then I'd go into the Army as cannon fodder. Compared with those options, ROTC (Reserve Officer Training Corps) seemed a much better choice, and the Air Force looked way more appealing than the Army: it had more cachet and nicer blue uniforms. By signing up for ROTC at Fordham I avoided the Draft and would serve as an officer.

All the drills and ceremonies seemed silly, and the course in "Military Science" was surreal. I recall being appalled by the writing of Carl von Clausewitz, who had many aphorisms, of which the most famous is "War is the continuation of policy with other means." This struck me as dryly abstract: utterly disconnected from the horrors of war.

Yet there was the dark undertone of real war looming. Tensions with Russia were increasing: e.g. the Cuban missile crisis in 1963. The situation in Vietnam was looking increasingly worrisome.

In my heart I had an utter abhorrence of war. I do not know where that comes from. I know I was conceived accidentally: my father was already in the war in Europe, but was allowed to come home briefly for his own father's funeral. He returned to the war, leaving my mother to discover she was carrying an unplanned child. She of course had no idea whether she would ever see her husband again. I suspect she was intensely anxious all during my gestation and after my birth in August of 1944. The war would rage on for almost another year; she and I would not see my dad till early 1946.

Growing up I heard war glorified on TV and in movies. I was always horrified at the violence between men. In early 1961, while still in high school, I'd been impressed by President Eisenhower's warning about the rising power of the "military-industrial complex." Ike had been the Supreme Allied Commander during WW2, yet even such a pro-military man could see a growing danger in war becoming Big Business.

So now I found myself wearing a military uniform while reading and hearing about all the protests growing about America's involvement in Vietnam. I struggled with my own conscience. I could not imagine killing anyone or treating anyone as an "enemy."

I knew some people were able to avoid the draft on the grounds of being "Conscientious Objectors," but that required being an active part of a religious sect like the Quakers who had a long history of resistance to war. Catholics decidedly did not qualify.

There were two other ways I might have avoided military service:

1. by declaring to the Draft Board that I was gay: that was unthinkable because I would have deeply hurt and confused my parents, and been ostracized by much of society;
2. by fleeing to Canada. Ironically I did not even know about this option back then. Even if I had known, I would not have chosen to hurt and disappoint my parents in that shameful way. It would have been viewed as cowardice and disloyalty.

The war was quite controversial on the Fordham campus with anti-war protests being inspired by two Jesuits, Philip and Daniel Berrigan, who were quite active in the growing anti-war movement. Most of my fellow students did not appear to feel any moral objections to the military, but were in the same draft risk as I. I did not sense any who shared my repugnance about war.

At the beginning of 3rd year (Sep '64), we in ROTC were required to enter the "Advance Corps" by signing a legally binding contract that we would serve at least 4 years immediately after graduating (plus an additional year for flight training).

I recall writing in my journal (a new practice emulating Dag Hammarskjold) a heartfelt if somewhat melodramatic declaration: *"This is your baptism by fire. You must taste your antithesis."*

The die was cast for my next 7 years: 2 years of "Advanced ROTC" then 5 years of active duty. I wondered what adventures - and possibly horrors - awaited me.

Chapter 4 - Trying to Fly in the Closet

During the first 2 years of ROTC, they gave us all a battery of physical and mental tests and told me I qualified for pilot training. Unlike others, being a pilot had never crossed my mind. Still, it had a certain romantic appeal. The carrot they dangled was "free" lessons at a nearby civilian airport (Teterboro, New Jersey) during 4th year. Full of excitement and dread, I drove to Teterboro one fall afternoon in 1965 and met my instructor. He congenially greeted me and escorted me to a single-engine Piper 140 and had me take the left (pilot's) seat. Soon he had me taxiing, and then we were on the runway. He confidently guided me to steer with my feet while advancing the throttle. Suddenly we were airborne. Yikes! I was both thrilled and terrified. It felt utterly different than being a passenger in a commercial airliner: there was nothing but us in this tiny, flimsy machine with the earth rapidly dropping away underneath us. He pointed toward Manhattan looming large just across the Hudson: "Head there." "Really?" I obeyed. I thought back to how scary it had been to be at the top of the Empire State Building a few years earlier. Now we were making a lazy circle around it, but 3 times higher. It was dizzying, intoxicating. I don't remember much as we headed back, and he easily landed. With wobbly legs I climbed out and shook his hand. We made plans for Lesson 2. I was hooked.

Thus began my 14 year career with flying: 6 years in the Air Force and another 8 years as a free-lance pilot in the Bay area. Mostly I worked as an instructor in similar small aircraft, as well as brief stints as a commuter pilot flying the Piper Navajo out of SFO, and a traffic reporter on KCBS radio.

Piper Navajo: twin 10-passenger commuter

My greatest growth during those 5 Air Force years was realizing that I was not a sissy-boy after all, and ironically, I came to fully embrace being gay.

Going through the rigors of Air Force pilot training was an intense year in the sometimes scorching desert heat near Phoenix. Statistically we knew ahead of time that only about two-thirds of us would succeed in earning our wings. The others sadly would "wash out." I was determined to make it.

It was very demanding both physically and mentally. We had academic classes to learn aeronautics, aircraft systems, and meteorology, and were grilled and tested intensively.

We also had lots of physical conditioning: jogging and calisthenics to be stronger and more fit. I was way out of shape when we started, and found exercising in the desert heat very daunting. We also needed to be prepared to "bail out" in a serious emergency. So we trained in "parachute landing falls" by jumping off progressively higher platforms into a sawdust pit. We began off a low platform and worked our way up to about 10 feet. It was exhausting to keep jumping and rolling in the prescribed way to let the whole body absorb the impact of the fall.

The actual flight training was both grueling and thrilling. Every flight begins with a very careful "pre-flight inspection" which is a sacred ritual for every pilot: walking around the aircraft making sure it appears airworthy. Doing that in the desert sun and heat (40-50C or 104-122F) wearing a full flight suit was literally draining. By the time I'd climb into the cockpit I'd be soaked with sweat. Once airborne, the air conditioning would pump out refreshing cool air but also cause a chill in those wet clothes.

Of course we initially flew with an instructor, who was both teacher and evaluator. We knew at any point we could fail to live up to the standards and be washed out. So there was perpetual performance anxiety among all of us.

We worked our way up from a single-engine prop Cessna for 6 weeks to a twin engine jet, the T-37, training for 4 months, then finally to the incredibly sleek and sexy supersonic twin engine trainer, the T-38.

I started pilot training feeling inadequate and intimidated, then gradually began to see that my skills were on a par with all of my manly straight classmates. I also came to really love flying. There is an indescribable exhilaration to taking off solo, which is well described in a famous poem:

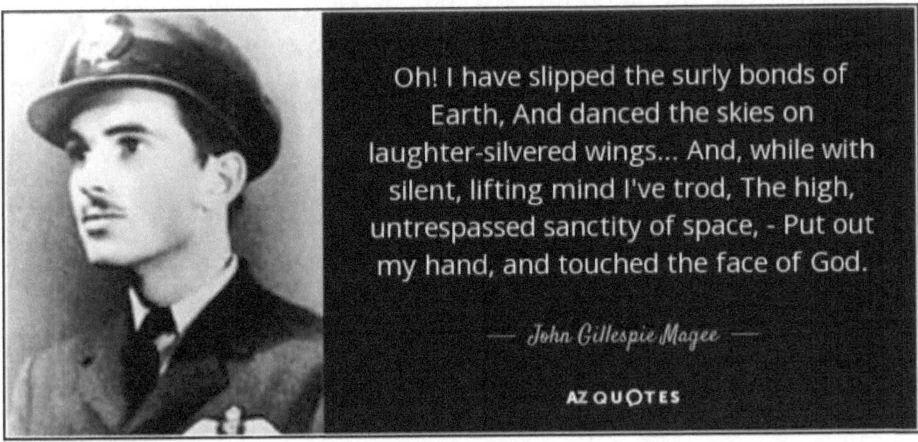

Something magical occurred once I transitioned into the T-38s. During the first 6 months I felt I was climbing into a machine and learning to manipulate it: to direct it to go where I wanted. Suddenly I had a new feeling: as though I was strapping the aircraft *onto ME* and *I was flying* with its assistance. It was a palpable difference: *I was flying!* I was now at ease in the air. I had found *my* wings.

Near the end of training, we learned 4-ship formation aerobatics in the supersonic T38s, which required great finesse and team coordination on the part of the lead pilot: if his movements are at all abrupt it is very difficult for his wingmen to follow him. I regularly received sincere compliments from my classmates for how smoothly I led and how clearly I communicated. Their obvious respect for me eradicated all my early years of shame about being deficient in masculinity. Inwardly I knew my sissy sensitivity was my secret weapon in this arena.

Those were the loneliest years of my life

In New York, it had been quite easy to find other men for at least a quick, anonymous wank in men's rooms. Now I was at an air base 25 miles from Phoenix, where the cruising scene required learning new rules. The only public toilets were in the Greyhound bus depot and a couple of movie theaters. It was slim pickings. Phoenix is very much a car-city. Most streets are 3-lanes wide. Downtown empties out after the workday ends, leaving the otherwise deserted streets to single men circling around, and around and around the same few blocks in the downtown core. I surmised it was like street cruising except with a car. If two men were attracted they'd pull off onto a side street. One would join the other to make a plan for where to go and what to do. A frequent unsubtle opener was, "What are you into?" I found this unnerving: not as anonymous as I was used to. Once I got hustled by a guy my own age. "No thanks", I said, "no hard feelings." Some of my discomfort was that my license plate could identify me, and the sticker on my windshield marked me as an Air Force member. I did find one porn theater better suited to my usual MO. Things were not as overt there as at my sleazy Duffield in Brooklyn: no sex in the aisles. It was straight porn and presumably mostly straight guys there for a solo wank. But the washroom was sometimes "fruitful." I met a sweet guy my age (23) there one winter afternoon. He offered to drive us up to park on South Mountain to make out. It was beautiful to look down on the twinkling lights of the sprawling city from this perch. I vividly remember us getting the windows all steamy listening to The Doors' throbbing lyrics, "Come on, baby, light my fire!" It was my first and only taste of an American teenage rite of passage: car sex. See YouTube for a hot video.

Before then, I hid being gay for fear of being shamed and/or ostracized. In the military the stakes were much higher. I held a Top Secret Security Clearance, so I feared my activities may be scrutinized for any signs of being a security risk. We gays were viewed as an easy target for blackmail. Any whiff of suspicion might have resulted in a humiliating Dishonorable Discharge.

So I was both super-lonely and super-paranoid. I would drive great distances away from base to look for some fleeting connections: usually the same quickies in public toilets and the back of movie theaters, where I had learned in high school to look for other lonely men. These exchanges were mostly furtive and functional: all of us were in deep shame.

On base, I was super-guarded. Still, all these men did need to shower, and that did afford at least a quick peek at other men in their full naked glory. In those situations, guys of all persuasions almost always sneak furtive glances at one another's endowments. It's not a sign of attraction so much as curiosity: measuring ourselves up, as it were. From my high school years cruising toilets and public showers I had honed the skill of looking out the sides of my eyes while appearing to look straight ahead. This skill was especially needed in these supposedly straight showers. Once in a while, usually at a gym, there would be a hint of deliberate homo-erotic energy. Guys would soap themselves up enough to be a bit fluffed...all quite nonchalantly, of course. If only two were present, that body language could become a dialog: each gradually showing a hint of higher arousal while pretending not to notice the other's equally growing enthusiasm. Only once or twice I experienced sharing full on masturbation (of course at a safe distance and without eye contact.). Sometimes on the way out while drying off there would be a wry smile or brief nod of acknowledgement.

Electrifying Love

I longed for deeper, more meaningful connections, and was at a loss. Yet my intention was strong, and gradually I began some semblance of dating. My first heart-opening experience came quite unexpectedly in the depth of winter near the Arctic Circle. I was on a Temporary Duty 2-week assignment at the base near Fairbanks, Alaska. It was February, 1969. The first week the daily *high* was minus 35F (-37.2C) and the nightly low minus 55F (-48C)...astoundingly cold. My exhalations condensed into frost on my face; inhalations caused my nostrils to almost stick together. Our nightly missions (it was almost always dark) were to circle at high altitude for up to 8 hours intercepting "intelligence" from Russia. Up in front all we pilots did was drive around in circles: not very exciting... except we were often flying *inside* the Aurora Borealis, which was indescribably beautiful and electrifying (literally hair-raising: we often experienced Saint Elmo's fire dancing on our windscreen and all the hair on my body stood on end). This image comes close to what I remember, except at 35,000 feet we were inside and surrounded those amazing, waving curtails of light.

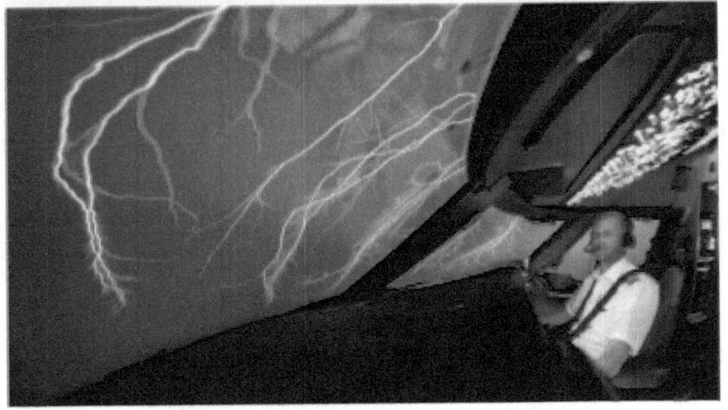

BACK DOWN ON EARTH after such an astounding experience, the base seemed hopelessly boring. I took the base bus into Fairbanks to look for... what?... some sort of human contact. "Downtown" consisted of a few blocks of tired shops and was utterly deserted. What sane person would be out in such frigid weather? So I resorted to my old standby: the movies. I have no recollection of what the show was, but the small theater was packed (obviously the most exciting thing in town.) I strode up and down the aisle looking for a likely seat, and spied one in the last row next to a nice looking lad. I was much more interested in him than the film. I felt sparks between us like Saint Elmo; was it just my imagination? My heart raced. I nonchalantly and ever so gently let my knee rest against his. He didn't pull away. Did he notice? Then his knee pressed into mine so subtly I feared it was my imagination. I got more daring and put my hands on my knees in such a way that my pinky now touched his knee...surges of electricity. After excruciatingly long seconds passed, he did the same. Our pinkies touched. I was trying to not breathe too hard lest I alert those next to us about the ecstatic surges of energy I was feeling. I don't recall how long we lingered in this loving and hidden pinky *pas de deux*. I could stand the tension no longer and got up to go to the toilet. I hoped he would follow me and we'd have the usual quick, functional exchange. I waited...and waited. He did not arrive. Bereft I walked out and found him shyly smiling in the lobby. "Hi, I'm Jim." My heart was so in my throat I could barely stammer, "Tom" offering my hand. My memory (going back 50+ years) is short on details. I know I felt instantly comfortable and safe. I vaguely recall a late-night greasy spoon, and talking for hours over cigarettes and bad coffee. "Would you like to come home with me? I think my roommates are out." Sure! This was a first: we'd exchanged our real names and I was going home with him. I'd always been terrified of either getting caught or put into some sexually compromising situation. Suddenly with this younger man (I was 24 and he was 22 and a student at the University of Alaska) I felt utter trust and safety. The night is a blur of exquisitely tender passion. My heart burst open; I sensed his did as well. Alas, like Cinderella, the witching hour arrived and I had to return to my base and my job. Riding the Air Force bus the 40 minutes back to the base was surreal. Alone in back, I wept not knowing why...only that my heart and soul had been seen and met and touched in ways I had never even dared to imagine. ***My life would never be the same.***

Jim gave me his number, and we agreed to meet again. I concocted a story to tell my crew. Four of us, pilot, co-pilot (me), navigator, and boom-operator flew as a team. We had flown up from our regular base in northern Maine and were normally always together in the barracks and for meals. So I needed to explain my eagerness to spend more time in town. They readily bought my story that I'd met a girl I had the hots for. They cheered me on. I was able to get away again a couple of days later, which was near the end of our two-week sojourn there. Jim and I knew our second meeting would be our last for the foreseeable future. We lived 4,000 miles apart at a time when phone calls to Alaska were $2.50/minute (roughly $25/min in today's dollars) and letters took forever. We wanted to spend the whole night together, but he did not have privacy at home. We met for a meal and got better acquainted, then decided to rent a motel room. Worried that the desk clerk would spot us as two homos and turn us away, Jim made up a story that "the heater in our cabin was busted" and we needed emergency quarters for the night. No problem! We had a night to ourselves and the whole next morning: how luxurious! All I clearly remember is 2 dams bursting... breaking down life-long barriers of intense loneliness (maybe for him, too) with touch and talk and stillness and wreaths of cigarette smoke. We were both heavy smokers, and the fire of our love seemed to require lots of smoke as well. Love it was: a mysterious meeting of kindred souls. Or was it "merely" that intense loneliness finally, fleetingly, being abated? It was nourishing and intoxicating to be together, and also unimaginable how so soon we'd have to part for who knows how long? We spoke bravely of writing and staying in touch. We treasured each second, each touch and kiss and word. Over breakfast at another greasy spoon (did Fairbanks offer anything else?) there was a palpable pain of anticipating parting. We were both bereft. In public we dared not show any affection. I think we shook hands as I headed to the blue base bus. This time I was too sad to cry. I stifled a scream that was both a yelp of joy and wail of anguish all at once.

Back at the base my crew was sympathetic and eager for stories, which I kept to myself. The next day we pre-flighted the plane in frigid cold. Actually it had "warmed up" to minus 20F (-29C.) which felt almost balmy. Fortunately, it was not my turn to do the flying. All I had to do was handle the radios, landing gear, and flaps on takeoff. It was a good thing: tears streamed down my face, which I tried to hide. I was returning to the lonely life on an isolated base at the very northern tip of Maine, almost in Quebec, where there was not a soul with whom I could confide this life-changing, heart-exploding experience.

I soon sent Jim a letter then eagerly awaiting a reply, which took maybe a month. It was so good to hear from him and so hard to hear he'd gone into a deep depression after I left. I quickly wrote back with an upbeat assurance that we'd find ways to connect... somewhere, somehow. His family lived in Colorado, and he did visit them. He only had a few more years at the U of A and I a few more of USAF: our separation would not last forever. I wanted to save his letter, the only tangible remnant of our connection. Yet I was so paranoid about it being found that I carefully cut out his name and address and then hid it under the mat in my car.

Weeks went by with no further word from him, then months. The agony of not hearing from him was made so much worse by not being able to share any of this intense ecstasy/agony with another human anywhere. I had to find the inner resources to bear this pain and uncertainty which gradually morphed into abject grief: he must have died... some calamity...or maybe even by his own hand?... or maybe lung cancer? I struggled to comprehend.

After about 6 months, suddenly a letter appeared. He was deeply apologetic, saying he'd been paralyzed by our separation and his ensuing depression. He was now eager to resume our correspondence. I eagerly replied and enthusiastically agreed... and never heard another word. What became of Jim was a painful mystery.

I know he forever changed my life... *in a very good way*. I could no longer deny it: "I AM Gay!" All those tortured years of pretending to myself that I am straight were over. I realized *I can truly **love** another man*, and that is my path. I did not know where it would lead, yet I knew the strength of my love for Jim was *my capacity to love*. I've never doubted that since: what a gift. I pray that Jim went on to find love equal to the huge heart he shared with me.

Over 50 years later, as I look back on the all-too-brief encounter with Jim, I realize he was a major healer for me. After a decade of heartless sex, Jim gently guided me into the experience of ***being whole***: my genitals, heart and soul were all one... at last. Knowing that was possible, I was never again fully satisfied with quick, functional, transactional encounters. He taught me that I am capable of so much more.

Because of Jim, my own Gay Liberation had begun. Years later I learned the Stonewall Rebellion had happened that same spring in June 1969.

MY NEWFOUND SELF-ACCEPTANCE of being gay had one big hitch. By this point in 1969, I had been in an ostensible love relationship with Andrea, my college roommate's sister, for over 4 years. We were totally platonic and very long-distance. When I "got my wings" a year earlier, she joined my parents in flying to Phoenix to pin them on. I began visiting her in Pittsburgh where she was in grad school at Duquesne University. To all appearances, we were engaged, though no words to that effect had been spoken. During one of those visits in late 1968, a few months before my life-changing encounter with Jim, we went to see Zeffirelli's Romeo & Juliet. I noticed I was salivating for all the young guys in tights and cod pieces, while feeling zero lust for the woman next to me I'd been dating for several years. "What's wrong with this picture?" I pondered, having no idea how to proceed, yet knowing the situation was untenable. A few months later when Jim rocked my world, I resolved (gulp) to end this inauthentic romance... but how and when? That summer I had a couple of weeks leave and visited my beloved great aunt's cottage in the Thousand Islands. I invited Andrea to join me. She came up on the bus. We had a few sweet days there hanging out in a relaxed way. One evening as we sat in adjoining rocking chairs on the porch, I took a deep breath and said, "Andrea, I've come to an important realization (pregnant pause) I'm realizing I'm not really a suitable husband and father for you. I'm not sure I can explain it; it's just an intuitively felt sense I need to express." She was understandably baffled and distressed. There was no way I could comfort her except to say very sincerely "I'm very sorry." We followed through with our plans for me to drive her home to Massachusetts en route to my new job at Loring AFB in northern Maine. Mostly we drove in silence. What could either of us say? Great sadness hung in the air like a very dark cloud... in stark contrast to the passing pastoral summer scenery in Vermont and New Hampshire. I dropped her off at her parents' as planned. We shared a sad good-bye hug. It was one of the hardest things I've ever done. I really did love her. I simply felt no lust for her. We both knew that, even though I was still too new at embracing my gayness to be able to voice it to her.

We had been "pen pals" for several years. So we maintained that tradition of exchanging hand-written letters, though they became fewer and farther between. I really wanted her to know I loved her, so I showed my love in my letters. In the mid-70s I was feeling secure enough in my new gay life that I was able to come out to her and her brother Paul by letter,

while sparing her the details of my erotic life. She took it somewhat gracefully, though still clearly nursing a broken heart.

A few years later, I was glad to learn she'd met a man she planned to marry. They went on to raise two daughters in Pittsburgh and had what sounds like a happy life. Her husband died young, in his 50s. Andrea continued living in their house raising their daughters, and then alone after the girls grew up and left home. The last few years, she struggled with lung cancer, which finally took her in the fall of 2022. We had maintained a thread of loving connection all those years, exchanging at least birthday and Christmas greetings. I always signed my letters "with love;" she never did.

All these decades later, having known many men who suppressed or denied their gayness and married women and fathered children only to ultimately break all their hearts by coming out gay in later life, I know it took real guts to end my inauthentic romance with Andrea before making any commitments I could not keep. Tears still come to my eyes knowing I broke her heart. Yet I also know my choice to end "us" was the most loving thing I could have done.

SO FAR I'VE ONLY DESCRIBED the first 2 of my 5 years in the Air Force. It got easier after that because I was at peace with being gay. I knew I could endure the remaining 3 years of "putting in my time," and hiding my sexuality, because I knew that eventually I'd be free to be the real me... whoever that turned out to be. I longed for a time when I could be fully a gay man... openly and proudly... free of shame and guilt.

Still, those Air Force years felt painfully inauthentic, not just in terms of my sexuality, but also my qualms about the military in general and warfare in particular. Many of my civilian peers were actively protesting the war before and during my time in Viet Nam. My sympathies were very much with them, yet I felt trapped in my commitment and unable to express my misgivings. I felt stifled and yearned to breathe free. I detested Nixon for many reasons, especially for his determination to find "peace with honor." I remember writing in my journal "Is there any honor left?"

Those 5 years helped me realize I was a man-among-men. My masculinity measured up. Younger readers may not fully appreciate how extremely binary our culture was in the 50s and 60s when I grew up. Anyone with a penis was expected and pressured to conform to the rigid stereotype portrayed in the media at the time by actors like John Wayne and Ronald Reagan: strong, tight-hipped, tight-lipped, tight-assed, tough, athletic, unemotional (except for anger), competitive. **I was none of those.** Yet I proved myself to be the equal of other men by becoming a really good pilot.

A few years earlier, struggling with the prospect of being in the military, I had the insight that "I need to taste my antithesis." I was aware of the aphorism that "in order to understand someone, we have to walk a mile in their shoes."

By the end of my 5 years living and working closely with mostly[18] straight men, I came to no longer fear them. I could begin to relate *as equals* from a place of knowing my own worthiness. I now can and do love straight men with full, mutual respect. What strikes me as ironic is that, by diving completely into the straight male world, I was finally able to appreciate my gay gifts and celebrate them.

Being an Air Force Pilot

My job in northern Maine was to co-pilot KC-135 tankers, which were kept "on alert" along with B-52 bombers, ready to launch nuclear attacks on Russia if/when the President pushed the proverbial "button." We rotated one week "on alert" and one week off. "On alert," several bomber and tanker crews lived confined to dorms at the edge of the runway, where we ate and slept and were prepared to literally run to our aircraft (which had been "cocked" so as to be ready for immediate take-off). We had to be ready to taxi within 6 minutes of hearing the horn (at any time of day or night).

DURING THOSE LONG, boring weeks on alert, while many watched TV sports and gabbed about who knows what, I took an interest in reading *Psychology Today*. In university I had been oblivious to the field of psych, and suddenly I found it fascinating. I enrolled in a remote undergrad course in Psych 101 offered through *Psychology Today* magazine.

Perusing the base library, I stumbled upon an odd science fiction novel that further informed my perspective on physical intimacy. *Stranger In A Strange Land* describes the discoveries about human culture made by an extraterrestrial visitor. The scene that most spoke to me was his sexual encounter. He was repelled by the way humans violently bang their bodies together. Where he came from, when two beings wished to become intimate they became very still in close proximity, then let the energy boundaries dissolve so they could melt into one another. They simply communed in utter stillness. Several years later, when I began to explore Tantra, I was reminded of that. It deeply resonated with my soul. Maybe I came into this life knowing that quality of intimacy.

THINGS IN VIETNAM WERE heating up. Johnson had chosen not to run for a second term in 1968 knowing how unpopular the war was. Nixon was now determined to win that war. I knew my turn would come. I pondered how I would respond if I received orders to Vietnam that involved me dropping bombs or shooting guns. As I listened to my heart I realized I'd have to refuse those orders and take the consequences: a court martial and almost certain imprisonment. My soul was unambiguous: that would be my choice.

Sure enough in the spring of 1970 I received an envelope with my written orders. Taking a very big breath, I nervously opened it: yes I was going to Vietnam; no I would not be bombing or shooting. I'd be flying reconnaissance in the venerable EC-47 (better known in civilian life as the Douglas DC3). I decided that fine line was enough to allow me to accept the

orders.

So in September, 1970, I packed my car for the long drive from northern Maine to Alexandria, LA, the home of England Air Force Base, to train in my new machine.

Thousands of these barebones aircraft had been credited with helping win WW2 as transports of troops and supplies, then were made most famous during the Berlin Airlift in 1948-49, and were the backbone of many domestic airlines in the 1930s and 40s.

Still, it felt like a come-down for me to be assigned to these relics. I saw myself as a "jet jockey," who had trained in those sleek supersonic Talons and then flown the first 4-engine commercial jet airliner, the Boeing 707, in its military tanker configuration as the KC-135. I quickly was humbled by the lack of automation in these ancient contraptions. For example, gear and flaps had to be pumped up and down hydraulically with long handles in the cockpit. The side windows actually slid open... what a concept! Cruising speed was all of about 135 knots: about a quarter of what I was used to.

Having tasted fully integrated erotic love for the first time in Alaska 18 months earlier, I was struggling to find ways to both express and hide my sexuality. My explorations needed to remain clandestine. During my month of training in Louisiana, I now knew I would not be satisfied with sexual quickies: I preferred to have some sort of real relationship, however brief it might be. Happily I met a very nice fellow... again at the movies. Tony was a bit of a southern belle, and somewhat stereotypical as a hairdresser. I found him quite easy-going (in part due to his pot use, to which he introduced me). He was not the love of my life, yet we had a sweetly cuddly connection I found quite nourishing. We both knew our time was limited. When it was time to part there were no promises of keeping it going; we both seemed to accept we were together "for a time."

Vietnam was even more lonely than Maine: there was nowhere to go. We were completely confined to the base, the perimeter of which was protected from the Viet Cong by soldiers from the Republic of Korea. I had now been promoted to Captain and the left seat: Aircraft Commander. Our missions were always the same: climb to 10,000 feet and take navigational directions for 7 hours from the radio operators in the back, who were spying on the Viet Cong, learning their location to call in air strikes. It was a pretty boring job, but remarkably safe, given we were in a war zone. The Viet Cong only had a few "big guns" capable of reaching our altitude, and we knew where they were. I felt guilty taking the extra $45/month "combat pay." (Yes, $45, or around $350 in today's currency.) We generally flew five days a week.

We flew wearing a full parachute over our "flak jacket," a survival vest equipped with a .45 caliber pistol, ammo, rations, water purifier and other gear for surviving in the jungle after "bailing out" of a crippled aircraft. I knew in my soul I would never be able to use the pistol: I would choose being killed over killing. Still, I was hesitant to leave it behind for fear someone would question its absence. Instead I left the ammo behind: my quiet way of expressing my pacifism.

The most exciting part of my job was when I was serving as an Instructor Pilot. Most of the new pilots coming over were also transitioning from much more modern aircraft. So we all needed additional practice at our base, which had a perpetual crosswind. By far the biggest challenge with this beast was maintaining directional control during crosswind landings. I discovered I had a natural gift for helping my students remain calm in a very anxiety-provoking learning situation. By some combination of skill, luck, and grace, I was the only instructor who never had a student do a ground-loop (a sudden U-turn, which can damage landing gear, or even wingtips and propellers, as well putting a big dent in the pilots' ego.) Avoiding such embarrassment earned me great respect from my colleagues, and gave my self-esteem a big boost.

Non-duty time was pretty boring. We pilots, all young officers, were housed together. Playing bridge was the most popular way to while away the long hours. I was struck by how odd it was: 4 healthy young men sitting around a small card table in very close proximity but not touching at all. The talk was also mostly inane. It felt to me like a kind of pseudo-intimacy. I wished we could be more real and authentic. At least in university we could discuss philosophy and current events. Here, there seemed an unspoken taboo against any meaningful conversation. I found several of the men attractive. Almost all had wives or girlfriends back home. I, too, offered straight credentials by referring to letters from Andrea.

I did develop one special friendship, which in contemporary jargon might be called a bromance. Don was a very sweet and gentle southern lad. He had dark hair and mustache, and soulful brown eyes. He did have a wife back home, yet seemed eager to have a special friend. We never got even remotely erotic, yet our long walks and talks were full of "sweet nothings" the way young lovers are: just being together was all we wanted. I was learning the many nuances of homo-erotic love. My new-found comfort with my gayness allowed me to love Don with no need for physicality. Our hearts were open to one another without the trappings of romance. I was sad to not be free to be authentic about my gayness with him.

Mike: High Romance Down Under

A built-in "relief-valve" that was provided to all the GIs in Vietnam was the famous "R&R" (for Rest and Recuperation). After 6 months "in country" each of us got to board a government-paid commercial jet for a week in 1 of 4 destinations: Honolulu (where all the married men rendezvoused with their wives), Hong Kong, Tokyo, or Sydney. I had a strong intuition Sidney would be my best chance of finding gay romantic/erotic sustenance. One advantage of having been a budding queer boy in the Big Apple is that my gaydar was well-honed. I quickly sussed out Sydney and surmised that the King's Cross would be its Times Square: the sleazy night-life part of town. I was right. I didn't really know how to meet a likely lad except to walk the streets, which I did... for hours. I walked by a couple of bars that seemed to be all men, but I was too nervous to go in. Actually it was partly revulsion left over from my parents' alcoholism: even the smell was (and still is) a turn-off, and the energy of people boozed up is quite repulsive.

I noticed a cute boy walking by. We both turned to notice one another, then each walked on. I circled back; so did he. Still I was unable to make contact, so we did that dance a few more times until we both laughed at its absurdity. We said Hi and continued walking together around the neighborhood making small talk. Mike was a "bar man," newly 21. I was the older man at 26. I did feel older; he was adorably boyish. Being a Sagittarius and a bar man, he definitely had the gift-of-gab: we hit it off immediately.

I invited him to my hotel, and we also hit it off in bed right away with wonderfully playful affectionate ways of connecting. We ended up spending the night curled up together... heaven. I would be in town for 5 more nights, and he was as eager to reconnect as I was. He did need to work, so I went sight-seeing on my own during the afternoons, then we'd meet for dinner and drinks each evening. Yes, drinks: he was after-all a bar man, so alcohol and smoking were a big part of his life. He knew his way around good restaurants and fine wines and especially loved cognac. So I lived on the wild side for a while with him.

Our connection was light and playful; we shared lots of warmth and humor. There was sweet tenderness between us as well, especially as the week was drawing to a close. I was able to say with confidence I'd like to write and come visit again. He liked that.

Sydney was hardly the bastion of queerdom in 1971 that it is today. Gay Lib had decidedly NOT arrived. One night after a particularly late dinner and too many cognacs, we were weaving our way arm-in-arm back to my hotel in The Cross. Quite a few individual women were standing in doorways. "Want a gurrrl?" one purred. Mike and I smiled and gestured to our interwoven arms in reply. "Ugh! Bloody poofters!" she exclaimed in utter disgust. We laughed and proudly walked on.

One of the fun things Mike and I shared was seeing the musical **Hair** in Sydney. It was truly life-changing. My military life beginning with pilot training in 1967-8 had taken me out of the popular culture. My only contact was pop tunes on my car radio. Even that was enough to tell me there was a groundswell of social change happening, but it was in far-off places like San Francisco. *Hair* gave me a concentrated look into the "sex, drugs, and rock'n'roll" many of my peers were exploring. I found the counter-culture values very appealing. These kids were rebelling in ways I had never dared. I envied their freedom. They looked like they were having fun, which seems far removed from my very dutiful military life. For the whole next decade I soaked up *Hair*. I saw the film version, bought the album and memorized all the songs by playing them so often. It was a clarion call to a freer life.

It was hard to leave and go back to the war. I was elated... in puppy love. I would not be able to hide my elation back at the base, so I turned Mike into Michelle so I could rave about what a wonderful time I had. Really all I had to do was change the name: then I could tell most of what we did. It was so freeing to finally be dating a man (even if I had to pretend he was a she for public disclosure). We actually did begin to exchange letters, which I asked him to sign just "M" so any spies would not know I had a boyfriend.

By a happy set of circumstances, Air Force policy supported us. I had been entitled to one month of "leave" per year and had not been able to take all I was owed. Regulation required they give it all to me before the end of my 5 years. What that meant was that, for the next 6 months, I was able to take 1 week of leave per month and fly "space available" for free on those same R&R flights: 4,000 miles each way to see my boyfriend. Joy!

The visits were fun at first, and certainly a welcome break from the boredom of my piloting life in Vietnam. Yes, piloting in a war zone did get boring. I am aware of how ironic that is, and how blessed and protected I was. Thinking back, I realize I romanticized Mike and tried to make him partner material, which he really was not. Our lives were totally different. Besides being 5 years older, I had a deeply philosophical university education and a sincere longing for spiritual growth. Mike was a good-hearted and fun working class barman, who did not have much vision for his life beyond that work.

So we had six visits, a total of one week each over the course of six months and wrote letters a bit in between. Each visit, the connection between us felt a bit less intense: it became routine... less and less alive.

When my Vietnam tour was ending at the end of 1971, I would complete my five-year commitment and return to civilian life to go where and do what? My future life was a blank slate. Mike and I talked bravely about staying in touch. He would not be able to come to the US because he had been arrested for cruising an undercover entrapment cop. He had a felony on his record and could not get a passport... at 21.

Once I was back in the US, I both ached for the sweet, cuddly togetherness we shared and was aware I wanted even more to stay home and not cross the Pacific yet again. Our letter writing dwindled and petered out. I grieved, not so much for Mike himself, but for the loss of a dream that we might be one another's true love. I still remember him fondly and know we were good for each other for that brief time.

Decades later I had a client who worked for the Australian Consulate. I asked him to try to locate Mike: I knew his full legal name and date of birth. There was no record. I suspect that, like so many of our generation, he did not survive the 80s AIDS massacre. My heart aches to imagine his young life ending way too soon... like way too many.

My two brief love relationships during my Air Force years began to teach me about love.

Jim touched my heart at an astoundingly deep level. He had a soulful quality that resonated with my own soul in ways that still surprise me. Glimpsing such deep love so briefly, then having it mysteriously disappear, really did break my heart open. He helped me escape from my prison of confusion about my sexual orientation and created instant self-acceptance of being gay. In addition, he gave me a sweet taste of my heart's deepest longing. Mike, on the other hand, was a fun companion for a wonderfully romantic fling. I was sad to realize he was not my equal as a life partner, as much as I wished he were.

I was becoming aware of longing for a real love relationship, but I had no idea where or how to find him. Throughout my five years in the Air Force I kept reading that Berkeley was the epicenter of free speech and free love. San Francisco was becoming the gay Mecca. The flower children celebrated the Summer of Love there in 1967. It was becoming a hippie hangout, which strongly attracted me. I had also seen the wonderful Dustin Hoffman film, *The Graduate* with music by Simon and Garfunkel, which strongly spoke to my own struggle at that point in my life. Ben, the protagonist, was almost 21 and newly graduated from university. At home with his parents, he was feeling alienated from their shallow, materialistic lives that were focused on looking and acting successful. I strongly identified with Ben's uncertainty about who he was and where his life was going: only knowing the values he was raised with were not his own. That was me, too. The film's many scenes in San Francisco and Berkeley had a magnetic pull. Clearly the Bay Area was where I needed to be to begin to find my true self.

The Middle Years - A Sexual / Spiritual Growth Spurt

Note: This phase of my life contains many details. There is a risk of getting lost in the trees and losing the view of the forest. If you'd find an overview helpful, I invite you to return to the **Introduction.**

Chapter 5 - Flying Free! (1972-1979)

———

In December 1971, on my way home from Vietnam, I stopped off for a few days in Honolulu. It was great to be back in civilian life and attire. Of course I began cruising. I met a fellow whom I found friendly, if not at all sexy. We had some good conversation. I learned Bob lived in San Francisco, and he invited me to look him up once I got there.

Finally free of the Air Force, at last I could leave behind all my sense of obligation to my family and country. I'd been living others' agendas for way too long.

I was ready to find my *real wings.*

While visiting my parents in Brooklyn, I went to see *The Boys in the Band* [19] to get a glimpse of "gay life." Having just spent 5 years in the uber-masculine environment of the military, I found the campy, bitchy behavior of the characters beyond off-putting. "Is THAT gay life? Yuck!" I did not yet know who I would be as an openly gay man, but I knew for sure I would not be like them: they all seemed deeply wounded and neurotic.

After explaining to my parents I was going to the Bay Area for flight training to become a flight instructor, I packed my car and headed west. After searching rental ads in SF, I surmised that rents were better in Berkeley. I had been charmed by its images in *The Graduate*, so I drove back east across the Bay Bridge.

I found the low-rise, low-density, almost small town feeling much more appealing than gritty SF. I rented a cozy studio in an old house near campus that had a real wood-burning fireplace...wow! Brooklyn was never like this. I delighted in the hippie vibes in the south campus, Telegraph Avenue area.

After a few weeks of flight training to qualify as an Instructor Pilot, I got a job teaching people to fly private aircraft like Pipers and Cessnas at the nearby Concord airport... the very same type of single-engine trainer I had taken off in on that fateful flight over Manhattan over six years earlier. Now it would be my turn to terrify and thrill prospective new pilots with their own version of that experience. After my year in Vietnam getting new pilots comfortable with the wild challenges of cross-wind landings in the C-47, teaching folks to land these toys was child's play. I was a natural instructor; students really liked learning with me. Yet I knew flying was not my life's work. I was ready to find what it was.

I was eager to start meeting gay men and was at a loss about how. My old technique of cruising toilets was, uh, fruitless. It did not seem to be the way gay guys were meeting in Gay Mecca. Then I remembered Bob, whom I'd met in Honolulu. He was happy to hear from me and introduce me to his circle of friends, which included an older fellow who owned a bath house in North Beach. I was intrigued and nervous about going. Just inside the entrance was a life-sized replica of Michaelangelo's iconic *David.* I appreciated that touch of class and not-subtle hint of what awaited within. I liked it immediately. Having spent many horny hours loitering in the showers and steam room at the Saint George in Brooklyn years earlier, where the cruising was furtive and rarely involved actual touch, I was happy to feel safe to look and even touch other men luxuriously soaping themselves in the shower or languidly lounging in the sauna. Men communicated their interest, or lack thereof, much more openly and directly. There were little rooms for lingering rendezvous, the length of which was by mutual consent. When either man felt complete, it was perfectly okay to simply bid farewell and either resume hunting or go home satiated, or disappointed. I really liked the sense of permission to be openly desirous. This was totally new and quite intoxicating.

I learned there were several bath houses in the city, and enjoyed exploring them all. One thing I quickly learned about myself: I was only interested in 1-on-1 play. Seeing groups of men groping was a turn-off. If I was interacting with a guy in the shower or sauna and another man intruded, I would leave. I vaguely knew I was vetting guys as prospective partners. I had to feel chemistry plus a certain soulfulness like I had experienced with Jim in Fairbanks three years earlier. That all-too-fleeting encounter became my benchmark. No one came close.

Dave, the bath house impresario, had a large circle of gay friends who were eager to share the delights of his large sailboat. How perfect: I loved getting out on the water, and this was a perfect way to meet other gay men. Dave was pushing 50, and his entourage ranged in age from a few of us 20-somethings to some much more "mature." I quickly noticed a generational divide. The older men's behavior often resembled that campy bitchiness I had recoiled from in **The Boys in the Band**. I surmised the older gays were more terribly wounded from the intense oppression they had grown up with. We who were younger were spared at least some of that. A new day had dawned, and we felt way more free than they had been. We were more able to be out and proud.

My revulsion at the "old queens'" demeanor softened a bit, though it and they still remained repulsive. I did not see any role models among the older gays. I definitely wanted to be a different kind of gay man, and my peers tacitly concurred: we rarely saw that pattern in our own gay male generation.[20]

I met my guru in a toilet.

I was also hungry for more meaning in my life. Leaving Catholicism behind at 19 left a void in my spirit: I had had a real sense of devotion to God, and for almost a decade had no way to express that.

You may recall: throughout my closeted gay life since my early teens, one of the only ways I'd found men to play with sexually was in public toilets. For many men back then, that was our secret meeting place. We had developed ways to show interest in one another without offending men who were simply there to relieve themselves.

So it was that I made my way to the Berkeley Public Library: to do different research than most patrons. There I had the great good fortune to find a hippie man with long pony-tail, bushy beard, and bright twinkly eyes. He did not have the shameful vibe that most bathroom cruisers had. He looked happy... even radiant. So I departed from my usual perfunctory exchange. After we had (euphemistically) shaken hands, I asked if he might like to go out for a coffee. In a sexy southern drawl he said he didn't actually drink coffee, but he'd be open to going for a tea. Right away I knew he was a different kind of guy than I'd ever met. Over tea I quickly learned that David was on an intensely spiritual path. He had a guru named Sant Kirpal Singh, and was a strict vegetarian who practiced yoga and meditation with great devotion. This was all very new to me. I felt strongly intrigued. He matched my eagerness to learn with an equal enthusiasm to share his experiences.

Soon thereafter, I visited his spartan, immaculately clean studio apartment on the north side of the campus. He was a live-in caretaker for an art gallery there. I was charmed by the vibe. His guru's photo was prominently displayed on a small altar with a candle and flowers.

The kindness and compassion obvious in his guru's photo was matched by David's own gentle energy. The inscription under the photo particularly resonated:

"Each embodied soul is a drop in the Ocean of Consciousness."

Those words thrilled my soul. Something inside me cried *Yes!* Yet my mind did not understand. David gave me some erudite lessons in eastern mysticism. I began to get my first glimmer that "God" is not far-off or judgmental, but is one and the same with our very own soul. What a radical

concept.

Over the course of several visits, David went on to show me some basic hatha yoga, teach me how to be vegetarian and still get enough protein, and the rudiments of meditation. I was very attracted to him on every level, and would happily have been lovers. So I was saddened that he never wanted to share erotic energy again: he had taken a vow of celibacy as part of his path. Nevertheless we became spiritual friends.

Above and beyond what David taught me overtly, it was actually his energy, his soulful presence, that was the most powerful teaching. Being around him I invariably felt uplifted in a way I had never experienced. He was loving me much more deeply than any sex I had ever had, yet we were not being sexual. I was implicitly learning a subtle kind of love: without attachment and without sex. By witnessing his devotion to his guru, and feeling the palpable blessing of his own presence, I was getting my first taste of a spiritual energy transmission. For that reason, I acknowledge David as my "first guru." On the down side, by choosing celibacy as a prerequisite on his spiritual path, he was perpetuating the sex-negative attitude I had been taught my whole life.

An inner voice said *No! Sex can be, must be, an integral part of my spiritual journey.* I yearned to learn how.

I met a spiritual brother in a gay bar.

It took over a year in the Bay Area for me to muster the courage to enter a gay bar. My alcoholic family had so turned me off to alcohol that just entering a bar was repulsive. Yet I was hungry to meet other gay men. So I began going to *The White Horse*, right on the Oakland-Berkeley line. It was (and still is) the oldest gay bar in the US. I would nurse my fruit juice (how appropriate, as I was trying to embrace being a "fruit") and hug the walls in painful shyness. The one redeeming feature (besides the fireplace, which did create a warm vibe) was the dance floor. My only experience with dances was in high school, where the boys were expected to go over and ask a girl to dance. I assumed this was the way it was done here, but no one approached me and I was too shy to approach anyone, even though some of the guys looked pretty cute.

After several lonely visits, there was one guy who stood out because he was willing to dance without a partner, and he actually looked like he was having fun. He had long, shaggy hair and a bushy beard (a major attraction after 16 years of clean-shaven Catholic school and another five in the military). Like David, he had bright eyes and even a big, bright smile. I loved watching him dance.

Finally, when he took a break from dancing, I took a big breath and went over and mumbled an opening line: "Were you in the Navy?" I have no idea where that came from. He laughed and said no, he'd avoided the military. Happily he seemed to want to keep talking, then invited me to dance. His ease and enthusiasm on the dance floor overcame my awkwardness: I began to loosen up and actually have fun. "Fun": what a concept. I was 28 and had rarely experienced anything I'd call "fun." Eric and I hit it off. I found him sexy, and hoped we could get it on. We agreed to meet a few days later, but he showed no interest in anything carnal. We talked. I was quite struck by his intelligence and keen interest in many things. Even more, I was struck by a quality I'd never experienced in my Catholic and military background: he talked about his *feelings*, his emotions, and even expressed them. Wow! When describing something sad, he actually cried. I realized I had much to learn from this younger man. He was 23 at the time: five years younger than I. We began getting together with some frequency, sometimes for meals, sometimes a walk and talk, and sometimes at the *White Horse* to delight in dancing. Our friendship had many of the elements of a romance, except touch. That saddened me.

We had met in February, 1973. Spring happened early, and Easter was approaching. Eric was Jewish, yet seemed interested in Easter. The day before, he invited me to join him on Easter Sunday morning to attend the Reverend Cecil Williams' Glide Memorial Church in the Tenderloin District in San Francisco. To my surprise and delight, he asked if he could sleep with me that night. I was excited and nervous, hoping we'd finally get it on. We were very cordial in bed, talking freely, but still not sharing touch. He fell asleep quickly; I was too excited to sleep. When dawn broke, birds began to chirp, and our eyes met in a new way. Neither of us spoke. We smiled and gazed deeply for an amazingly long time. It was way more intimate than any sex I'd ever had. My heart felt so full of love. We dressed and ate and rode BART into SF to partake in a mostly Black, very high energy service with lots of gospel singing and Cecil's evangelical preaching, which raised the roof. I was as high as a kite. Catholic Mass was never like this!

I was falling in love with Eric. I found him, like Jim in Alaska and Mike in Sydney, very attractive in body and soul, which brought up an aching yearning... for what? I longed to somehow merge with them. Yet each one was unavailable for merging, and I found this deeply painful. I was feeling a depth and breadth of love with Eric that went beyond anything I had ever known, even though it did not include being sexual. I both accepted the limitations of each of these beautiful connections, and continued to long for an integration of sex and spirit. For example, I often wished to have a partner with whom to explore being both sexual and meditative or prayerful...maybe at the same time.

I journaled (emulating Dag Hammarskjold):

The aching beauty of friendship

The deep need for fusion

The awareness of its impossibility

The recognition of the tremendous value of shared solitude:

A mirror to see the self more clearly,

A vision of expanded horizons,

An impetus to further growth.

Even though we were not in any sort of romantic involvement, my heart was aching to express my love to Eric. I bought a large poster of Picasso's beautiful bouquet, and inscribed it with the title "Flowers that Will Not Wilt," and a

quote from Dag:

"Every deed, and every relationship,

is surrounded by an atmosphere of silence.

Friendship needs no words.

It is solitude delivered from the anguish of loneliness."

Then I added,

"Yet the deep need to communicate,

once and for always, to celebrate and affirm

the moment of total and absolute sharing:

You are my friend and I love you."

Meditation: Beginning a New Way of Life.

Also that spring, in April 1973, my budding interest in meditation led me to be initiated into Transcendental Meditation. Even though meditation was mostly unheard of in the West, I had experienced some quiet contemplations at Catholic retreats with my Dad, and also had been drawn at times to sitting quietly in an empty church during my teens. So when I saw a poster for *Transcendental Meditation* I was immediately drawn. It definitely seemed exotic. After an initial group orientation, after paying the required $75, which was a lot of money back then, we were given an appointment for an individual initiation, and instructed to bring a plain white cloth and a flower. The initiation had the quality of a secret ritual. In a small room with my instructor, I was told I'd receive a secret mantra which was chosen just for me, and was admonished never to reveal it, or it would lose its effect. The instructor created a simple altar with my white cloth and flower and small photo of the Maharishi.[21] He had me sit facing the altar then whispered the mantra in my ear, and instructed me to silently repeat for several minutes, and to let go of any other thoughts that arose. Then he invited me to come out of the meditation with a deep breath. In the debriefing he asked, "Was it easy?" Yes. Then I was told to practice for 20 minutes twice a day, preferably before meals.

I loved sitting quietly for 20 minutes twice a day. My evening meditations, after a tense day teaching flying in a cramped, noisy cockpit, were amazing: "just sitting" and repeating my mantra, I felt my tense muscles unwinding, and my mind quieting down. I invariably got up refreshed. I was sold!

By then I had already logged thousands of hours of piloting time. I loved the feeling of being "above it all" in an airplane cockpit. It put our petty human concerns in perspective. Meditation had the same effect.

A few times, Eric was with me when it was time for my evening meditation. At first, he was highly skeptical, but somehow the peace I was experiencing assuaged his reservations. A couple of months later, he also was initiated. Then we often delighted in sitting together. The silent communing deepened our bond and took our loving brotherhood to a new level.

Shortly after that, in May, Eric gave me a copy of a mind-blowing book:

Be Here Now, by Baba Ram Dass.

The author conveyed his own ego-busting encounter with an Indian guru, Neem Karoli Baba, which opened his heart as it humbled his very proud PhD mind. A part of me yearned to have such a profound alteration of consciousness.

Peer-counseling Training

During our first year Eric and I took a peer-counseling training which was being offered *pro bono* by a retired psychologist named John Enright. Enright had concluded, after offering professional counseling over several decades, that most people come with minor emotional or psychological issues, and primarily need a sympathetic ear: someone who will fully hear them. So he set about teaching us lay folk the fundamentals of good listening:

- sit with an open posture facing the person speaking, e.g., arms and legs uncrossed;

- maintain eye contact with them;

● do not interrupt;

● even more important, do not react with facial expressions or sounds that express approval or disapproval. We all unconsciously seek approval, he said. If we convey that when someone is speaking, we'll subtly influence what they say, "shaping" their speaking to gain more approval. Stay neutral in face and voice.

● notice internal reactions or mentally going into one's own inner narrative, and practice "coming back" to being fully present with the speaker.

This took surprising discipline. It was like another form of meditation. I found being this fully heard was incredibly comforting. I realize how very rare that is in our culture. I've endeavored ever since to be present in that way with both friends and clients. It has enormously improved the quality of all my relationships. Sharing that skill with Eric has been one of our bonds ever since.

WHAT ABOUT DRUGS? AMONG people of my generation, my life has been surprisingly free of recreational substances. I owe that largely to my parents: they showed me that I did not want to live in an alcohol-induced numbness. I wanted to find a better way to relax and reduce stress. My Catholic schools were virtually drug-free, as was my experience among Air Force pilots. There was a fair bit of drinking in the Air Force which did not appeal in the least.

Berkeley in 1972 would have been the perfect opportunity to explore the drug scene: it was all right there. I did sample pot. Like alcohol, it made me low, not high. Magic mushrooms were somewhat interesting, but I definitely did not enjoy the coming down.

By 1973, I had read Ram Dass' realization that, after all his experiments with psilocybin and LSD and other hallucinogens, he realized they were not taking him to the deepest truths he had later found in meditation through his guru. Having been introduced by yoga and meditation that year, that path seemed much more appealing. What I love about meditation is how clear it makes my consciousness. Mental chatter subsides, leaving a clear sky of consciousness itself. Why would I want to introduce more clouds?

Quakers: Deep Silence

Eric had been attending the Quaker Meeting in North Berkeley, and asked if I'd like to go to their Sunday "Meeting for Worship". I was aware of my ancestral Quaker heritage, yet had never actually explored the only Christian sect which practices a kind of meditation. Their guiding principle in Meeting is *do not speak unless what you have to say is more powerful than silence.* Ideally they do not speak unless they are literally exploding, or "quaking." So people arrived and sat down at the appointed hour, and just sat. Nothing happened. No music. No preacher. Silence. Wow. It was like meditating, yet more powerful because there were about 50 of us sitting in silence together. After about 45 minutes, sometimes someone would stand and speak from their heart or soul about something in the spiritual realm, perhaps some insight they had. Then more silence for several minutes. Then maybe a few others would speak "from spirit."

When someone speaks from the heart, their words are few and feel very powerful. When people speak from the head or ego, they can often feel flat or even boring. The depth of wisdom expressed at Meeting was often much more profound than I'd ever heard from any pulpit. We went often.

I heard about another kind of meditation I wanted to check out. There was a Tibetan meditation center that offered Sunday dinners eaten in silence after their shared meditation practice. Eric eagerly accepted my invitation to check it out. We became regulars then Eric took a huge leap: he decided to move into their community and live like a monk. I wasn't ready for that, but cheered him on and continued going for some of the wonderful silent Sunday dinners.

That soulful connection that began in the spring of 1973 has endured now for half a century, despite Eric's having moved away from the Bay Area a few years later. That love bond led us to become chosen brothers. I had always longed for a brother. He had only one, who was straight and difficult for him to get along with. So we met an aching need in one another's lives and still do. We email and speak very regularly: at least several times a month.

Gay Pride

The first few years in Berkeley were wonderfully liberating for me in many ways. After being required during 16 years of Catholic schools and then 5 years in the Air Force to keep my hair short and my face clean-shaven, and to wear a jacket and tie, I found it incredibly freeing to let my hair and beard grow. Longer hair and facial hair were becoming permissible and even fashionable, as were open collars and casual clothes. I fancied myself a neo-hippie. One of the most liberating things was marching in Gay Pride Parades and anti-war protests on Market Street in San Francisco, wearing my Air Force flight jacket festooned with gay insignia in both events.

Opening Up to Women and Straight Men

In my hunger to discover more about new ways to live, I joined a weekend event called "**A Possible Dream**" that I'd seen posted at one of the Berkeley churches. There I met many men and women who, like me, were yearning to make big changes in their lives, either around work, or relationships, or spirituality. For the first time since dating my college roommate Paul's sister, Andrea, I met some women I could be friends with. One of them, Susan, was especially easy to talk with. For the first time in my life I found myself yearning to not hide being gay. I was so tired of hiding. **It was time to live authentically.** Still, actually saying the words, "I am gay" was SO hard! I did, and she was wonderfully supportive and accepting. I met her husband and found him quite attractive. Alas, he really was straight. I was certainly aware my whole being vibrated differently around him: an inner excitement I did not feel with Susan. With her I felt warm, not hot.

Susan introduced me to several of her women friends who readily liked me. My gayness was possibly even an asset: they knew I was not going to be coming on to them. We felt safe with one another. I was surprised after so many years of having zero female friends to suddenly have several. One of them I found especially attractive: she was quite pretty with long blond hair. Nancy had a certain poise, a kind of dignity that seemed to mirror my own. She could also be quite clear and direct. She began attending the peer counseling training with Eric and me, which deepened our friendship. She had been married and now seemed to be happily single. Nancy knew I was gay, so I felt safe proposing we share some non-sexual touch like holding hands and clothed cuddling. We both loved it. We began spending more time together and things were feeling more romantic between us in some ways. In time, we kind of developed a crush on each other, and both wanted to share some more physical and even erotic connection. I was curious to explore with her, and thought she understood there would be limits. Ever so gradually we moved beyond cuddling to kissing and even sharing masturbation with one another.

Because of our shared experience with peer counseling, and some therapy she had done after her divorce, we began actively processing one another's emotions. At first, it felt wonderful to regularly listen to her, and have her welcoming my expressing ever-deeper emotions, which was very new territory for me. Then things gradually morphed: she began expressing anger at me, with full-on affect, like getting beet-red and yelling at me. My little boy, who had felt wonderfully safe with her, was suddenly terrified. To her credit, she was able to turn off her raging and become a caring listener, inviting me to express what I was feeling, which was mostly terror and great sadness. I never felt angry at her. At first, she comforted my fearful and sad little boy. Then she got angry *that I was not getting angry.* This made me feel crazy. Yet I did gradually let myself feel and express anger to her, which was very new. I hated the feeling of being in turmoil yet persevered for a few months.

What finally made me throw in the towel was learning that she had a hidden

agenda for where it might lead. She was gradually getting the hots for me. Then suddenly, in a burst of furious anger she revealed she had been secretly hoping I would turn into a sexual animal like her former husband, who used to literally chase her around the bedroom and force sex on her (which she clearly loved.) I was horrified she expected that from me. I was also deeply hurt.

Again, to her credit, Nancy wanted to process all that with me. We tried for a while, but

I totally shut down. I no longer felt safe. It had begun to seem as though we had created an endless anger machine. If that was her idea of an intimate relationship, perpetual intense emotional processing, I wanted no part of it. Having practiced meditation for a couple of years by then, I wrote in my farewell that our relationship had begun to drain me of energy, that our anger sessions devastated me, and that the regular recurrence of anger was a sign to me of some fundamental incompatibility. "I'd rather not be in a relationship than be in such an anger factory. I seek a life of quietness and simplicity, and value close relationships that enhance those states." I felt intensely sad to be breaking up: as though I had somehow failed...a sense of cowardly defeat. I imagined she would view it that way and despise me.

She wrote a long letter expressing her disappointment and sadness that I had made a unilateral decision to break up. I wrote my own great loss and gratitude for all the wonderful things we had shared. We met one more time, outside on the university campus on a sunny day "to return keys and tooth brushes." Seeing her walking toward me with blond hair glistening in the sunlight, she looked both radiant and incredibly frail.

Afterwards I journaled my vivid impressions:

"the dreaded moment

visions now of all the good things

all that has joined us together

filled with love and loss and wishing-it-weren't so

we walk in silence

sharing the last quiet moments

with trembling tears and a few stifled sobs

'I've never known such joy

as I've felt from your smiling face, Nancy.

I've never known such peace

as I've found by your side.

But neither have I ever known so much pain

as I've felt in your rejections

nor such fear

as when seeing your angry face.'

'I hope you won't hate me.'

'I don't hate you.'

'I hope someday you can look back kindly on all this.'

'I do now.'

a tearful hug

'I appreciate you.

Please remember that.'

an exchange of keys and toothbrush

a lingering silent look

between sad eyes

and loving hearts

'Thank you.'

'Good bye.'"

My tentative and tender gradual opening to intimacy with women closed for the next 20 years. I would not allow myself to be that vulnerable again! I stopped trusting women's ability to "just be friends."

I was questioning the model of primary relationship. I felt reluctant to again "put all my eggs into one basket" or receive all of another's eggs. I journaled that, "in spite of a number of warm, close relationships, my life is essentially solitary. Moments can be shared, feelings (which are inherently momentary) can be shared. These brief experiences of intimacy and communion are surely life's most exquisite joy. But to hold a bird is to kill it: to cling to intimacy is to destroy it. It must come and go freely, bringing occasional respite from life's solitary journey. Even in close relating, therefore, non-attachment is the attitude to seek."

Looking back I am amazed I was having such insights before turning 30. I realize my too-solitary childhood taught me that the only one I can always trust is myself.

I'm glad I navigated away from Nancy, even though we truly loved one another, and it broke both our hearts. She was too immersed in her emotions, and viewed intimacy through that lens of sharing all the ups/downs of one another's psyches. I realized then (later confirmed with others) that I want partners who are able to mostly manage their own emotions and not need to dump them on their partner. That was a major insight that has served me well ever since. When I'm feeling intense emotions now, I find ways to process them away from the person first: I journal, yell, pound my pillow, and/or talk it over with trusted others. Only after my inner storms have calmed do I share the nuggets of what I've been experiencing with the person involved. I endeavor to follow the principles of ***Compassionate (aka Non-violent) Communications*** and/or ***Authentic Relating***

(see **Resources** for details).

It was around that time that I saw a greeting card in a shop that completely resonated. It read:

"Love consists in this

that two solitudes

protect and touch

and greet each other."

The author was the German poet Rainer Maria Rilke. I very much agree with his views on the nature of intimate relating.

I was also realizing I wanted to develop more gay male friendships and erotic relationships. So my brief foray into having girl*friends* suddenly ceased. Gay men became my whole focus in terms of erotic intimacy. I was more aware, after loving Nancy so heartfully yet not feeling any lust for her, that lust and love are independent. It is definitely possible to have one without the other. I learned I can love women more like brother-sister love. My hope was to meet men where I could experience lust **and** love together.

Healing my Fear of Straight Men

Coming out with Susan, Nancy, and these other women, I was eager to tell more people. I heard about the Berkeley Men's Center, and dropped in to their weekly "rap group." I learned a new ongoing group was forming and went to the initial session. Having hidden my sexuality around men all through high school, college, and the Air Force (13 years in total) I longed to be open with other men, and I was terrified of being bullied and ostracized. It took all my courage to say out loud to all these unknown men, "I am gay." To my amazement, no one batted an eyelash. We began meeting every week, and I discovered I was the Pink Sheep. Unlike a Black Sheep that is ostracized, I felt warmly welcomed. I found it profoundly healing to not only feel accepted among these wonderfully open and conscious straight men, but to eventually feel genuinely respected and loved. We continued meeting for several years, sharing the trials and triumph of our lives and loves. Now, 40 years later, we still connect whenever I visit the Bay Area. I am "uncle" to some of their (now grown) kids. Two of the men have told me in recent years that knowing me made it way easier to love and accept their own queer children. Wow! My initial trepidation was so far off-base.

Becoming more fully embodied

through sensual (non-sexual) massage,

Hatha Yoga, and Tantra

MANY YEARS BEFORE, as a kid, I remember watching movies of cultures like Italy where people routinely share affectionate touch. I was so aware that it was not part of my family or culture. Men never touched except to shake hands. Adult women would only want a peck on the cheek as a greeting or parting. With neither gender was there ever ANY sustained touch like hugs or cuddling. I knew I was terribly touch-deprived.

Decades later, in that same transformative year of 1973 (as I was entering "Saturn Return"), I answered an ad in a free newspaper for a weekend workshop in "Esalen Massage" which was described as sensual and nude, but not sexual, for men and women. It seemed like a huge leap, and I was eager. The event was, of course, in the Haight-Ashbury neighborhood of San Francisco: the epicenter of the "Summer of Love" a few years earlier. The area had a distinctly hippie vibe. Judith welcomed us warmly into a classic SF flat, and said matter-of-factly that we'd be nude all day and not having sex. "Guys," she said comfortingly, "you might get erections at times, and that's okay. Genitals won't be included in our massage: every other part of the body will be the focus of our caring touch." Given that my penis had been almost the only part of me that had received any touch during the previous 2 decades, this reversal felt astounding. I discovered that many if not most parts of my body could experience as much pleasure as my magic wand.

She had taken some massage training at Esalen recently and was eager to pass on the blissful touch she had experienced there. Given how generally touch-deprived I'd been all my life, the kind of slow, laid-back, all-body caressing we shared that weekend was a huge epiphany for my body, heart, and soul. I felt like I was giving and receiving love for the first time in my life, and it was with a dozen total strangers of diverse ages and genders. I discovered that touch can be a profound language unto itself. Even more importantly, *I realized I have a gift for touch.*

I also saw that *touch is the universal language of love*. Strangers who had the right intention were able to open up and share what felt like truly loving energy. It's not about waiting for the "right" person: opening the heart and expressing love through the hands is a choice anyone can make with anyone else. I realized what I had been missing: the simple and utterly natural experience of caring human touch—the gift of giving as well as receiving tactile nourishment. After that discovery in 1973, at the age of 29, my life blossomed. My unconscious starvation became conscious fulfillment. It was truly an epiphany: a life-altering experience.

I continued training with Judith in a six-week course she offered in Berkeley, not far from where I lived. Then I began offering simple massages to friends: shoulder rubs, foot massage, facials. They loved it, and loved me for giving them that gift. I felt like I was the one receiving the gift: it was such a pleasure to connect with others in such a hands-on, non-verbal way. I sensed immediately that the contact put us both "in touch" with ourselves at a level not found in ordinary social conversation. Touch is such a powerful yet gentle way to bypass mental chatter and get to another dimension. I realized many, if not most, people in our culture are starving for caring touch. Many, like me, come from touch-averse families. Much of North America is a touch-phobic culture. I believe the level of violence and stress in our world is a direct result of touch deprivation.

People were reporting feeling so much better on so many levels (physically, emotionally, and spiritually). I felt inspired to take further training so I could offer professional massage, which I did in 1980. My passion became my profession: offering nurturing, sensual, holistic massage like I learned with Judith was my wonderfully satisfying and delightful livelihood for the following 40 years till 2020.

The contrast between this kind of full-body, nurturing touch and the kind of genital-only sex I had been experiencing became glaring. The latter looked paltry in comparison. Yet I also knew I still wanted to engage in genital sex: just not such a limited form.

As if on cue, in late 1974, I met another gay teacher in another public toilet, this time on the University of California Berkeley campus. Hans worked in the library, and enjoyed his breaks by playing in the stalls. Like David, his bright energy intrigued me. He had been a refugee from East Germany, and seemed much older than his 40 years. Maybe his stressful early life had aged him prematurely. Maybe his German Catholicism had contributed to his extreme propriety. Still, he had a playful side and was sincerely spiritual. He had been exploring non-Christian mystical paths, and had an eclectic approach to the metaphysical.

Hans felt more to me like a spiritual big brother than a lover. Even though we met cruising in a bathroom, and I enjoyed playing with his hefty, intact cock, I found his German Catholic rectitude way too similar to the repressive atmosphere I was trying to escape. I did not feel the potential to be sexual lovers. So I limited our physicality to cuddling, though I sensed he wanted more. Still we enjoyed being spiritual buddies. Together we practiced some yoga and enjoyed singing devotional songs on LP records by Paramahansa Yogananda. We went to see films about Da Free John and Alan Watts: two gifted teachers of eastern mysticism.

Then he invited me to a weekend workshop on Tantra for gay men - another major epiphany. The year was 1975. The teacher, Stan Russell[22], was straight, and usually taught Tantra to men and women. Yet he was totally comfortable and cool teaching a room full of queer men one sunny Saturday near the Rockridge BART station. Stan led us through a gentle series of exercises that were mostly non-verbal: simple, clothed touch that was slow and meditative, sharing breathing, a gradual mutual undressing, some quiet gazing, and equally quiet nude hugs. Men sometimes were erect and often not. Our energy was more relaxed than sexual, despite the naked touching.

He explained that, in Tantra[23], the slow whole-body focus moves the sexual energy out toward the periphery and up through the subtle spine to awaken love and spiritual connectedness... within ourselves and with each other... and ultimately with the divine itself. I felt it! It was the completion of what had been missing in Judith's wonderful massage instruction. Finally, I could be naked with men and connect my whole self with their whole selves. From that experience, I realized the kind of quick, goal-oriented sex that I had been experiencing in casual encounters would no longer satisfy me. *I wanted my whole body, heart, and soul engaged.*

The furtive fumbling of my youth seemed by comparison like fast food: it sort of satisfied a primal hunger, yet did not provide any real nourishment. "Getting off" ceased to be a high priority for me. I became much more interested in the journey of erotic intimacy than any sort of goal. Eros became an adventure, an exploration into the mysteries of our very life force. This was my first taste of true intimacy that felt both erotic *and* spiritual. It resonated with my soul.

In hindsight, I also sense these "discoveries" were re-awakening something I already knew in my soul from previous lives. They were a confirmation of a deeply held, barely conscious awareness. As I look back now, some 50 years later, it seems obvious to me that I came into this world with a soul understanding of how eros and spirit are one. My mission in this lifetime has been to "remember" what I already knew, and to spread that awareness among queer men.

Hans also introduced me to a whimsically playful, mystical poem by the linguistic trickster, James Broughton. The Song of the Godbody sings of a sinewy, sensual divinity expressing itself in all flesh. I loved it. Little did I know James would become a mentor and dear friend a few years later.

By 1976, my life was becoming quite full with other involvements. I spent less and less time with Hans, which I suspect was a big disappointment for him. Sometime in the early 80s, I heard that he had contracted AIDS and gone home to Germany. I had no way to reach him, except through prayers. I suspect, like so many others, he died way too young.

Having been introduced to Hatha Yoga by Yogi David in the early 70s, I felt a curiosity, even a hunger, to delve more thoroughly into this curiously alluring practice of self-care which held out the promise of both better physical health and even "higher consciousness." In 1975, I researched teacher training programs and found a very reputable one in San Francisco at what was then called *The Institute for Yoga Teacher Education*[24]. After enrolling in their two-year program, it quickly became apparent that my body was so tight I would need a much longer period to begin to unravel the knots accumulated over 30 years of stressful, and mostly sedentary living.

My mind was keen to understand how what I was learning experientially in yoga and meditation practice was being understood in western psychology. That led me to discover the California Institute of Integral Studies. I enrolled in 1976 in their Master's program in East-West Psychology. Between these two programs I was immersing myself in a comprehensive body-mind make-over. The wonderful irony is that the "GI Bill[25]" paid for most of my studies. I felt very blessed by this opportunity. Even though I was continuing to support myself with piloting, I knew I was in training for some sort of new profession, although the exact parameters of that remained vague for some time.

Right around the time I was beginning all that training in a very holistic lifestyle (and possible future career), I took a job for a start-up cargo airline flying DC-3s out of the Oakland Airport. It seemed like an ideal part-time job as I had been "Type Rated" in that vintage aircraft after flying hundreds of hours in them in Vietnam. By an odd twist of fate, the company went bankrupt just as I was completing their training and about to start on the job. The very silver lining for me was that being laid off qualified me to receive Unemployment Insurance for a whole year, which allowed me to focus on my new studies and practices. What grace!

Someone told me about *What Color Is Your Parachute*, which was newly published right there in Berkeley and has gone on to become a total classic: published in dozens of languages and revised annually since 1975. It proved to be invaluable in helping me get a clearer vision of what sort of work I was creating for myself. One of its key recommendations: instead of looking to fit yourself into an existing job (like a cog in a wheel), "find a **need** and fill it." In other words, *invent a job* that exactly suits your own unique skills, interests and passions. I took that advice to heart, and am so glad to have followed that sage advice. My "career" is unique to me.

Sexual Healing

As I explored the ancient Yoga tradition, I resonated with the attitude that sexual energy is inherently sacred because it is the Life Force in concentrated form. From Yogi David onward I deepened my value that sexuality can be treated with reverence, which in turn imbues all of life with sacredness. The crucial word is *can*. Just as food can be mindlessly wolfed down while watching flicks, so sex can be just a momentary satisfaction of hunger, like scratching an itch. Or *it can be a sacrament*. **Intention is everything!** This attitude of savoring sex as a sacrament is radically different from the Catholic repression I grew up with. I was learning that Tantra views sexuality as the gateway to higher consciousness. The quieting of the mind that sex creates can give a glimpse of what lies beyond the ever-chattering egoic "discursive mind."

My explorations of sensual touch through massage and my initial glimpses of the explicit connection between the sexual and spiritual from Tantra led me to want to explore full-body erotic-spiritual massage. That began informally in my bath house adventures. Throughout the 70s, "the baths" were my major way of meeting gay men and having sex: I found them much more appealing than the bars and toilets. The baths were free of alcohol and smoke, and were a safe place to be with other men who were also looking for sexual contact. For many years I made at least a weekly visit to one of the many bath houses in the Bay Area. Looking back I can see I was hoping for more than quick sex: I was hoping to meet a man I found sexually attractive, *and* with whom I shared spiritual values as with David and Hans.

I was always cautious: spent lots of time observing a man before showing any interest. I was looking for signs of a kindred spirit: someone more interested in being sensual and affectionate than hard-core sexual. I limited my interaction to either mutual masturbation (in the showers or steam room) or maybe oral sex. I never felt comfortable exploring anal sex: it seemed way too intimate for a casual encounter. I had a strong sense I'd want to know and deeply love someone before that kind of penetrative sex. Part of my caution was awareness of Sexually Transmitted Diseases. Even before the advent of AIDS, I sensed that manual contact was the least risky. Once the AIDS epidemic exploded I became even more cautious. Now, decades later, I am profoundly grateful to have come through that horrific period unscathed, except for the emotional devastation of losing way too many friends way too young.

After my initiation into Esalen massage with Judith and intro the rudiments of Tantra with Stan Russel, I began bringing massage oil with me. My chosen way to introduce slow, sensual touch to a stranger was in the steam room or sauna. If initial eye contact or body language suggested there may be some mutual attraction, I would slowly initiate gentle touch, usually of his outer thigh. His response informed how I proceeded: always avoiding the genitals for a while letting him know I am full-body-oriented. Men's body language in those situations is usually eloquent and trustworthy. If he seemed relaxed and open I would offer an extended massage in one of our rooms. What was striking for me about those encounters is how rarely the massage turned into full-on sex: most guys seemed to be both surprised and grateful for this kind of contact. Many commented that it was a relief to not have to perform sexually... that caring touch was more important for them. I found that very affirming.

Gradually, my sexuality was evolving from using others to "get off," to a genuine desire to serve others by giving pleasure. I wanted them to experience the kind of full-body, heart and soul fulfillment I had begun to savor. Years later, I heard the term "sexual healing." I had already come to understand healing to mean making whole and complete. Now I was experiencing becoming more whole and complete erotically, and was happy to offer that to others. This was a precursor to the Sexual Healing I would begin to offer two decades later as a trained Sacred Intimate.

Even though I enjoyed some wonderfully loving exchanges with men in the baths, either I or they did not seem to feel the urge to take it outside into an ongoing relationship. Maybe we were all kids in a candy store: there were so many available men to sample, few wanted to settle down to a steady diet of just one fella. Maybe tomorrow someone even cuter, hotter, etc. would appear. I was aware of being caught up in the feeding frenzy, even as a strong part of me did yearn to find Mr. Right instead of always settling for Mr. Right Away.

During my explorations in bars & baths in the 70s, my empathic awareness (or projection) was that most men were quite lonely: "looking for love in all the wrong places." I imagined sex for many was a quick fix (kind of like fast food) for a much deeper need for quality intimacy and real love. I yearned to find and share more whole-hearted kinds of intimacy. That yearning led, a few years later, to beginning to offer weekend workshops.

Chapter 6 - Soaring Higher - (1976-1982 to the present)

My initial experiences with meditation that began in 1973 with *Transcendental Meditation* were very positive. I was finding my mind more quiet and my body more relaxed. This was especially palpable when I would get home from a stressful day of teaching people to pilot small aircraft. The cramped cockpit is noisy. The student is nervous. There is some danger in giving a novice the controls to practice landings: the instructor has to be ever-ready to intervene in a split second to prevent a bad landing. In the evenings, after many hours in that setting, my body would be in knots. After my 20 minutes of meditation, my mind and body were way more relaxed and spacious. I loved it.

Yet I resented the TM requirement that students never share their mantra. It was supposedly custom-crafted for each student. I suspected that the requirement was more a scheme to make money than about my "custom mantra." I had paid what, at the time, seemed like a large sum for this practice, and I resented not being able to share this wisdom with friends.

During the 1970s as I explored Yoga and Meditation at different schools, I was blessed to meet many inspiring teachers. By far the most amazing was Baba[26] Muktananda. In the course of a single evening in his presence my life was forever blessed with a new awareness.

In 1976 I began hearing about a meditation guru in town, and many people, who knew I was already exploring Yoga and practicing Transcendental Meditation, began telling me *I had to experience Baba.* I resisted the idea of a "guru." Yet the messages became relentless. I remembered David's utter devotion to his beloved Sant Kirpal Singh. Something in me yearned for that kind of guide/mentor. Yet whom could I trust?

Finally when I heard he was about to leave the Bay Area to continue his world tour, I swallowed my pride or resistance (I fancied myself as a "self-made yogi") and went to the ashram his devotees had set up. It was in a seedy section of the East Bay; I later learned they had transformed a run-down brothel into a temple of devotion.

I rushed in from a busy day of teaching flying and was welcomed by a hostess, who explained I should put my shoes in the rack and join the chanting already in progress by standing among the men on the right side of the hall. Women were on the left. There were probably 200 people chanting a liturgical chant in an unknown language I later learned was Sanskrit. I was mesmerized by the mysterious chant. The man I stood next to shared his chanting book and clearly knew the words. The meaning was a mystery, and the feeling I got was of deep comfort...almost familiarity. As a Catholic boy, singing in Latin was my favorite part of the "High Mass," and this was similar: something was happening that my mind did not comprehend, yet my soul savored.

When that chant ended, everyone sat cross-legged on the floor. I was glad I had been practicing yoga for 3 years: I could sit fairly comfortably. Then we began a very slow, melodic intonation of words written in large letters over the empty chair in front:

Om Namah Shivaya

Again I had no idea of the meaning, and again I felt a profound comfort. I also realized to my delight that this must be their main mantra which was being shared with me, who had not yet donated a dime to enter. I liked that generosity.

The empty chair in front was gently lit in pale blue lights. Flowers adorned a side table, and a photo of a nearly naked man was on the other side table. I closed my eyes and joined in the melodic chanting of *Om Namah Shivaya*. After a while I heard rustlings and looked up to see an orange-clad man walking slowly down the center aisle. People were bowing. My resistance flared: "Hrmph! He's a guru?" He seemed to be waddling oddly. I again closed my eyes, drawn inward by the mesmerizing music and words: **Om Namah Shivaya.**

What I next experienced made no sense to my skeptical mind. With my eyes closed I "saw" ruby-red light[27] emanating from this man now seated in the chair in front. One of the red rays shone straight into my heart. *I felt bathed in love!* My mind questioned "how can he love me? we haven't even met!" Yet the feeling was so palpable: a depth and strength of love that was way more powerful than any I'd ever experienced. After that blissful chant ended, we were invited to sit in silence and use that mantra as the focus of meditation. They explained it translates as "I bow to God within." I liked that it had such a beautiful meaning, and I settled into deep stillness.

After a few minutes in silence we were invited to line up to greet "Baba" in a practice called *darshan*, a Sanskrit word meaning "to see." By being close to Baba and looking into his eyes we could experience his deeply peaceful presence. We could also ask Baba a question. I was nervous: what would I ask? For the preceding several weeks I had been preparing to move back to Brooklyn to care for my mother, who was going down hill quickly from her metastasized breast cancer. When my turn came I bowed like the others then stammered, "Baba I ask your blessing on my visit to New York." He nodded and brushed me with his wand of peacock feathers, as he was doing with everyone. Yet I felt specially blessed and happy to have had this brief "audience" with this strange man.

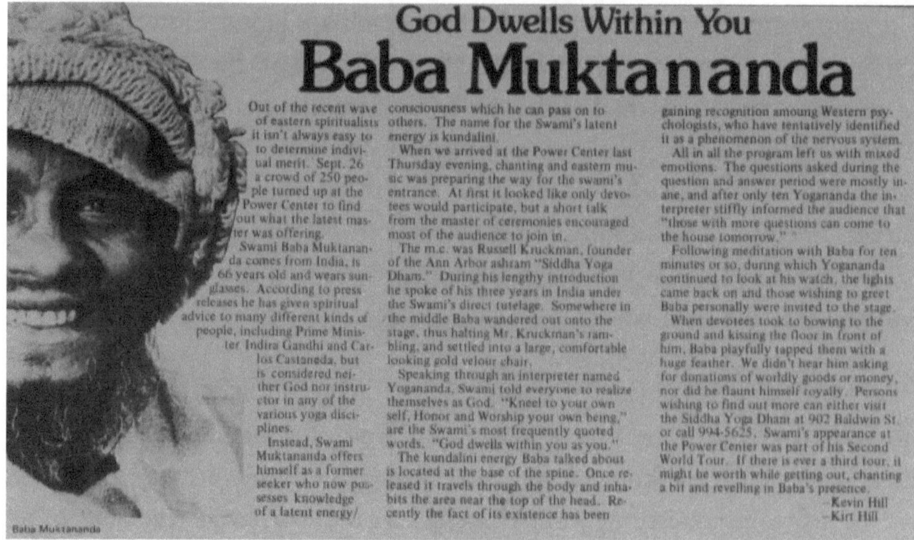

God Dwells Within You
Baba Muktananda

Out of the recent wave of eastern spiritualists it isn't always easy to to determine individual merit. Sept. 26 a crowd of 250 people turned up at the Power Center to find out what the latest master was offering.

Swami Baba Muktananda comes from India, is 66 years old and wears sunglasses. According to press releases he has given spiritual advice to many different kinds of people, including Prime Minister Indira Gandhi and Carlos Castaneda, but is considered neither God nor instructor in any of the various yoga disciplines.

Instead, Swami Muktananda offers himself as a former seeker who now possesses knowledge of a latent energy/ consciousness which he can pass on to others. The name for the Swami's latent energy is kundalini.

When we arrived at the Power Center last Thursday evening, chanting and eastern music was preparing the way for the swami's entrance. At first it looked like only devotees would participate, but a short talk from the master of ceremonies encouraged most of the audience to join in.

The m.c. was Russell Kruckman, founder of the Ann Arbor ashram "Siddha Yoga Dham." During his lengthy introduction he spoke of his three years in India under the Swami's direct tutelage. Somewhere in the middle Baba wandered out onto the stage, thus halting Mr. Kruckman's rambling, and settled into a large, comfortable looking gold velour chair.

Speaking through an interpreter named Yogananda, Swami told everyone to realize themselves as God. "Kneel to your own self, Honor and Worship your own being," are the Swami's most frequently quoted words. "God dwells within you as you."

The kundalini energy Baba talked about is located at the base of the spine. Once released it travels through the body and inhabits the area near the top of the head. Recently the fact of its existence has been gaining recognition among Western psychologists, who have tentatively identified it as a phenomenon of the nervous system.

All in all the program left us with mixed emotions. The questions asked during the question and answer period were mostly inane, and after only ten Yogananda the interpreter stiffly informed the audience that "those with more questions can come to the house tomorrow."

Following meditation with Baba for ten minutes or so, during which Yogananda continued to look at his watch, the lights came back on and those wishing to greet Baba personally were invited to the stage.

When devotees took to bowing to the ground and kissing the floor in front of him, Baba playfully tapped them with a huge feather. We didn't hear him asking for donations of worldly goods or money, nor did he flaunt himself royally. Persons wishing to find out more can either visit the Siddha Yoga Dham at 902 Baldwin St. or call 994-5625. Swami's appearance at the Power Center was part of his Second World Tour. If there is ever a third tour, it might be worth while getting out, chanting a bit and revelling in Baba's presence.

—Kevin Hill
—Kirt Hill

Baba Muktananda

A FEW DAYS LATER, WHILE I was still putting my affairs in order in Berkeley I got the sad news Mom had passed: on Holy Thursday before Easter. During my time back home for Mom's funeral and helping my Dad adjust to his new single life, I saw a big poster with Baba's image, inviting **"Be With Baba!"** He was at another of his ashrams about 2 hours north of Manhattan. I signed up for a weekend Intensive (for Mothers' Day: how appropriate!) to dive deeper into this new world of Baba's mysterious energy. Having had such a powerful first encounter with Baba Muktananda, my earlier skepticism was replaced by intrigue. Who was this orange-clad man, and what might I learn with him? During that weekend, several hundred of us experienced Baba's chanting and meditation in greater depth.

The Intensive was designed to give each participant a deep dive into many spiritual practices. There were 4 segments: morning and afternoon both Saturday and Sunday, and each was similar. They began with talks by people who had experienced the power of Baba's Shakti and were able to articulate its effect on their lives. They were invariably eloquent. Then we would do some chanting of one of Baba's mantras[28], which tended to open the heart. Then Baba would come in and give a brief talk and sometimes take questions. Then after a break for toileting and a snack we would spend around 20 minutes chanting the slow version of Om Namah Shivaya, which was done "call-and-response" style with a lead group of musicians playing a harmonium and sometimes a tamboura. I always found this chant mesmerizing in the best possible way: it quieted my mind and opened my heart. Then we were invited to sit for an hour of meditation using the mantra to further quiet the mind. We were taught to use the mantra as a vehicle to replace mental chatter: to take us into the state of pure awareness. We could let the mantra go while the chatter was quiet, and use it again whenever chatter disrupted the inner stillness.

During that hour, Baba would walk around between the rows of meditators giving Shaktipat[29]. This usually involved some brief physical touch, or sometimes simply brushing with peacock feathers, or sometimes eye contact or a few words. Each person seemed to get their own special blessing. The room would feel charged with vibrant energy: Baba's Shakti. It was understood to potentially awaken the "kundalini" (the normally dormant energy curled up "like a snake" in the base of the spine.) This awakening could create a rising up of the energy through the subtle spine through the chakras and eventually to the crown. As each chakra was awakened it could create many spontaneous and unpredictable inner or outer manifestations in the meditator. Some people's bodies moved into yoga postures or mudras (hand positions). The sound effects could be amusing or even alarming: laughing, crying, chirping, barking, roaring. Internally, people might feel a variety of emotions, have visions, or feel expanded states of awareness. It was all understood to be part of a purification process culminating (perhaps over many lifetimes) in the experience of Pure Consciousness and Pure Love.

For me, each of the 4 sessions was powerful in different ways. What I remember most vividly from nearly 50 years ago was the indescribable energy I felt whenever Baba was near me. It was as though my own energy field expanded dramatically. My heart expanded and my mind quieted. Sometimes my breathing got quite rapid. On Saturday, I recall Baba brushing me with peacock feathers, which smelled divine. Once he gently kicked the base of my spine from behind while resting the feathers on my head for a long while. It was blissful. Another time he pinched the bridge of my nose.

The Sunday morning session was momentous. I had been crying: a combination of some ancient grief and huge gratitude. I felt or saw him coming closer and had the courage to open my eyes. As I looked up at him, he looked down at me with the utmost tenderness and love... like he was seeing all the suffering I'd experienced over countless lifetimes and acknowledging it with utter compassion. Then in English he clearly said, "Happy? Happy?" I nodded yes: I felt ecstatically happy despite all that grief which had suddenly evaporated. After he moved on, I began sobbing even deeper, yet the feeling completely shifted. The grief was replaced by immense love. My heart was suddenly enormous and embraced everyone everywhere throughout time. As I experienced my heart overflowing with love, the tears became an expression of that love... for the many people I had known personally (family and friends) and then for unknown strangers. I began to glimpse the power of his core message:

"God dwells within you. See God in each other."

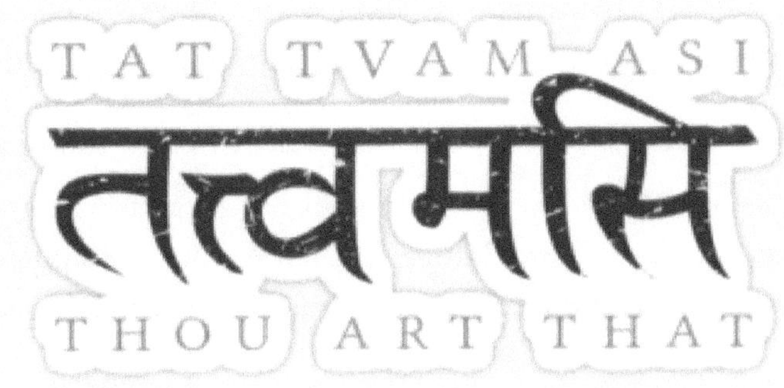

DURING THE LUNCH BREAK, I sat under a tree by the water. My mind was utterly still: no thoughts at all. This was totally new and unfamiliar. I was silently aware of how unusual it felt, and wondered whether I had lost the capacity to think. So I inwardly recited my address and phone number just to make sure. Indeed I could still think, then I continued sitting in that total at-one-ment with my surroundings for a timeless while.

The afternoon session felt different. I was tired from having gotten up too early, and from the huge catharsis I had in the morning. My legs were tired of sitting cross-legged on the floor. So I opted for one of the chairs along the side of the room. This gave me a whole different perspective. This time, when Baba was walking among the people sitting on the floor, I watched. Again I was moved to tears seeing the immense love he was showering on each person. I found myself comparing him with Christ or the saints. I was really romanticizing his saintliness. As he completed making his rounds he stood silently in the back of the room surveying the other-worldly scene of all these people moving and sounding in seemingly bizarre ways. At one point I saw (and almost heard) him lift one hip and let out an almost silent fart. Wow: that wonderfully punctured my romantic balloon! He's human, too. He farts and even shits! That was a really profound teaching for me that the divine and human are completely coexisting, in him, and by extension in each of us.

Those two sessions that Sunday in May perfectly complemented one another. The first was sublime, divine rapture, and the second was fully realizing that divinity is showing up in each of our very human, and mortal bodies.

Baba brought a rare gift to the west: the ancient (and traditionally secret) direct transmission of his *Shakti*.[30] He did not speak to the intellect. His verbal teachings were almost child-like in their eloquent simplicity. Instead, he intentionally emanated an energy that transformed each person differently.

His direct transmission powerfully and completely opened my heart and deepened my awareness that all of manifest existence is an outward expression of the same universal divine consciousness, which goes by many names in many traditions and is all the same One. He taught that in India the name **Shiva** represents that primorial pure consciousness.

Change your vision.
Go deeper and deeper
into meditation to where
the state of extraordinary
ecstasy awaits you. When
you reach that state, you
will become it. You will
know: "I am That."

~Baba Muktananda

I CONTINUED BEING WITH Baba each time he visited California until his passing in 1982. And I have continued to practice meditation using the mantra he so freely shared with everyone[31]: ***Om Namah Shivaya ~*** I bow to the divine Universal Consciousness deep in the heart (mine and everyone's).

I also continue to practice other "limbs" of yoga, including *asanas* (postures/ movements), *pranayama* (breathing in deliberate ways to change energy flow), *kirtan* (chanting many sacred mantras and names of God/dess).

I met Baba during the period when I was preparing to teach yoga and offer holistic massage like what I had learned with Judith. The mind quieting and heart opening I experienced with Baba, along with his core teaching to "See God in each other," gave me a perfect template for my future work. As I began teaching yoga and offering massage a few years later, my strong intention was to guide people into a more embodied, and centered in their heart. I wanted them to feel seen by me as the divine Self they were, and to feel universal love coming through my hands to their hearts. What a wonderful job! I loved loving people for a living. I cannot imagine more fulfilling work."

My favorite part of teaching yoga was the savasana ("corpse pose") at the end of each class. I would enter a meditative state myself. Then, as I led people into a meditative state, I was able to speak to their hearts and souls, and convey some simple message that affirmed and honored the pure consciousness they each were at the deepest level. One simple technique I often used, after guiding them in being aware of their whole body, was to invite them to simply observe the breath. Then begin to notice the transition from the exhale to the inhale, and observe the usually very brief pause between those 2 phases. In that moment, I pointed out, there are no thoughts; there is only awareness itself. Being aware of awareness is the essence of meditation: it is a glimpse of our deepest pure Self.

Looking back on the impact of Baba's teachings and *Shakti,* I can see more clearly how revolutionary it was for me. Like most Christians, I had been taught that I and all humans are fundamentally flawed by "Original Sin." I understood that God was utterly separate from me. "He" was off somewhere judging me and everyone, and that I have to look outside myself for God and for divine love. I mistakenly understood that I/we need to be "forgiven" through the Church in order to be"redeemed" and be worthy of God's love.

Baba's message completely turned that around: "God dwells within you. Bow to your own Self. Worship your own Self. You are That (divine pure Consciousness)... See God in Each Other." He echoed the teachings of Ram Dass' guru, Neem Karoli Baba, "Love Everyone. Serve Everyone. Remember God."

After decades of meditation, I see that "Remember God dwelling within" comes first. Only when I am tuned into that divine inner frequency am I aware of my Self[32] as love. Only then can I hope to "Love Everyone. Serve Everyone" and "See God in Each Other."

What I now understand is that humans' "original sin" is to live in *the illusion* that the thoughts in our heads are who we are. I have come to believe our brilliant front brain, our neo-cortex, is nothing more than a binary computer. It operates by making distinctions: between this and that, up and down, dark and light, good and bad, friend and foe, beautiful and ugly, attractive and repulsive. That is how I now understand the story of Adam and Eve's fall: they ate the fruit of the tree of knowledge of good and evil. They became trapped in dualistic thinking, which is indeed hell on earth.

Now, over four decades later, the shift of consciousness Baba initiated continues to deepen. My mind is more quiet. My heart is more open than before meeting Baba. I generally feel love for myself and others as manifestations of the same divine pure Consciousness. I feel incredibly fortunate to have been guided to this astounding Guru.

Meditation practices, of which there are many, can shift our awareness out of the binary brain and into the holistic heart, which sees the connections between all of us seemingly separate entities.

(Learn more about the Meditation in **Resources** and **Experiential Practices**)

Chapter 7 (1976) - Unhinged by Michael then major epiphany

Early in 1976, shortly before meeting Baba, I met Michael in a public men's room. We were both there to simply relieve ourselves. Yet we made eye contact and both smiled, which is a radical departure in men's rooms. Straight guys don't smile for fear of being thought gay. Gay guys don't smile because cruising and casual sex are Serious Stuff. So it seemed Michael and I both knew instantly that we had a different kind of connection to explore.

He was around my age and lived only about a mile from me in Berkeley. We began kind of dating: a nice surprise. We didn't start out getting sexual: a rarity among gay men. Over a few weeks we moved from going for coffee to cuddling, kissing, and gradually into sweetly affectionate erotic play. Not since Jim in Alaska and Mike in Sydney had I felt such comfort and connection. Looking back I can see his energy evoked the kind of pre-sexual affectionate genital touch my cousin Paul and I had shared when I was only 8. We were boys loving one another's "exposed tip of the heart."

That safety and openness led me to quickly fall in love. It was really a childhood crush. Since the onset of puberty, I had semi-consciously covered over my vulnerable and playful child self to put on the persona of an adult, and I had completely lost touch with my little Tommy. Michael changed that quite suddenly.

When little Tommy suddenly burst forth, I felt unhinged. I vividly remember one evening when I was in a class in San Francisco, feeling completely confused internally, unable to concentrate on the class, leaving early. Riding BART back to Berkeley, I wrote out my inner turmoil:

"Feeling very disconnected - mentally very scattered - physically high energy - feeling hyper-alert - mentally overloaded - 'TILT!' - too much going on - where is the 'real me'?...

"Is this a 'psychotic episode'? a 'nervous breakdown'? I'm certainly not 'myself' - whoever *that* is!... Feel sad, but without tears - more like empty. There's nothing that feels 'right.'

My dear mother was becoming more ill with cancer. I flew home for a brief visit, which confirmed my sense of urgently needing to move back to be with her and my dad. During my time away, and upon my return a week later, things had shifted for Michael. Afterwards, I digested my feelings in this journal's summary:

"Dear Michael,

"Meeting you and the period since has been the most emotionally tumultuous experience of my life. It's been amazing and puzzling throughout. I don't understand much of what has happened.

"What I get is that I 'fell in love' with you. I had thought myself too sensible and 'mature' for such a 'childish' response. The little boy in me was instantly turned on to you. He felt safer with you. He gloried in the warmth of your affection. I (the Adult me) have kept my little boy locked up far inside me for many years—so long, in fact, that I had forgotten he was there. Very rationally I 'knew' he could never have the kind of love he craves, so I've cut him off from myself so as not to feel his sadness and disappointment.

"Something about you—the gentleness of our touch, the kindness in your eyes—made him trust you very quickly. My little Tommy came bursting out from that deep inside place to love you. It felt beautiful. I felt whole again—having Tommy alive and active and loving."

It was in that state that I went to New York. And from that point on, nothing felt the same: it was all disappointing, confusing, and very painful. In New York, my imagination generated countless fantasies about how it might be between us. My return from NY was filled with eager expectations of being with Michael again. But from his tone on the phone, I sensed something was different. It felt like a coolness—almost an indifference. Tommy got scared. I was very disappointed that Michael didn't come over that first night—really hurt.

Our time together the next night felt pleasant on the surface, but deeper there was a vague feeling of strain. Something wasn't right. The sex we shared felt somewhat mechanical—in contrast to the joyous spontaneity I had felt with him just over a week earlier.

> "The following day was sheer hell: incessant thoughts of you—sad, worried thoughts—feeling of confusion and loss. Hence my need to talk to you that night.

> "As I've told you, I greatly appreciated your sympathetic listening to me, and your honest response. That helped my Adult, but Tommy was plunged into even greater sadness."

Michael had burst my bubble. I digested the intensity of this experience into this poem:

the Child in me

is a little boy of three or four

shy, timid, joyful, playful

he is comfortable with Adults

but distant

know they won't play or love him enough

they are to be gotten along with

he is shy among his peers

is easily hurt by their roughness and cruelty

often plays by himself

all the while wishing for a brother all his own

a brother to love and be loved by

to be with day and night

to touch without feeling scared

to be touched by

someone to trust completely

to feel totally at-one-with

the Child in me doesn't show himself much anymore

he has given way to my Adult

a reasonable, kind man

who doesn't get too close to anyone

my Child still waits and watches for his brother

once in a while someone comes close enough to touch him

and he awakes

and his eyes open wide with joy and love and hope

and he reaches out with all his strength to touch that person

to love him

to hold him

to play with him day and night

when that person pulls away

the Child in me is very sad

all the world is black

there is no joy

no play

no love

no touching

he wakes at night

yearning for his brother who is not there

he aches

and feels empty

and alone

and he cries.

————————

A WEEK AFTER BEING "unhinged" by Michael, I had my first encounter with Baba: on Spring Equinox, 1976. It radically shifted my perspective - about Michael, and about life and love.

A week later I journaled:

> "Feeling pain all day about Michael: a sense now of how exploitative my feelings toward him have been - plugging him into my pre-adolescent fantasy of a mate - the idealized lover - somebody 'just for me...me...me!!!'

That's hardly love. I haven't been able to love Michael at all: there's been so much shit of mine (and his?) in the way. I'm beginning to see him now for himself, instead of for me, as a being much like myself: struggling to get clear of the garbage.

How can we love each other? Can we share ourselves at any level? Can we be really open with each other? Can we relate on a higher level?"

(Then I quote Kahlil Gibran) *"Your pain is the breaking of the shell that encloses your understanding."*

About another week later, after a particularly insightful meditation about Michael, and very much under the influence of Baba's universal love, this poem flowed out:

love desires, yearns passionately, is never fulfilled.

                         Love asks nothing, being totally fulfilled.

love is intense

    joy-sorrow

    pleasure-pain

    together-separate

    ever-changing

    ever anxious

    Love is blissful, eternal union, unchanging, ever peaceful.

love feels a separation: reaches out for closeness in body and emotion

                         Love feels no separation:

relating to all "others" as manifestations of one's Self.

love makes distinctions among whom it can love.

Love is without distinction: for all beings unreservedly

love is selfish, a taking, an attachment.

Love is self-less: giving without attachment.

Love knows that ultimately that giver and receiver are One.

The confluence of meeting and falling in with Michael, my mother's dying, and meeting Baba, all during the first few months of 1976, as I was approaching 32, brought two major heart openings that connected my chakras. First, my inner Tommy has been a *conscious* part of me ever since. I (my Adult self) am his devoted parent and friend. I protect "him" from people whose energy feels harmful, as Nancy's did. Only when I am with someone I feel totally safe with, on both Adult and Child levels (as I did with Michael, however briefly) do I open to let others love my beautiful boy self. Second, Baba shifted my understanding. In my early life, I kept looking *outside* for love - again as with Michael. Since being with Baba, I feel the source of love is *inside* my own heart. I now know Love is *who I am.*

My strong intention and frequent experience is to **"See God in Each Other."** Ever since, I have been able, in varying degrees, to experience sharing love with very many people in many kinds of relationships: lovers, friends, family, neighbors, store clerks, and even passing strangers. I now know we are all That Love, even when they do not experience it. What a blessing!

This period was a major turning point in my intimate explorations. Henceforth I would always be aware of both my very young self as well as my wise old soul, and insist on expressing and honoring *all of me* in every intimate involvement. Everything from this point onward was simply a deepening embodiment of these insights. No longer would I be driven by my lust. My abiding desire going forward has been to offer love, and not the lower-case selfish love in my poem above, but the upper-case universal Love. *This integration was the central epiphany of this whole lifetime.*

A few years later, a woman friend gave me a sweet birthday card containing a poem that touched my heart, because my soul felt fully seen and affirmed.

The Children of Happiness are not like ordinary children.

They are usually little girls, but sometimes little boys are born with the signs.

You can tell one of the Children of Happiness by the way it is different.

A Child of Happiness always seems like an old soul living in a new body,

and her face is very serious until she smiles,

and then the sun lights up the world.

You look at the eyes of a Child of Happiness

and you know the child knows everything that is truly important.

Children of Happiness always look not quite the same as other children.

They have strong, straight legs and walk with purpose.

They laugh as do all children, and they play as do all children,
they talk child

talk as do all children, but they are different, they are blessed,
they are

special, they are sacred.

They are to be cherished and protected,

even at the risk of your life.

They will know sadness, but will overcome it.

They will know alienation

for they see past and through this reality.

They will Endure where others cannot.

They will Survive where others cannot.

They will know love even when it is not shown to them.

They spend their lives trying to communicate

the love they know.

- Anne Cameron

` `*Daughters of Copper Woman*"

Chapter 8 (1976-79) - Exploring Marriage-like Partnership with Kyle

Some straight friends helped me connect with a very sweet and loving potential partner. One of the men in my Berkeley Men's Group was dating a woman who had a gay friend. So of course: they decided *we must be a match*. My dear mother had passed away in the spring of 1976, and I spent about 6 weeks back in Brooklyn being of support to my dad and helping sort out mom's affairs. I was feeling particularly hungry for a loving partner when I returned to Berkeley, and that is when I got introduced to Kyle. I really liked him. At first he seemed like someone I could settle down with. He was sweet and kind. He worked as a preschool teacher. He also loved to work with his hands and had a burning desire to buy a "fixer-upper" and renovate it. I had always been a renter, and my childhood dream was to live in my own home; so Kyle's fantasy ignited my own. Looking for, buying, and renovating an old Edwardian on Harper Street in the flats of Berkeley (near Ashby BART) became our "baby." We scraped together a down-payment with a bit of help from my dad and Kyle's doctor-uncle, who also co-signed our mortgage. Suddenly, right around my 33rd birthday, Kyle and I, along with his uncle and the bank, had title to a decidedly run down "diamond in the rough."

Kyle and I rolled up our sleeves and went to work. It was fun. Kyle had grown up in a single-family house in southern California, and his father was handy. Kyle inherited his father's savvy, and I was his eager apprentice. We were a good team with tools. Alas I gradually found we did not have much else in common. My real passions in those days were my yoga, meditation, sensual massage, and playing with the boys in the baths. Kyle was a "one-man man." . Monogamy was certainly the model I was raised on, so I pressured myself to "settle down" and be satisfied with this genuinely lovely guy, but I got bored in bed. Kyle's idea of how to relax after a hard day of renovations was to smoke a joint and sit side-by-side masturbating. That did not satisfy me at all. From my alcoholic family I had become allergic to chemical alterations of consciousness. Kyle's "high" seemed quite low to me. I got much higher from my yoga and meditation, which did not seem to attract him. We tried for a couple of years to craft a satisfying love, even working with a gay therapist.

In the spring of 1979, I gave up. It was not working for me. I was realizing yet again that I need *both* solitude and intimacy. Living together was depriving me of the former. I'm a very independent Leo, who prefers intimacy in small doses with gaps in between to come "home" to myself.

The marriage model was the ubiquitous template I was raised with by family, media, and the Church. It makes some sense for raising children, though the nuclear family is far too small a unit. It really requires an extended family to work well. "It takes a village."

Ironically, my mother's aphorism, "There is safety in numbers," led me to observe that monogamous marriage tends to isolate the couple. My parents were one another's only real friends. When Mom died, my Dad was emotionally lost, even though he moved close to his brother and sister-in-law. I've seen that among many of my straight friends as well.

Seeing that, I vowed to never become totally emotionally dependent on one person: they may leave or die. I've cultivated a rich network of "chosen family."

For queer people, monogamy and marriage are merely options. What I love about being queer is that we can free ourselves from that cultural template and invent our own kinds of relationships that meet the unique needs of each of the people involved.

Kyle and I sadly discovered our needs did not coincide. He was understandably hurt and furious. I knew I genuinely loved Kyle. He was caught in all-or-nothing thinking and pushed me away. I sincerely wanted to maintain some form of loving relationship, and he was adamantly opposed.

Fortunately the aptly named legal "Limited Partnership" agreement his uncle had required us to draw up set out clearly how to dissolve our financial involvement. Of course, the emotional disentanglement was way more complex, but at least we weren't fighting over finances.

A few months earlier my Dad had passed away and left me enough cash to buy out their equity and take over the mortgage. Suddenly I had a huge (2,200 square foot) three-bedroom house and no way to pay the mortgage. The obvious solution: bring in roommates. By my 35th birthday I was a landlord. It has proven to be a financial boon for which I will always thank Kyle.

The most tragic aspect of all this: Kyle became lonely living alone. A few years later in the early 80s, he violated his own values by going to the baths (once!) and having unprotected sex (once!) and promptly contracted AIDS. It was heart-breaking to hear he was infected. It was 1985 and I knew too well his prognosis. Yet there was a slight silver lining for me. For several years after our breakup he was too angry to have anything to do with me. I had tried to maintain a loving friendship, alas, to no avail. When I heard he was ill with AIDS, I reached out in writing saying, "Kyle, I love you and want to be of whatever support I can." To my great relief he called, and the tone in his voice told me his heart was suddenly wide open again! He welcomed me to be part of his care circle who nursed him through his inexorable wasting away. It was so very sad to watch. Tears still well up as I remember his and our profound grief. I'll always remember helping him eat what turned out to be his last meal. His mind was clear. His heart was open. He was very present. There was huge tenderness in the giving and receiving. The next morning I heard he passed that night. He was 36.

Similar tragic stories were playing out all over: young men were shriveling up and wasting away - dying way too young. Many were disowned by their families, who were learning all at once that *they were gay and had AIDS*. Many felt abandoned by our governments, who stood by and did way too little.

Experiencing so much tragic premature dying among gay brothers made it even more clear to me that I would be foolish to put all my love eggs in one basket. So many of us queer men were in so much emotional anguish (loss of loved ones, fear of our own demise) that the only sensible way to relate was with many and not focus on any one exclusively. Also because sex was now potentially lethal, I and others began to explore and discover other ways of being loving and intimate. We gradually morphed into a community of non-sexual lovers who were learning to relate more from the heart and less from the groin.

That model has informed my love life ever since: heart connection first, sexual expression an optional extra with one or a very few safe partners (safe emotionally as well as medically). That prepared me for what came next.

Chapter 9 (1979) - Finding "the faeries"

In the summer of 1979, on a bulletin board in San Francisco, I was thrilled to read *"The Call"* put out by Harry Hay, John Burnside, and Don Kilhefner to gather as a tribe of loving men in the desert of Arizona for a weekend celebrating our queer love. Here is that eloquent invitation:

A CALL TO
Gay Brothers
A SPIRITUAL CONFERENCE
FOR RADICAL FAIRIES
TO BE HELD LABOR DAY WEEKEND
AUGUST 31-SEPTEMBER 1,2, 1979
AT A DESERT SANCTUARY NEAR TUCSON
• exploring breakthroughs in gay consciousness
• sharing gay visions
• the spiritual dimensions of gayness
$50 REGISTRATION INCLUDES FOOD, LODGING, POOL
SPIRITUAL CONFERENCE FOR RADICAL FAIRIES
P.O. BOX 1414, LOS ANGELES, CALIF. 90028
for more detailed information see reverse side

SPIRITUAL CONFERENCE FOR RADICAL FAIRIES
A Call to Gay Brothers

It's in the air. Heard everywhere. At the World Symposium on Humanity the talk is about "New Age Politics"—beyond Left and Right—a synthesis of the political and spiritual movements of the past two decades. Sitting in the Kiva at Lama, high in the Sangre de Cristos Mountains of northern New Mexico, Ram Dass talks about the need for "conscious beings" assuming responsibilities for social and political change—a radical Circle of Dharma. In the holy halls of academia, the temple prositutes are whispering about a "paradigm shift"—something new is happening in our society with more and more people living and perceiving their lives differently—and they haven't figured out yet how to contain it. Deep in Oregon's lush Umpqua forest, at the annual fairy-like gathering of the Rainbow Family Tribe, late into the night people talk about the merging of political consciousness and spiritual consciousness—an interest in healing society rather than championing exclusive claims to "rightness."

"New Age politics is a politics in which we learn to assume personal and collective responsibility for the ways we treat one another, and nature, and ourselves. A politics in which we assume this responsibility not out of a sense of grim duty, but out of a sense of real, virtually untapped possibility."
Mark Satin

Does all of this political/spiritual ferment have any relevance to gay men? Is there a gay vision of New Age society? Is a "paradigm shift" in gay consciousness also manifesting itself? The answer to all the questions is: YES!

And many gay brothers are feeling the need to come together . . .

To share new insights about ourselves;
To dance in the moonlight;
To renew our oaths against patriarchy/corporations/ racism;
To hold, protect, nurture and caress one another;
To talk about the politics of gay enspiritment/the enspiritment of gay politics;
To find the healing place inside our hearts;
To become Inspirer/Listener as we share new breakthroughs in how we perceive gay consciousness;
To soar like an eagle;
To re-discover/re-invent our myths;
To talk about gay living/loving alternatives;
To experience the groundedness of the calemus root;
To share our gay visions;
To sing, sing, sing;
TO EVOKE A GREAT FAIRY CIRCLE.

The Call goes out to gay brothers everywhere—poet, Sufi, musician, revolutionary, shaman, heretic, community organizer, farmer, artist, healer, city dweller, Buddhist, dancer, magician, political activist, yogi—whoever you have become since the last time we came together.

The Call goes out to all who know that there is more to us than hetero-imitation. To all who are ready to move on. To all who have broken through and are ready to share those breakthroughs with your fairy brothers.

"The term 'spiritual' represents the accumulation of all experiential consciousness from the division of the first cells in the primeval slime, down through all evolution, to your and our latest insights of Gay Consciousness just a minute ago. What else can we call this overwhelmingly magnificent inheritance—other than spiritual."
Harry Hay

The gathering is to be called, among other names, "A SPIRITUAL CONFERENCE FOR RADICAL FAIRIES." It will be held over the Labor Day weekend, August 31-September 1 & 2, 1979.

The conference site is a comfortable ashram located in the beautiful Sonora desert of southern Arizona—Don Juan country—near Tucson.

There will be a conference fee of $50 to cover the cost of vegetarian meals, lodging, and other incidental expenses involved in putting on the gathering. No one will be denied participation in the conference because of inability to pay.

Pre-registration is required. In order to pre-register, simply send a note with your name, complete address, and phone number to:

SPIRITUAL CONFERENCE FOR RADICAL FAIRIES
P.O. Box 1414
Los Angeles, CA. 90028

A $25 deposit is requested with your pre-registration. More detailed information about the conference schedule and logistics will be provided to you upon pre-registration.

Transportation pooling, whenever possible, will be facilitated for conference participants.

"Come forth, o children,
under the stars,
And take your fill of love!
I am above you and in you.
My ecstasy is in yours.
My joy is to see your joy."
A. Crowley

The initial Call for the gathering is coming from: the Circle of Loving Companions/New Mexico; the Fairy Circle/Los Angeles; Treeroots Foundation/Berkeley; and the Sri Ram Ashram/Arizona.

Anyone interested in receiving additional information or getting involved in conference organizing can write to the mailing address above or connect with one of the following contact persons:

Harry Hay
Circle of Loving Companions/New Mexico
Phone: (505) 852-4404
or
Don Kilhefner
Gay Community Services Center/Los Angeles
Phone: (213) 876-5953

I DROVE FROM BERKELEY to Arizona with my housemate Hal and my dear friend Eric in my 1965 VW van which had a sliding canvas roof and "eyebrow windows": the perfect chariot for a legendary quest. Hal dubbed it "Percy," short for Percival, the knight who went on endless quests.

About 200 of us spanning 3 generations of gay men traveled from all over North America and found our way to a desert sanctuary near Benson, in eastern Arizona, on a hot Labor Day weekend for a 3-day and night encampment. Under that blazing sun, we sought refuge from the scorching sand in the wondrously cooling swimming pool: what an oasis! Imagine dozens of naked men being silly, frolicking like boys, evoking the erotic in a playful way like diving under water to blow bubbles on one another's magic wands. At other times, we smeared mud all over our naked bodies, revealed our wounds in "heart circles," raised our voices in traditional pagan or indigenous chants, shared sacred ceremonies, danced under the moonlight, and were passionate in full-bodied ways that invited our hearts and souls to dance together.

Under Harry's fatherly guidance, we were encouraged to move beyond the objectification that was the norm in the new urban gay landscape, and instead, embrace "subject-subject consciousness" to discover the inner beauty underneath even the homely or wrinkled among us.

That event was a life-changing experience. The energy was so much more uplifting than the bars and baths of San Francisco. At "the tubs" the guys took sex very seriously: there was a job to do (or get). Men sized each other up to see who had the biggest qualifications.

Becoming Sequoia

A month earlier, I marked my 35th birthday at a yoga retreat with Baba Hari Das[33] at Mount Madonna near San Jose, California. Both he and Baba Muktananda would give people who requested one a "spiritual name." In both ashrams, many had taken Hindu names to signify their commitment to the path of yoga. I felt like I was becoming a different person, my real and authentic self, and Tom seemed old and tired. One afternoon, while meditating in a beautiful grove of stately redwoods, Sequoia came to me clearly. It sounded beautiful, having all the vowels and ending in "a" making it androgynous. For me, the sequoias convey timeless serenity. But the idea of taking their name as my own seemed completely audacious. I dismissed it immediately and continued my meditation. Still the idea intrigued me.

Harry's eloquent call was a clear invitation to step into a new version of me. I was excited arriving at the Sanctuary with my 2 dear friends. Among the first to arrive, we were greeted at the gate by Harry and John, who registered us, and invited us to sign our name on a key-ring "earring[34]." I followed the sudden impulse to write "Sequoia." It was a momentous choice. The whole weekend people met me as Sequoia. It was clear that I was beginning a new life.

Ever since, whenever I meet someone, invariably they are struck by the name, and often ask me to explain its origin. It gives me the perfect opening to speak about my deepest values. For example, I later learned that in Cherokee,[35] the name means "peacemaker." That became my guiding inspiration in teaching yoga and meditation beginning a few months later. Claiming my true spirit with a new name proved to be surprisingly empowering. Even all these decades later I still look upon claiming my "true name" as one of the most momentous choices I've ever made.

People usually find my name memorable, which can be awkward for me since I have a poor memory for names. It can be amusing if they can't quite remember. I've been called Sierra and Sonoma when in California, as well as Segovia, and even Saguaro when visiting Arizona.

Some of the new faeries offered small classes in their particularly favorite practices. My dear friend Eric offered a class in *"Loving Kindness Meditation"* or *Metta*, from the Buddhist tradition he was studying. I loved it immediately; it quickly became a regular part of my devotional practices along with meditation. Catholicism has a long tradition of praying "to God" for loved ones or even strangers. Buddhism drops the God part: one simply sends good wishes in a meditative way: first to oneself, then to specific people, then perhaps to "all sentient beings."

The phrases that stayed with me (there are many variations):

- *May... (*insert *I / you / (someone's name / all beings...)*

  ○ *Be Happy*

○ *Be Free From Suffering*

○ *Dwell in The Heart*

○ *Be Healed into Wholeness*

○ *Be At Peace*

● For a fuller explanation of how to practice Metta, see **Experiential Practices** or look online.

I continued attending and sometimes organizing and/or helping facilitate Faerie Gatherings quite regularly for a few years, but became less regular in the ensuing decades. While I have enjoyed the playfulness and open affection of the faeries, my soul is more satisfied by more grounded and structured containers like workshops, many of which I have taken and offered over those same decades.

Who are The Radical Faeries? I've sometimes called us "the queerest of the queer." Each one is unique. We share an appreciation of gender-fluidity, ritual, making music and dancing, being in nature, nudity whenever possible, playful eroticism, and offering a heartfelt "welcome home" to each one-of-a-kind rare gem who chooses to show up.

Before finding the Faeries, I had observed a striking uniformity in the physical appearance of young gay guys in the Bay Area, which became satirized as the "Castro Clone." The uniform included a stach, tight, button-fly torn jeans (preferably Levi's 501s), and a semi-opened shirt (preferably plaid) revealing toned pecs.

The Faeries were all ones that either could not or would not fit that mold. Being with the Faeries gave me even more permission to be my own unique creation. In the ensuing decades, I became ever more one-of-a-kind.

Meeting James, my eros-spirit mentor

A year later I went to another faerie gathering in the Rockies west of Denver where 200 of us shared many days and nights of song, dance, and deliciously loving hugs. There I met James Broughton and his much younger partner, Joel Singer. I was still an objectifying 35 year old; at first saw James as a wrinkled gray prune. "What can that handsome young guy see in that old dog," I wondered, then quickly discovered that James was a true delight. I learned through him that older men's love need not be predatory: it can be pure beneficence and blessing. My housemate Hal also bonded with James and Joel, and loved hosting dinners. So, back in Berkeley, the 4 of us and sometimes some other faeries enjoyed many convivial candle-lit evenings of good food and conversation.

Our friendship endured for 19 years until his passing in 1999. Knowing the end was approaching, I visited them in Port Townsend, WA, where they had lived for the last 10 years of James' life. I offered him some massage, which he happily accepted. The energy between us felt very loving with frequent eye contact. Concluding the massage, I straddled him naked and paraphrased one of his most iconic poems[36], "Is this it? Is this really it?" Without missing a beat, he replied "This is all there is, and it's perfect as it is." Those were our last words.

James was the author of the poem Hans had shared with me 5 years earlier, Song of the Godbody. To this day I revere James and that poem as one of the all-time great gifts I have received.

It was at that Colorado gathering that James was inspired to compose *"Shaman Psalm,"* which I continue to find a moving manifesto. (View text below). Soon after that, he & Joel collaborated to combine film footage from that gathering with *"Shaman Psalm,"* James' new poetic clarion call for men to truly love one another.

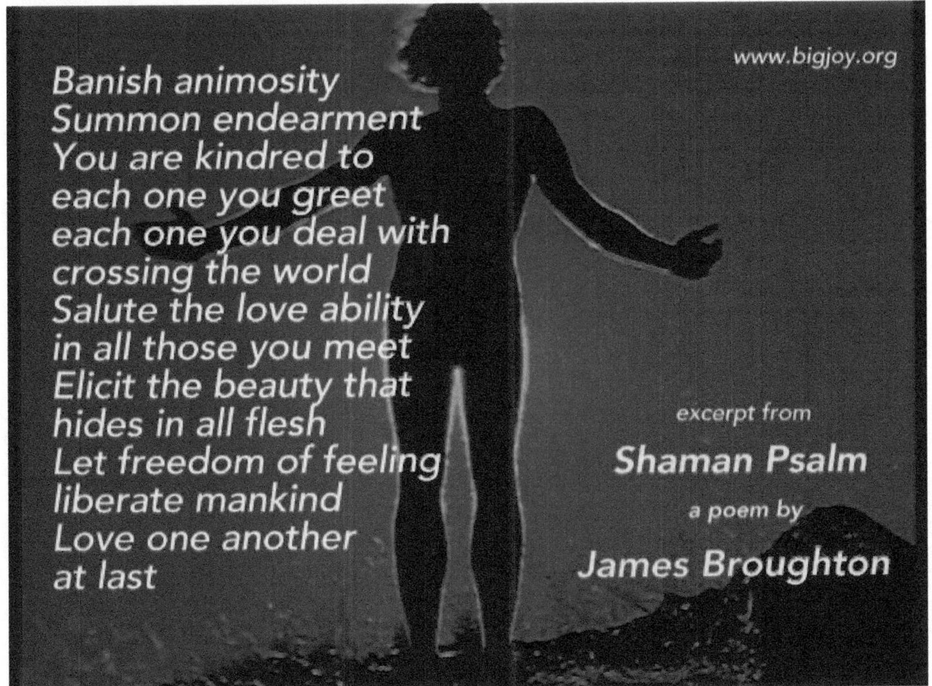

JAMES WAS THE AUTHOR of that one sentence I mentioned earlier, which had etched itself into my consciousness in a life-changing way:

"The penis is the exposed tip of the heart."

Up until reading that I had always experienced my own and others' penises as delightful toys: something to play with, not quite entirely attached to their owner. In this simple statement, James completely altered my view of my own and others' bodies. I suddenly realized the incredible vulnerability of our genitals, and that it is possible to touch, caress, and love another man's heart by the way I touch his penis. My erotic life was forever changed.

In retrospect, I can see that my youthful yearning to see and touch other men's genitals, which are always hidden from public view, is a deep desire to feel men's hearts, which are all too often hidden as well.

I bow in gratitude for the blessings of these mentors and to all who mentored them since ancient times: those who have carried the torch of men loving men even through the darkest of times.

May that light burn ever brighter for generations to come!

Chapter 10 - The 1980s: Continuing Healing the Eros-Spirit Split

1979 was a watershed year for me: I turned 35, broke up with Kyle and took over ownership of "Harper House," met the faeries and felt inspired to take the name Sequoia. I was becoming my real self. The modest inheritance from my dad gave me just enough of a financial cushion that I felt ready to let go of aviation as my livelihood. I bid farewell to my last flying students in December, and was ready when the new decade arrived to start a new life.

As the new decade began, my mentor at the yoga teacher training program insisted it was time to begin teaching yoga, even though after 5 years of training and practice I still felt like a beginner. Figuring that the gay men's community in SF was my natural constituency, I began postering the Castro area of San Francisco offering *Yoga for Gay Men*, rented a classroom in a neighborhood church and began offering weekly classes.

Being a flight instructor the whole previous decade had given me confidence as an instructor. My soul love of yoga also made me confident in teaching what I was learning, and my learning was deepening through the teaching.

I had observed that many of my gay brothers seemed to be caught up in a life lacking much spiritual direction. Many of us had fled lives of religious and social repression and were reveling in unbridled sexual explorations largely devoid of soul. I was finding so much heart-soul nourishment in yoga and meditation and was eager to share them with whoever answered my invitation to come together.

Tantra Massage: On-the-job Training

In the first 3 months of 1980, I took a California-certified massage training at the *Institute for Psycho-Structural Balancing*. It offered a very holistic approach to massage, which was very much in alignment with the Esalen-style massage I had learned 7 years earlier with Judith. It also aligned with Tantric philosophy, which views the body as a temple of the spirit. All through the 70s, I had been offering massage to friends quite often and getting rave reviews. So after completing that training I felt very ready to put my hands and heart to work.

There was a Finnish Sauna on Market Street not far from The Castro, where I had gone for massage a few times. Having become friendly with some of the massage staff and even doing a few exchanges, I applied to work there. By then the other masseurs happily recommended me. I was hired in spring of 1980. Teaching *Yoga for Gay Men* and offering holistic massage, both in the Castro, was a winning combination: my yoga students became instant massage clients and some of my massage clients began coming to my yoga classes. I was off and running!

The owner was a crusty old Finn: very traditional, from the old country. He wanted to run a respectable massage business, so he separated the men's sauna and massage from the women's. That way he figured there would be no hanky-panky. Ha! He seemed oblivious that he was a block from The Castro, and 90% of his male clients were gay. As soon as I started work there I realized most of the men were coming hoping for "a happy ending." That was a dilemma for me. While I spent years cruising places where getting off was the name of the game, here I felt I had more to offer than a mere hand job, and wanted to educate my brothers about the delights of the whole body, just as I had been educated many years earlier in Judith's Esalen massage training.

By then I had been practicing and studying yoga and Tantra theory. One of its premises is that sexual energy can be "cultivated" and refined so that it flows upward rather than being expelled through ejaculation. The advantage is that, instead of the momentary and fleeting pleasure of ejaculation, the practitioner can experience a variety of subtler delights as the sexual energy flows upward into the heart (expanded feelings of love) and into the "third eye" (deeper intuitive insights) and into the crown (a sense of the ultimate unity underlying the seeming differences perceived by the ordinary mind.)

With my background in yoga and Tantra, I intuitively created a sacred space in my tiny massage cubicle by lighting a candle and playing new age music. Judith's version of Esalen-style massage formed the basis of my own. Whereas massage therapy usually segments the body, working on different body parts without ever connecting them together, my style was all about the connecting by using long, flowing strokes, beginning at one foot and gliding up the leg, over the pelvis and on up the torso. I brought men's awareness to their chakras (energy centers) by holding any 2 of them (e.g. belly and heart, or heart and forehead) and inviting them to breathe that connection as I breathed with them, and encouraging them to let out sounds in order to express feelings and let go of stress. From my yoga practice I was aware how powerful stretching can be. So I did passive stretches as part of the massage, e.g. extending an arm upward and massaging all along that flank, armpit and arm to encourage more openness in the upper chest. With a knee bent, that leg can be opened outward or taken across the midline into a twist. So I was working on 3 levels of density: the subtle energy, the muscles as in traditional massage, and the bones through movement and stretching. My intention was to do yoga to my clients and then take them into the traditional "corpse pose" at the end, which I hoped would be a deeply meditative state. I'd quietly slip out of the room to leave them in that serene state for a few minutes then return and quietly check in about their experience. They were invariably amazed how deeply relaxed they had become.

Initially, when men were face-up I would flow around the genitals. I quickly realized this could create frustration and maybe even shame. So I began explaining the rationale for a Tantra massage: that it works intentionally with sexual energy to spread it into the whole body. "You can experience as much pleasure in every part of your body as in your penis. All you have to do is keep relaxing by breathing fully. I'll remind you. If you're comfortable with it, I'll also flow over your genitals and not linger there. I'll spread the energy everywhere. It does not matter if you're hard or soft. It's not about performance, but full-body pleasure. You'll be amazed."

Even though my male massage clients may initially have felt turned on genitally by being lovingly touched and caressed, as I continued to focus my attention and theirs on their entire body, gradually that sexual tension which had been localized in the genitals gave way to full-body relaxation and bliss. By the time they left they usually had forgotten that they had arrived horny. They hugged me in genuine gratitude for touching them at a deeper level: *touching their core and not just their cock*. Often they commented they'd never had their genitals touched without any expectation of getting hard: it was a huge relief to enjoy goal-free genital pleasure.

Observing this transformation repeatedly with many different men confirmed the validity of the Tantric metaphor of alchemy: these practices can turn the lead of mere sex into spiritual gold. I was teaching with my hands what I needed to learn: **that sex is the gateway to the heart and soul.**

I was continuing to study both western views of human sexuality as well as Tantric perspectives as part of my graduate work at the *California Institute of Integral Studies*. I learned that the Taoists in China had a similar view as the Tantrics in India: that sexual energy can be harnessed and transmuted with many physical, emotional, and spiritual benefits for the practitioner. Everything I was learning about sexual Tantra felt oddly familiar: as though I had already known this from previous lives and was simply being reminded of what I already deeply understood.

One of the Tantra teachers I studied was the very controversial Indian master, Bhagwan Shree Rajneesh, who later became known as Osho. One of the reasons he caused such a stir in the west is that he was unashamedly teaching the radical notion that sex and spirit are not antithetical: they are actually two ends of a spectrum of energy. They are the same energy vibrating at different frequencies, like the bass and treble notes on a keyboard or the varied colors of visible light in a rainbow. *They are inherently whole and one.* One of his most beautiful books is a succinct and poetic compilation of quotes from his many talks. It is entitled **Neo-Tantra**. I've read it many times and shared it with many friends and students, who invariably are moved by its simple eloquence in conveying this perspective. The link above is to a PDF we created for some of our Tantra courses. Osho observes that,

"Sex is not the ultimate in pleasure, it is just the beginning.

It is not the bliss supreme, but just an echo of it.[37]"

"If you remain aware, you will come to know that sex is not just sex.

Sex is the outermost layer: deep inside is love,

and even deeper is prayer,

and deepest is God himself.

Sex can become a cosmic experience.

Then it is Tantra.[38]"

I've read many erudite treatises on Tantra, and none conveys its essence with such clarity and simplicity.

Taking Tantra to the Baths

The Oakland Ashram of Baba Muktananda continued to be a spiritual haven for me, even after his death in 1982. Living only about a mile away made it easy to go at least once a week to immerse myself in Baba's rarified "Shakti" (spiritual energy) which permeated the place even though he was no longer physically present. One of the main spiritual practices there was devotional chanting or "kirtan." It was little known in the west back then, yet for me it was so familiar. From my very first taste[39] in March, 1976, it awakened something in me that my soul seems to have known for many lifetimes. A framed quote of Baba on the ashram wall read, *"Chanting the names of God is the highest state!"* To this day, that statement rings true. For me, kirtan is better than sex! In some ways it's like sex. There is a mysterious combination of rhythmic breathing accompanied by drumming, along with the vibration of my own and others' voices, and the gradual increase in the tempo to a crescendo that closely mimics sexual arousal and climax. I suspect this is quite intentional: it's like having sex with God! It's kind of a cliche that when people are at the peak of sexual orgasm they often cry out "Oh God!" In kirtan, an entire group is breathing together and essentially crying out again and again "Oh God!"... "Oh God!" The actual words may be in Sanskrit, some of the many names of the one divinity, such as Ram, Sita, or Shiva, but the meaning is the same: "Oh God!"[40]

So in those years I deepened my ways of massaging to *integrate sex and spirit*. Often my Saturday nights began at The Ashram with an ecstatic chant of *Hare Ram Hare Krishna* from 7-9 PM. Then I'd drive across the Bay Bridge to the baths, bringing my awakened kundalini and my massage oil. As I had been doing, when I'd meet a fellow I fancied I'd ply him with some gentle touch and invite him to receive my full-body massage, then see where the energy took us. In addition to wanting to give him pleasure, I intentionally directed his sexual energy upward through his chakras, hoping to awaken his kundalini as Baba had awakened mine. I had experienced energy transmission from Baba, and wanted to pass it on. To do this, I tuned into Earth and Sky and to Baba, and intended that those energies would come through my heart and hands. I approached these exchanges free of expectations, and was often pleasantly surprised by how things transpired. Men would sometimes open up and become quite affectionate, or meet me in trance-like gazing. It was a wonderful exercise in simply being present with another. My intention was to practice Baba's advice, *"See God in Each Other."* These encounters were continuing experiential learning for me about the endless variety of human sexual expression. Every man I was with was different.

DURING THAT TIME, GAY elder Christopher Isherwood gave a talk one evening in The Castro.

Christopher inspired me because he had been living for decades as both an actively gay man and an ardent practitioner of yoga. He lived in LA and had an ongoing spiritual mentorship with an Indian swami. In *My Guru and his Disciple,* his spiritual autobiography, he reflected on juggling sex and spirit. One story really touched my heart. For years, he had felt ashamed of his regular habit of playing sexually in the park. He had some sense this was "against the rules" for someone on a spiritual path. (Perhaps this guilt may have been a holdover from a repressive Christian family, but maybe that's just my projection.) One day he could not stand the sense of shame and guilt any longer and confessed to his guru that he had this long-standing habit. His guru looked at him with the utmost compassion and said , "See him as the Boy Krishna." Reading that was a balm to my soul. My own Baba had never spoken in any positive way about sexuality; he seemed to feel it was something to transcend. Here was another Indian guru essentially saying "see your sexual activities as a form of divine worship." What a liberation that was for me. From then on, my ministrations at the baths were offered with even greater fervor and devotion.

IN THE EARLY 80S, I continued to enjoy the faerie gatherings that were happening, mostly in various parts of California. In 1981 at the gathering in the mountains near San Diego I met a very soulful guy around my age named Steve who lived in LA. His birthday was the same as my mother's: July 15. While being thoroughly masculine in appearance and demeanor, he had a Cancerian gentleness that was almost maternal. I was very attracted, and saddened to learn he was partnered. He effortlessly touched my heart.

The next year there was interest building among the faeries to begin searching for land to create a "faerie sanctuary." A meeting was suggested. My house in Berkeley proved geographically central, so we agreed to meet there over the course of a weekend. Several LA faeries came north, including the faerie founder, Harry Hay, and his partner, John. Steve also came. "Be still, my heart!" During the meetings, Steve's beautiful, soulful presence. totally distracted me. During one of the breaks, we adjourned to a park and lay in the grass just gazing into one another's eyes for a timeless interlude. My heart and soul opened wide: feeling even more deeply touched, even though there was barely any physical touch between us. Alas, he made it clear he was still partnered. Yet it was also clear we had a profound connection.

The next year, at another San Diego gathering, there was Steve again. I was beyond happy to see him, and he seemed equally delighted. He let me know he was single: *green light!* We shared some wonderfully loving touch. He was literally "a man with a slow hand." We were totally on the same wavelength, and quickly fell in love. We wrote and visited back and forth as often as our work and lives allowed. Every 2-3 weeks, I'd ride an overnight bus to LA, or he would bus up to Berkeley. Our times together were deliciously relaxed and nurturing, leaving me feeling "at home" with him in a way I had longed for for a long time.

Then, after about 6 months, on one of my visits with him, he said he'd begun to feel troubled realizing in his heart that he was still in love with his former partner. He did not feel in integrity continuing to be involved with me. He needed to focus on finding resolution with his previous partner.

I was shocked...totally unprepared. It was like the ground had dropped out from under me: leaving me tumbling through space. On the train going home, I cried for hours. I wrote for hours in my journal every day and talked with friends, feeling utterly bereft. In a way it harkened back to the sudden disappearance and heartbreak I'd experienced with Jim in Alaska 14 years earlier. Except Steve was willing to talk by phone. He did make it clear why he was pulling away. I longed for any shred of contact, so I lived from phone call to phone call. Yet it seemed clear a door in his heart had closed to me. So our calls became fewer and farther between till finally he did not return a call. With a hugely heavy heart, I let him go.

Turning again to my beloved Kahlil Gibran, I found solace in his passage on pain:

> *Your pain is the breaking of the shell*
>
> *that encloses your understanding.*
>
> *Even as the stone of the fruit must break,*
>
> *that its heart may stand in the sun,*
>
> *so must you know pain.*

And could you keep your heart in wonder

at the daily miracles of your life

your pain would not seem less wondrous than your joy;

And you would accept the seasons of your heart,

even as you have always accepted the seasons that pass over your fields.

And you would watch with serenity through the winters of your grief.

Much of your pain is self-chosen.

It is the bitter potion by which the physician within you heals your sick self.

Therefore trust the physician, and drink his remedy in silence and tranquility:

For his hand, though heavy and hard, is guided

by the tender hand of the Unseen,

And the cup he brings, though it burn your lips,

has been fashioned of the clay

which the Potter has moistened

with His own sacred tears.

I trusted the wisdom of his words. My heart did take comfort. Life would go on. I began to see Life was teaching me (again!) about letting go of attachment to a specific source of love. The message was *never to stand on someone else's ground*: stay on my own ground and relate from there. Life kept insisting I look within.

Joseph Kramer and The Body Electric

In the early 80s I was delighted to meet a fellow-explorer on the path of integrating the erotic and spiritual. Joseph came to one of my early *Yoga for Gay Men* classes, and I learned that, like me, he was a "recovering Catholic." Indeed he had gone even farther by being briefly in seminary. We both lived in Berkeley and were both exploring the many offerings in Eastern mysticism available in that wonderful spiritual smorgasbord of the Bay Area in the 70s and 80s (and still.). Joseph invited me to join him for a weekend with Taoist Mantak Chia to learn about the *"Microcosmic Orbit"*: a way of circulating energy through the entire subtle body from root to crown. It was analogous to what I was learning of the chakras and kundalini through the Tantra tradition.

By the early 80s, Joseph and I were both horrified at how many of our gay brothers were getting sick and dying from a mysterious new disease. It seemed to be caused by exchanging bodily fluids in sex. We both wished to share what we were learning from eastern wisdom about ways of being with sexual energy that were not just about "getting off." Joe began offering evening and then weekend workshops incorporating what he learned with Mantak Chia and others. I was one of his early and eager students.

Around the same time I learned of another gay men's erotic offering called *"Intimate Explorations for Men"* being run by Floyd and Jim out of their beautiful home in Marin, on the north side of the Golden Gate. Jim had already been exploring the path of Sufism, and had studied in Turkey with traditional Sufi masters. He brought back what he was learning and combined it with what Floyd had been learning with more western teachers of conscious eroticism. Their events were a rich potpourri of men loving men. One of the exercises I most vividly remember: we were paired up at random, and invited to take turns tenderly planting "baby kisses" on our partner's face for several minutes. This was quite a radical departure for most of us from the ways we typically kissed another man. It took us into a whole different state of consciousness that was remarkably sweet and intimate without being genitally sexual.

The more I explored these "gourmet" forms of erotic intimacy, the less ordinary sex seemed satisfying. I became increasingly eager to share what I was learning. My opportunity came during one of my graduate courses, called *"Cross-cultural Healing,"* offered by a wonderful Basque woman named Angeles Arrien. Angie taught about the importance of healing rituals and the essence of how to create them. Our course assignment was to create an actual healing ritual with real people and write up a report about it. Inspired by her, as well as by what I was learning of yoga, massage, Taoism, and Tantra, I created a weekend event encompassing those practices, and offered it to fellow faeries as well as my yoga students. I reserved *The Lotus Sutra*, a day spa in Cotati, about an hour north of SF. A group of about 10 of us was able to take over the whole place for a Friday night, stay overnight, and all day/evening on Saturday. It was perfect, with a group space, sauna, outdoor hot tub in an enclosed yard suitable for nude yoga and sun-bathing, and a massage room with 4 tables. We created a loving circle of brothers to care for one another through shared yoga, heartful speaking, and hours of luxurious full-body touch. It was a big hit, and I was on fire about this formula. James and Joel were 2 of the participants, and encouraged me to create more such events. Angie was very supportive and approving of my healing ritual. It became the prototype for the weekends I began co-creating with Doug Fraser 5 years later. Stay tuned.

The next year, I became completely immersed in my Master's thesis, exploring whether and how people with AIDS might benefit by learning to thoroughly relax through simple practices drawn from yoga and meditation.

Around then Joseph had formalized his workshops in *Taoist Erotic Massage* and opened **The Body Electric School**.[41] I enrolled in several of his weekends, which were profoundly healing for me in a new way. Unlike the calm, meditative Tantric Massage I had been developing based on my earlier Esalen-style training, Joseph has synthesized a much more high-energy type of massage intended to replicate the intense arousal of conventional sexual stimulation without the usual ejaculatory release. Instead he taught "The Big Draw": a combination of a rapid "charging breath" coupled with unconventional genital strokes to raise energy without triggering ejaculation, followed by tensing the body while holding the breath for 10-30 seconds. The "release" that followed moved the sexual energy in entirely different ways that were unique to each man each time. For me, it moved the energy first up into my belly chakra, triggering strong laughing and/or crying, then further up into my heart chakra creating blissfully loving and peaceful feelings. I had long ago disconnected my genitals from my heart through all the casual masturbatory sex I had had in quick, casual encounters. It was as though there was a solid wall between my cock and my heart. To my amazement, this Taoist Erotic Massage reunited them. I felt whole, and had the direct experience of what James had written: "The penis is the exposed tip of the heart." Having my genitals lovingly touched was what I had been missing my whole life. My mother had viewed them with distaste, and my furtive sexual partners had used them for their own arousal.

I greatly appreciated and valued what Joe was offering. He wanted to create safe sexual alternatives for gay men in the face of the AIDS epidemic and more broadly to bring the ancient wisdom of the Tantric and Taoist traditions to gay men's lives. He seemed to value my presence and invited me to assist at many of his weekend events. That was a whole other way to learn: to witness dozens of men in high states of arousal deliberately channeling that sexual energy in new ways to open their own erotic bodies for their unique healing integration. It was beautiful to witness and to lend supportive energy to the participants.

What I saw over and over every spring and fall in Seattle and Vancouver was a room full of men, who arrived as strangers, full of hope, excitement and apprehension undergoing a personal and collective transformation. After 2 very full days, we had melted into a puddle of blissful relaxation and bonding, without the use of any substances.

I loved the role of Assistant. We were typically a team of 4 supporting the facilitator by providing supplies to the massage tables as needed and serving as a communications link between individual participants and the facilitator. In addition, during the actual massage sessions, which usually lasted 60-90 minutes, we were encouraged to offer an additional pair of skilled and caring hands to each duo, and to do it in a way that was both supportive and unobtrusive. Ideally we were to offer touch that augmented what the masseur was doing. I delighted in surveying the room and sensing when a particular duo could use an extra shot of energy and love. Sometimes my input would also inspire the masseur to expand his repertoire.

The experience was also a voyeur's delight: a room full of around 30 naked men in varying states of arousal delighting in pleasuring one another was a wonder to behold. It was hard at times not to be distracted by my attraction to certain men. I vividly remember being so taken by one participant that I was unconsciously giving him extra attention. Finally the instructor had to quietly remind me to share my love equally with everyone. To my happy surprise, that lovely guy and I went on to become fellow Tantra explorers and life-long friends.

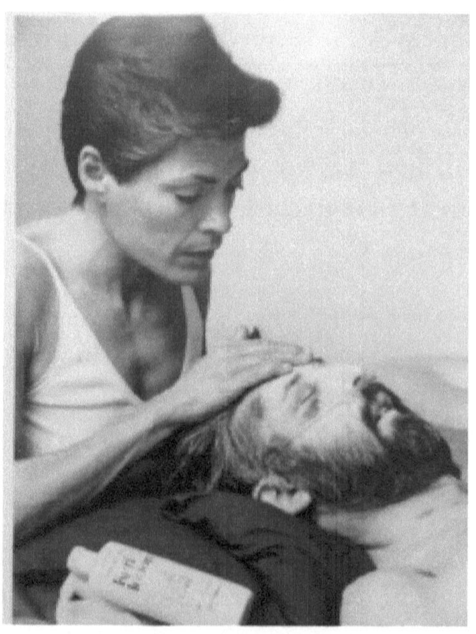

JOSEPH'S *Body Electric School* also began offering a state-approved holistic (non-sexual) 100-hour massage training to men and women. The main instructor was an inspiring woman named Irene Smith. Irene had a colorful sexual history herself, and was very at ease teaching full-body sensual massage to groups of gay men. The AIDS epidemic was exploding, and San Francisco was one of the epicenters. Irene saw that gay men who were living with and dying from AIDS were being treated as pariahs, not only by straight culture, but right within the gay male community. They were literally "untouchables." She pioneered a program to offer caring touch to men on Ward 5B at SF General[42], which was essentially a palliative care hospice. I was so inspired by her vision and dedication that I offered to assist her in her incredibly compassionate volunteer work. She had cleared things with the nursing staff so that we could show up for an evening and go from room to room, quietly asking the occupants, "Is there anything you'd like in the way of caring touch?" Men almost always replied with an eager "Yes, please!" They often seemed starving for caring touch. Most of them were quite young. Too many had been abandoned by lovers, friends and family. They had become infected with a still-mysterious illness that seemed to be passed on through sexual contact. Touch had been their death sentence. Our intention was to offer the kind of subtle, non-sexual, yet sensually satisfying touch I had begun learning a decade early from Judith, and through my explorations of Tantra. I found it both incredibly moving and astoundingly heart-breaking to see so many beautiful young men (I was then 40, and most were younger than I) withering, shriveling, literally wasting away. Many were starving to death because their extreme diarrhea prevented them from retaining enough nourishment to support life.

What I was learning even more fully in this situation than when I'd been making my massage rounds at the baths is that sex is often not the real need. The deeper need that touch can fulfill is for love. Touch is our first language. We knew in our first hours of life whether or not we were being loved by the quality of touch we received. During our sexually active years, many people conflate their life-long needs for loving touch with their desire for sexual stimulation. They look to sex for a more primal need. Now, near the end of their lives, these men were not hungry for hot sex: they craved feeling loved and cared for. We were able to provide that level of primal comfort...right up into their final hours. It was so sad and also so beautiful.

As much as I treasured being able to offer that kind of caring touch, I also found it draining to keep looking death in the face over and over. After about 6 months, I had to stop. Other volunteers were joining our team, and I was more than willing to take a break.

Irene kept going. She was astounding to me. Even after the intense dying in the 80s subsided, Irene founded *Everflowing*, and continued offering and teaching others how to offer that kind of compassionate touch to those nearing the end of their lives in hospice settings. She was the nearest thing to a saint I have ever met: so utterly real and from the heart.

I last visited with Irene in 2014. She passed in 2021 of cancer, surrounded by those she had taught to offer compassionate touch. I will always treasure what I learned with her. I vividly remember her teaching:

"Our arms and hands are an extension of our heart.

Touch is the language of love."

Embracing the healing power of anger

IRENE HAD BEEN A PROTEGE of Elisabeth Kübler-Ross, who is most known for her description of Five Stages of Dying. In addition to cultivating her incredibly compassionate approach to comforting the dying, Irene also learned some emotional release techniques from EKR.

While she and I were collaborating on Ward 5B, she told me of a one-day workshop she would be offering on anger release. I knew somewhere inside I must have a lot of bottled up anger which I had never been allowed to express as a child. I trusted Irene and heard my inner voice tell me it's time to take the lid off that long-sealed container. A dozen men and women joined Irene one Saturday morning knowing only that we'd spend the day exploring anger. The morning felt pretty tame, as Irene talked theory about the body-mind connection. She had learned that anger is at its root a fundamentally benign energy our body activates when it feels it is time to make a drastic change. The shadow side is that it is too often expressed in aggressive and destructive ways, or bottled up corrosively, or turned inward in self-destructive ways.

Irene was going to have us take turns on a mattress, doing some seemingly simple movements coordinated with breathing. When it was our turn on the mattress, we were surrounded and supported by the rest of the group sitting on the floor watching. We were to kneel facing a stack of phone books with

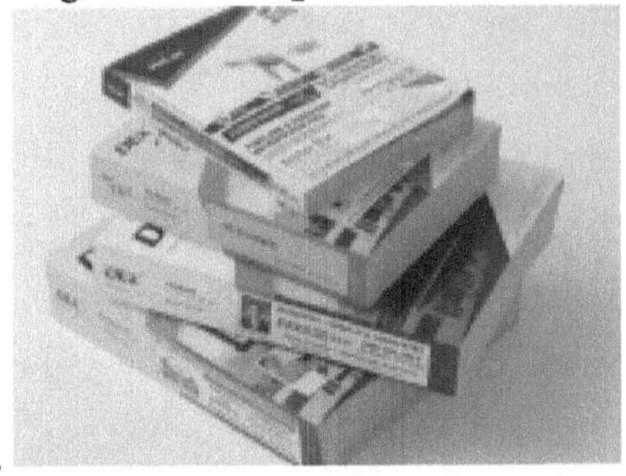

a meter-long rubber hose in our two hands.

The simple movement:

- inhale fully while kneeling up tall and raising the hose high overhead;

- exhale letting out any sound and coming down hitting the phone books as hard as we could.

- Repeat over and over.

Invariably, the person doing the movement and sound would become more emotionally intense. A larger energy would emerge with louder sounds and more forceful striking of the stack. We were allowed to curse and swear if it helped us access our rage. The magnitude and intensity was surprisingly safe to witness because it was being directed at these inanimate objects within the safe container of our shared intention.

Watching I felt a bit detached: "Wow, they have so much rage. I'm not feeling that and never have." I doubted I'd get very emotional. Wrong! When my turn came, I followed the instructions. It felt powerfully liberating to have total permission to make these huge, seemingly violent movements and sounds. Each time I did it, and heard Irene's gentle encouragement, my energy got bigger, and my movements and sounds more intense. The phone books suddenly became my father. There was no particular image or memory: more like a global animosity for all the ways he failed me. Not only had he been physically absent for much of my first eight years, even after coming back home he was emotionally absent with all his drinking. I got louder and more forceful. Pages went flying! Tears came as well. Rage and sadness were one big ball of energy. Suddenly I collapsed into tears. The rage was gone. In its place I felt incredible sadness *for him*. I sensed how emotionally absent his own alcoholic father must have been, and how much horror he must have witnessed in Europe and Korea in those two wars. I could see clearly that his drinking was his self-medication to numb all the pain he must have been carrying. I felt immense love for him, and appreciation for his sincere efforts to be a good father. My heart broke open in love. Even though he had died several years earlier, I felt I could communicate my love and appreciation to his spirit.

That was a powerful catharsis. I still feel amazed how it transformed frozen unconscious rage into compassion and love. Now writing about it 40 years later, tears of love are again flowing. Not only did that Saturday afternoon with Irene heal my long-fraught relationship with my father. It also taught me not to fear my own anger. I now experience it as a powerful force for change that can be harnessed constructively.

I COMPLETED MY MASTER'S in June of 1986, and, as if by magic, met Doug Fraser that fall. We had heard of each other by seeing our respective display ads in the gay classifieds. When we met in the stairwell of the Central YMCA in SF, we stood talking for at least 90 minutes. We discovered that we shared a similar vision about offering events for our gay brothers combining conscious movement and touch to connect more fully with ourselves and one another. Amazing!

Within a few weeks, we met several more times and laid out the specifics. We surveyed possible weekend retreat sites, reserved them, and began publicizing our new offerings through our respective networks. It felt like an idea whose time had come. Our first *"Light Touch Retreat"* was in January, 1987, at the Marin Headlands, a retreat center run by the Golden Gate National Recreation Area. A month later, at a Faerie Gathering at Breitenbush Hot Springs east of Portland, I offered a sampler of the kinds of touch we had done at *Light Touch*. One of the faeries who lived in Seattle urged me to bring *Light Touch* there. I said, "Sure! Find me a place!"

Brian was very well-connected. He found and booked Doe Bay Village[43], an aging, hippie resort on Orcas Island, and handled the publicity and registration in the Seattle area. Doug had grown up in British Columbia, and asked his old friend, Eric, in Vancouver to serve a similar role handling PR and admin. On Father's Day weekend that year we launched the first of almost 10 years of *Light Touch Retreats* twice a year at that spectacular venue.

Neither Doug nor I had been to Orcas when we took the ferry there that June. I was blown away by the beauty of the San Juan Islands. I had only been to Seattle once before: on the way to Vietnam. Now I was getting a look at this astoundingly gorgeous topography: I knew I needed to live somewhere in this beautiful part of the world.

Doug and I were a dream team. We worked hand-in-glove. Even though we were wonderfully friendly, we were never socially friends or lovers: our shared work was our passion and our baby. It felt like some kind of fate or karma that drew us together. I never remember a moment of friction.

A couple of years later, Doug told me he'd heard of a magical hot springs in northern New Mexico he thought would be another possible site for our work. He and his partner drove down to check it out and gave an enthusiastic thumbs-up. So in the summer of 1991, we began offering *Light Touch* at Bodhi Manda Zen Center. It was indeed magical: located in a red sandstone canyon carved from a million-year-old volcano called Jemez (hay'-mez) Mountain, it was a verdant valley in an otherwise arid desert. The hot springs were right on the grounds: warm water bubbling right up from Mother Earth. Because it was a Zen monastery in a tranquil canyon, it was astoundingly peaceful: a real get-away to explore connecting more deeply with our bodies, hearts and souls and with our Mother.

Part of the magic was Hosen, a Zen Abbess who was, and still is (!), the spiritual director as well as the very warm host. Hosen has been there in that role since 1980, when she was around 30! She has dedicated her life to welcoming spiritual seekers to savor this special sanctuary.

Doug and I kept a full schedule of retreats for several years: every spring and fall in northern California, Orcas, and then also at Jemez Springs. It was super-fun and fulfilling. Sadly however, death was stalking Doug. He had been infected with AIDS and was slowly going downhill. I vividly remember the closing circle at our 1994 retreat at Bodhi when he announced he was sensing that this would be his last retreat: his energy was waning. We were all bereft: he was greatly loved. A year later his partner let me know the end was near. I flew to SF, and took turns with several who loved him keeping all-night vigils in his room at SF General as he struggled with the ravages of AIDS. It was painful to witness his suffering, feeling there was so little comfort I could offer. Yet we both knew the language of touch, and I did the best I could to minimize his suffering. Tears well up now remembering those nights, and how lost I felt after he passed. A couple of the regular participants at *Light Touch* pitched in during the next few years to help me keep the retreats going. I am forever grateful for their support.

James Broughton and Joel were early, enthusiastic participants at our retreats. I always prevailed upon James to read some of his inspiring poetry. After he read *Shaman Psalm* one weekend I asked his permission to reprint it as a handout, and he heartily agreed. Later he gave me several copies of the original calligraphed edition, along with a hand-written note authorizing me to make copies for handouts. So I know I have his complete permission to share the poem with you here.

Shaman Psalm ~ a poem by James Broughton

From the book Special Deliveries.

Listen Brothers Listen

The alarms are on fire

The oracles are strangled

Hear the pious vultures

condemning your existence

Hear the greedy warheads

calling for your death

Quick while there's time

Take heed Take heart

Claim your innocence

Proclaim your fellowship

Reach to each other

Connect one another

and hold

Rescue your lifeline

Defy the destroyers

Defy the fat vandals

They cry for a nation

of castrated bigots

They promise a reward

of disaster and shame

Defy them Deny them

Quick while there's hope

Renovate man

Insist on your brotherhood

Insist on humanity

Love one another

and live

Release your mind from

the handcuffs of guilt

Take off your blinders

Focus your insight

Take off the bandages

that infect your fears

See your wounds heal when

you know your birthright

Men are not foes

Men are born loving

welcome being tingled by

the touch of devotion

Honor one another

or lose

Come Brothers Waken

Uproot hostility

Root out the hypocrites

Warm up your phoenix

to arouse a new era

Disarm the cutthroats

Sever the loggerheads

Offset the history

of torment and curse

Man is the species

endangered by man

Quick while there's time

Abandon your rivalries

or mourn

Deflate pugnacity

Magnify friendliness

Off with your mask

Off with your face

Dump the false guides

who travel the warpaths

Uncover your loving

Discover surrender

Rise in your essence to

the tender occasion

Unwrap your radiance

and brighten your crew

Value one another

or fall

Come forth unabashed

Come out unbuttoned

Bury belligerence

Resurrect frolic

Only through body can

you clasp the divine

Only through body can

you dance with the god

In every man's hand

the gift of compassion

In every man's hand

the beloved connection

Trust one another

or drown

Banish animosity

Summon endearment

You are kindred to

each one you greet

each one you deal with

crossing the world

Salute the love ability

in all those you meet

Elicit the beauty that

hides in all flesh

Let freedom of feeling

liberate mankind

Love one another

at last

Hold nothing back

Hold nothing in

Romp and commingle

out in the open

Parade your peculiar

Shine your monkey

Rout the sourpuss

Outrage the prig

Quick while there's room

revel in foolhardy

Keep fancies tickled

Grow fond of caress

Go forthright together

or fail

Affirm your affection

Be laughing in wisdom

You are a miracle

dismissed as a moron

You are a godbody

avoiding holiness

Claim your dimension

Insist on redemption

Love between men will

anachronize war

bring joy into office

and erogenate peace

Accept one another

and win

Relish new comrades

Freshen new dreams

Speak from the heart

Sing from the phallus

Keep holy bounce in

your intimate ballgames

Sexual fervor can

leap over galaxy

outburst the sun

football the moon

Give way to love

Give love its way

Ripen one another

or rot

Extend your vision

Stretch your exuberance

Offer your body to

the risks of delight

where soul can run naked

spirit jump high

Taste the divine on

the lips of lover

Savor the divine on

the thigh of a friend

Treasure the divinity

that ignites the orgasm

Surprise the eagles

and soar

Let the weapons rust

Let the powers crumble

Open your fists

into embraces

Open your armslength

into loving circles

Be champions of hug

Be warriors of kiss

Prove in beatitude

a new breed of man

Prove that comradeship

is the crown of the gods

Cherish one another

and thrive

Listen Brothers Listen

The alarms are too late

This is the hour for

amorous revolt

Dare to take hold

Dare to take over

Be heroes of harmony

in bedfellow bliss

Man must love man

or war is forever

Outnumber the hawks

Outdistance the angels

Love one another

or die

I love that this poem connects the erotic, emotional, personal, political, and spiritual dimensions together. I've read it countless times at our many weekend retreats, and I invariably get choked up at some of the lines, especially, "Man must love man or war is forever." I especially treasure the love I share with many straight men. Sex is not the glue: it is love itself that is the bond. May we men learn to "love one another at last," and to love all humans as family!

MY OWN LIFE WAS UNDERGOING major changes. The late 80s saw two major completions for me. In 1986, I completed all the schooling I had first undertaken in 1975: yoga teacher training and a Masters in East/West Psychology. In early 1987, my dear Kyle had left this world. The Bay Area had never seemed like it would be my long-term home. It was a fantastic place to find myself, but by the late 80s I was feeling drawn north. I longed for 4 seasons and had seen enough of the Pacific Northwest to feel a magnetic attraction.

In 1986, the summer I completed my Masters, Vancouver had invited the world to come for its Expo. I happily accepted. It was truly love at first sight. July in Vancouver was, and still is, stunning. The temperatures are a balmy 70s F /20s C with low humidity, few bugs, and gorgeous blue skies to frame the snow-capped, forested mountains by the sea. Stunning is an understatement.

The next summer I treated myself to a train ride across Canada from Vancouver to Toronto,

which led to meeting a larger-than-life man who swept me off my feet. I was already intoxicated by Canada, having loved the Thousand Islands area of the Saint Lawrence River as a kid. We met at the Kingston Men's Conference and continued getting acquainted through long phone calls. That quickly turned into a passionate, long-distance romance: the phone wires must have been sizzling. Early on, we began calling each other "Babe."

He was a holistic doctor who was totally enthused about my work, and apparently about me. The next spring he flew out to Orcas, ostensibly to experience **Light Touch** for himself. That turned out to be a pretext, albeit sincere. I was in full facilitator mode, trying to treat him just like any other participant: not wanting the other guys to know I had a crush on one of them. I would not have had any private moments with him on my own, but he was a cheeky suitor. The first night at the end of the opening evening, as I was turning out lights and tidying the workshop space, he seductively said, "Can I come give you a good-night kiss?" I suspect I blushed as I stammered, "Uh, sure." Well, his forwardness continued. One kiss led to another and another and ...

For the rest of the weekend, it was really hard to pretend he was just another one of the guys. I'm not sure how obvious we were. It was fun: almost naughty.

Then, a couple of months later, in January, I flew to Ottawa where he lived to sample the winter in the frozen north. The heat of his love kept me warm, and my own infatuation with Canada convinced me I'd love it there. So in the spring of 1988, preparing to give him and Ottawa a try, I packed up a camper and headed across the continent. It was an exciting time: a new life was beckoning. The Bay Area had been wonderful in so many ways and also utterly heart-breaking. Being in an epicenter of the AIDS crisis, and losing most of the beautiful kindred spirits I had met through the Faeries, was a grief was too huge to digest. I needed to get away.

Babe was wonderful, yet also somehow too much for me. What I had savored about him in small doses when we first met and were connecting long-distance became overwhelming when we were together non-stop. His intensity was like drinking from a fire hose. His often huge emotional swings began to feel like a dizzying roller-coaster to me. The meditative calm of my meditation practice was too agitated: I knew within a couple of weeks that we were not a good match. Yet I did not want to give up so easily, and tried to convince myself we could make it work.

He was wonderfully helpful with Canadian Immigration: long before there was any recognition of same-sex relationships, we had to concoct a tall tale that I would be working for him as a stress-management specialist. By some kind of luck and grace we were able to get me a year-long work permit, during which time I initiated the longer process of applying for "Landed Immigrant" status, the Canadian version of the American "green card."

Babe and I did share many fun adventures. We both loved to dance and to be out in nature. He was very involved with *Re-evaluation Co-counseling*, which I took to immediately, as it dovetailed nicely with my earlier peer counseling training. He had a wonderful circle of friends of all genders and sexual orientations, who all welcomed me warmly. He and Ottawa treated me really well.

Yet I knew it was not home. The climate is similarly extreme. Summers are hot, humid and buggy. Winters are beautifully bright and blue but also brutally cold. I loved ice-skating on the Rideau Canal. In between there are long months of dark, gray, wet, and mud. The only months I truly enjoyed were May and September. By late 1989, I was realizing my future was back out west. Having seen Vancouver, nowhere else would do. I let Babe and all my new friends know I'd be heading west again by summer. I was surprised how surprised he was. He did not see that coming and was deeply saddened. I realized I'd been keeping my dissatisfactions with our relationship largely to myself: not wanting to rock the boat, knowing he was prone to bouts of depression. Now our emotions could not be avoided. We did try to talk things over and be honest about our feelings. Yet nothing we said or did made me want to stay. To our mutual friends, I made my decision sound more about the weather and my love of the west coast, which truly was a major factor. So Babe and I put on a brave public face. He even came to my going-away party and we danced up a storm. In June, exactly 2 years after I'd arrived, I packed up my camper and headed west to Vancouver.

So the 1980s were a time of huge growth and transformation for me. I experienced great delights through eros-spirit integration experiences with many amazing teachers, launched 40 years of offering holistic and Tantric massage, both individually and in retreats, and experienced inexpressible grief confronting how ephemeral our mortal lives are. I explored and relocated to Canada, and am still in love with Vancouver decades after my first infatuation.

If sex and death are indeed life's two biggest teachers, I experienced huge lessons in both during that decade. I began to learn that death can come at any time, and to savor each day, each hour, each breath, and each moment of loving connection with another.

I was also beginning to experience ever more deeply one of Tantra's most essential teachings: love is not *out there*. We must find love *inside first*. Indeed, the love in our own heart is Who We Are. Once we know that, then every person can become an embodiment of The Beloved.

Sounds great in theory, right? What about that asshole who (pick your pet peeve) ? Once someone asked the Dalai Lama, "How do you not hate the Chinese for what they've done?" He took a deep breath and sighed: "This is why we practice."

Chapter 11 - The 1990s: Diving deeper into Tantra with all genders

Again as in 1980, the new decade of the 1990s marked a major personal shift. This time I was finding "home" in Vancouver, Canada. I'd been searching for "home" for 55 years, and had been zeroing in, beginning with Expo in Vancouver in 1986. My sojourn in Ottawa showed me that, by and large, Canadians are a very kind and gentle people. On the surface they are more reserved than most Americans: there is a certain propriety and politeness. Once that surface reserve is crossed, there is an abiding warmth and loyalty I've found really comforting. I quickly felt more "at home" in Canada than in the U.S., and still do.

So in June, 1990, as I headed west, it felt very right. For me there is something more expansive about the consciousness on the west coast: all the way from California though coastal Oregon and Washington and on into "Beautiful British Columbia." The culture is much less bound by tradition. Innovation is normal. Quirkiness is, too. *All the fruits and nuts roll west,* a wry pundit observed. I am proudly both!

Just as Vancouver had welcomed the world with its Expo when I first visited in July, 1986, so again was it welcoming the queer world with the **Gay Games** in the summer of 1990 (30 min vid[1]). For me it was an amazing time to arrive in my new and future home. The city was full of queer folks walking arm in arm, often 4 or 5 abreast. It was intoxicating to experience so many of us from all over the world joyously celebrating life and gay love.

---

1. https://youtu.be/6d_zsXhDEHI

I was fortunate to already have several wonderful friends here from having offered **Light Touch Retreats** on Orcas Island the preceding 3 years. I felt very warmly welcomed by them as well. They formed the core of some of the classes and workshops I began offering. Some became massage clients themselves and/or referred friends. So I had a fairly instant professional and social life, which felt wonderful.

By then I had been granted my Landed Immigrant status, and was so incredibly grateful to know I could legally live and work in Canada the rest of my life.

Shortly after arriving I changed the name of my events to **Men In Touch**: wanting to be more inclusive of all men, no matter what their sexual preferences were. I wanted to create a safe place for men to explore being more open, vulnerable, and intimate in whatever ways each man wanted. In addition to the weekend retreats, which were held a few times a year, I began offering men's weekly classes in yoga and sharing non-sexual TLC.

Kenyth: my straight-but-not-narrow big brother

IN ADDITION TO OFFERING weekly classes in Vancouver, I began doing the same in Bellingham, WA, about 90 minutes south. I had sold my Berkeley house and purchased a 4-plex near Western Washington University, which has since become my retirement nest egg.

After postering around town, I got a call from a man who said he was intrigued by my classes. He did not actually want to attend, he said, so much as to meet the man who was bold and innovative enough to offer such classes. He invited me to meet him for lunch. I'm so glad I accepted his invitation.

He was 10 years older and a retired dean of Fairhaven College, a subdivision of Western Washington U. I found him to be a suave southern gentleman with a keen curiosity about all things erotic about all genders. He described himself as "straight but not narrow," and was keen to hear all about my gay life and erotic adventures and loves. He readily shared his own very full and varied love life. He'd been married multiple times and had 2 grown children. Now in his upper 50s with a full shock of wavy gray hair, bright eyes, and a lithe frame, it was easy to imagine women falling for him. He'd long since had a vasectomy so as to not have pregnancy worries with his many lovers. Some considered him a womanizer, but I quickly learned he really did **love** women, not merely use them for his own pleasure as too many men do. In general, he was serially monogamous and usually with women younger and less experienced.

We quickly discovered we had a shared passion for racquetball, and developed a pattern of weekly visits to one another's YMCA for a sweaty game, then adjourn for lunch and a catch-up about our intimate encounters. We developed a great love for one another. He actually bemoaned not being gay, saying that, if he were, he'd surely find me to be a wonderful partner. I was genuinely flattered, especially by his clear comfort in kissing on the lips when we'd meet and part company. He reported that people often mistook him for gay: he had a certain flair for colorful dress (sort of hippie-chic). He loved to dance and practice Tai Chi and Emilie Conrad Daoud's *Continuum* movement, so his posture and gait were much more fluid and graceful than most straight men. Kenyth became one of my dearest friends. In a sense, he was the big brother I never had. As we both had a background in psychology we were able to be skillful confidants for one another. Over the course of our 18 year friendship we were able to help each other weather some of the storms in our love lives. I could tell him anything, the highs and lows of my life, and he was invariably supportive. I felt seen and validated in a way I found wonderfully comforting. One of his mottos has greatly inspired me: ***"It's never too late to have a happy childhood!"***

I learned over time he had not had a happy childhood growing up in the Appalachian mountains of North Caroline with a cold, distant mother and an authoritarian father. His Southern Baptist upbringing had soured him on all religion. He was a confirmed agnostic, and looked upon my spiritual devotion with skeptical bemusement. It saddened me that he was missing the deep soul nourishment I experience in my spiritual practices. I observed he suffered from chronic anxiety, which he self-medicated with marijuana. I wished he could experience the deep comfort and well-being I regularly experience from meditation and devotional practices. Still, we respected our differences.

Where we met was in holding love of our fellow humans as a paramount value. Over the many years of our friendship, he went through several relationships with women. What was striking was that he truly loved each one. Even after they stopped being lovers, they invariably retained a loving friendship, albeit sometimes with a rocky period of transition from lovers to friends.

Fast forward to the spring of 2009: I heard about a workshop in Tucson called **Sexual Shamanism**. The term really resonated, as shamanism had been part of my studies for my Master's at CIIS. I understood it to consist of rituals designed to alter consciousness: to take people out of their ordinary egoic state into something deeper. I had never applied that term to my work even though it's what I had been doing for years. I had to go to learn more.

Years earlier, Kenyth had loaned me a book called *Women Who Love Sex*, by Gina Ogden. That may seem an odd book to offer a gay man, but Kenyth knew my erotic history very well. He knew that, unlike most gay or straight guys, my approach to eroticism was more Feminine: I was generally less inclined to rush toward climax and more inclined to explore sensual subtleties for extended periods with no particular goal in mind except heightened awareness and bliss. He suspected I'd resonate with these women who were writing about other women's erotic experiences. This was pretty radical, as most scholarly research about human sexuality was, ironically, conducted by men. Women's experiences were usually filtered through that male lens. This book was new.

At the last minute, as I was heading to the airport to fly to Tucson, I remembered Kenyth's book that had gathered dust for years and stuffed it into my backpack to read on the plane. I loved it.

Among the dozen or so of us aspiring or actual Sexual Shamans, one woman stood out. Francie and I were the elders in the room: unlike most of the participants, we were in our mid-60s. She was vibrantly alive. At lunch I struck up a conversation, told her about this unusual book, and asked if she might be interested to look at it. She was.

Two days later at our final dinner, we sat together. She was enthralled reading that book: it really spoke to her.

"Where did you find it?"

"Oh, a friend in Bellingham, Washington leant it to me."

"Bellingham? I used to live there! I worked at Fairhaven College."

"Really? My friend was the dean there a while back."

"What's his name?"

When I said his full name her eyes got huge. ***"You KNOW Kenyth Freeman?!?!"***

She was clearly gobsmacked and went on to tell me of a brief affair they'd had some 30 years earlier. Back then, she was both utterly smitten and crestfallen to learn he did not want to sire any more offspring, which was high on her priorities at that point. They sadly parted ways. She had secretly carried a torch for him all these years, all through a marriage, raising a son, a divorce and a few other men. None held a candle to the flame she had for him.

"Would you like me to put you two in touch?" I asked.

"Oh...only if he's, uh, *interested*," she cooed shyly and coyly.

I did. They visited soon thereafter, then Francie moved in and never left!

They reconnected and became the fulfillment of one another's mature love lives. Three months later they sweetly asked me to officiate at their backyard wedding with just their sons and me present as they read vows they'd each written. I had gotten "ordained" online and could legally sign their papers to file with the state.

Their knot was well tied. Over nearly two decades, I'd seen Kenyth go through a succession of younger women who were not his equal. He thought he liked that power over and being in an elder role with them; yet they also left some part of him unfulfilled. With Francie, he met his match. I think he was actually taken aback, maybe even a bit intimidated by her. He referred to her as "a force of nature."

I loved hearing about the depth of their love and passion. They were an amazing example of passionate, erotic love in later life. Kenyth was 75 when they reunited. Even though Francie was still busy as an artist, and Kenyth had many friends, they were very intentional about reserving "love days" every week. On those sacred days they spent some time in the morning doing emotional clearing of any frictions that may have arisen since their previous love day. Then they exchanged massage and practiced movements like tai chi or freeform dance to be fully embodied and relaxed. Only after all that warmup did they begin to explore erotic touch. While I am not privy to all the details, I know Kenyth built a sling suspended from the ceiling for Francie to relax in, allowing him to remain standing for intercourse. It was much more comfortable for both of them and allowed them to modulate the degree of arousal over an extended period, which created the optimum conditions for multiple orgasms for both of them. Their term for the entire process was "making love." Sometimes at the start they may not have felt all that loving, and by the end they were invariably immersed in profoundly satisfying love. I found their love life an inspiration.

Sadly a couple of years later, Kenyth began to show signs of rapid-onset dementia, which was diagnosed as Alzheimer's. It was both heartbreaking and inspiring to witness their devotion to one another as the disease began to rob Kenyth of his lifelong asset: his brilliant intellect. The beautiful part was seeing how, as his mind went off-line, his heart took center stage. He became the embodiment of love: with Francie and with many of us. With me, he was more demonstratively affectionate than ever, offering big wet kisses each time we met and parted...so sweet. Francie remained devoted till the very end: a huge gift to both of them. I'm happy to report that she and I remain very dear friends and fellow-explorers on this amazing path of conscious eroticism, seeking to learn ever more about where sex and spirit meet.

Sacred Intimacy and Sexual Healing

IN ADDITION TO RUNNING my own events, I felt very happy to publicize and assist at many *Body Electric* events in Vancouver and Seattle, which I always found inspiring, healing, and great fun.

The school had developed a number of week-long intensives with varying themes for men who had taken their introductory *Celebrating the Body Erotic*. In 1994, to mark my 50th birthday, I participated in *The Body Electric's* **"*Sacred Intimate Training*"** at Wildwood, a beautiful retreat site north of San Francisco that was dotted with Sequoia trees. The *Sacred Intimate Training* was the most advanced: it was intended to prepare men to serve as professional intimacy guides and healers. (Learn more about the *Sacred Intimate Training* in **Resources**)

One of the massage techniques we reviewed[44] that week was anal massage. This was done 2-on-1: a receiver, a masseur, and a support person whose job was to offer the client comforting additional touch and to serve as a communications link. Having the client face down in a face cradle, and loud music playing, made that role essential. The whole focus was on making the client completely and utterly comfortable throughout the massage.

When I was in the support role, the client was a burly guy (a "bear" in gay lingo) who had flown down from Alaska just for this event. As the masseur began massaging in the area of his anus, he began crying. I inquired whether there was anything he needed: no it's fine. As the masseur slowly and tenderly inserted a finger, the client began wailing. Again, I inquired whether there was anything he needed. He shook his head and gave a thumbs-up. Even the facilitator came over to check on him, and was reassured that the client was okay, despite his seeming anguish . We continued that way a long while: the masseur gently massaging his "rosebud," as it was termed, and I offering comforting, supplementary touch and words. Eventually, as the music subsided, we were guided to wind down and to maintain a meditative silence without further touching the client, to give him time to fully absorb and digest the experience. Finally, the facilitator invited all the clients to slowly come to sitting and to share with the 2 who had been touching him what he had experienced. Through more tears, this man said that the only other time his anus has been touched was when he was raped in his teens, roughly 20 years earlier. The physical and emotional pain had been intense; he had never shared it with anyone... until now. This, he said, had been profoundly healing. To be lovingly, consensually touched in that wounded place, and feel like he was in complete control, and to be able to emote so fully and freely, had allowed him to recover his power and his voice. He thanked us and hugged us again and again.

Joseph Kramer's vision that erotic intimacy can be profoundly sacred truly resonated with my soul. The whole experience was a transformative learning for me about the powerful potential of erotic intimacy to heal old wounds and experience new heights of loving connection.

My respect for this work grew enormously from that experience. I returned to Vancouver with a much fuller appreciation of the Sexual Healing potential of the massage work I was offering, which I was calling *Mystical Massage*. Up till then I had been offering optional genital integration into my massage, but had not been offering explicitly erotic massage, preferring to keep the energy more in the sensual realm without intentionally raising sexual energy. Not wanting to be confused with the people who offered a "rub and tug" experience, and undoubtedly feeling some shame about being seen as a sex worker, I felt I had something more to offer that was more gourmet than fast food. I hoped to uplift men's souls as well as their sex organs.

After completing *Sacred Intimate Training*, I felt a strong YES about giving clients the option of integrating sexual energy into the relaxing, full-body massage experience, to connect with all chakras. Offering *Tantra Massage* to truly affirm the healing power of that most primal energy allowed my clients to learn to move it consciously into the whole body, into all the chakras.

With most of my clients, the contact was one-way: they lay on my massage table receiving my lovingly erotic touch. I view my massage as "shamanic": a ritual to deliberately take my clients into an altered state of feeling more relaxed, whole, and alive. With some clients who wanted more interaction, I followed the model[45] we had used in the *Sacred Intimate Training*: getting them to articulate as clearly as possible what they wanted to experience *for their pleasure*, then expressing any boundaries I was feeling. We would negotiate ways of being together that attempted to affirm and honor who they were as erotic and spiritual beings. In order to minimize any confusion this level of intimacy might cause for them (or me), I maintained strict time/money boundaries: they would pay me for the amount of time I was giving them intimate touch. The exchange was clear.

My good friend and fellow Sacred Intimate, Don Shewey, has written about his journey with Sacred Intimacy in his own memoir. I love his description:

> "What does a Sacred Intimate do? I like to say that sacred intimates combine the roles of priest, prostitute, and psychotherapist. In other words, they approach sexuality with the understanding that it is related to soul work and to spirituality. They use mindfulness and integrity to help people identify, embrace, and practice desire as holy, sexual embodiment as an expression of the soul. They hold the body as sacred and view erotic energy as a crucial component of human life and spiritual health. Their primary intention is that of healing—and by healing I mean addressing not just the wounds to the spirit and the flesh caused by sexual abuse, addiction, or disease but also acknowledging that the fun and the pleasure, the vitality and the divine mystery of sex can have nourishing properties in and of themselves. That's a message that easily gets lost in a culture that is as ambivalent or sex-negative as ours."[46]

Flying Below the Radar

One real challenge facing anyone doing erotic work professionally is The Law! In virtually every known jurisdiction, touching genitals for pay is prostitution...period! There is no appreciation under the law for the healing power of Sacred Intimacy. Being all too aware of my legal risks, I kept a low profile by describing it on my website in more generic terms. Unlike most jurisdictions in the US, "Vansterdam" is pretty chill: unless someone filed a complaint with authorities, there was no real risk. They're not actively harassing people doing sex work except street workers. I was never really worried, and indeed was never hassled. Still it's been odd being an outlaw all these years. Of course it was really nothing new: the kinds of sex I was having in my teens and 20s in public toilets and parks and theaters was totally illegal as well.

Connecting more deeply with The Feminine

The next year, I returned to Wildwood for a new BE offering: *"The Cosmic Orgasm"* for all genders: an opportunity for some long-overdue reconnecting with women and The Feminine. Sensing that I had more to learn with women, *The Cosmic Orgasm* was an ideal container.

Twelve of us came together for a week at Wildwood, 6 women and 6 men. We were facilitated by Colin, the new owner of Body Electric, and his woman partner Selah. All of us were veterans of many BE events before, so this was an even more advanced training. We were quite diverse in terms of gender and sexual orientation. Some of us were "gender fluid." We were homo-, bi-, and hetero-sexual. All of us were open to exploring new territory. It was so liberating to have such a safe space to be with women. Witnessing women being so powerful in their erotic/spiritual aliveness was a stark contrast from the girls and women I was around in my youth, who were all living in subservience to men. Feeling a new respect, I formed lasting friendships with several, which continue decades later.

My most vivid memory: one of the women announced she loved shaving men's balls! She offered her services by the pool on several sunny afternoons. Wow! Talk about feeling vulnerable. What a great way to tackle castration anxiety. I signed up. It was astoundingly wonderful to experience this woman devotedly lathering my scrotum then tenderly shaving me. I felt utterly safe, cared for, and nurtured.

The friendships I formed with some of the women are still a treasure. Among them was Betty Martin, who was herself going through a huge life change that weekend. She had been a single mom, raising 3 kids and working as a chiropractor while living in an intentional community on Vashon Island near Seattle, WA. We developed a sweetly cuddly connection... my first since my ill-fated relationship with Nancy 20 years earlier. I found Betty to be a much more mature and grounded woman whom I could deeply trust.

She began developing a whole new line of work as a Sacred Intimate in Seattle, and a prolific educator about conscious sexuality. You'll soon read about her Wheel of Consent (see below), which I consider to be a truly pioneering practice of authentic communication in physical intimacy.

Later that same year, Selah and Colin invited me to assist at an all-gender *Celebrating the Body Erotic* weekend in Seattle. What a joy and turn-on to be with two dozen people of diverse genders and orientations truly celebrating our eros-spirit aliveness. Again I formed several long-term friendships with many of those very conscious beings.

As the decade progressed, I enjoyed many more weekends assisting at men's and all-gender CBEs. My own massage practice was thriving. In a way, my massage clients became "my lovers." I cut way back on visits to the baths, and those became less interesting and satisfying. Guiding my (mostly male) clients into sublime states of eros-spirit bliss was greatly fulfilling for me as well . More practice of my Tantra Massage led to more skill, and to deeper oceanic states of Oneness for my clients *and for me.* So when I did go to the baths, I found most men's goal-oriented genital focus not nearly as fulfilling as my client sessions.

A mid-life crisis.

The shadow side of my sex life during the 90s was increasing insecurity about my attractiveness. Erections had long-since ceased being "on-demand." In fact they were becoming downright elusive when playing with a new guy at the tubs. In that scene, it's all about getting hard and staying that way, which was never my long suit even in younger years.

When I hit 49 in 1993 and 50 was on the horizon, I had a classic mid-life crisis. I was convinced that at 50 I'd fall off a cliff and become totally invisible and undesirable in the world of gay cruising. Even though I'd learned so much about high-quality erotic connecting through all the experiences in workshops and with hundreds of clients, I still enjoyed "the thrill of the hunt" at the baths, which required that mysterious spark of instant mutual "chemistry." My increasingly wrinkled body and limp member made that ever less likely.

Since I did enjoy getting hard and being admired for my visible manhood. I tried little blue pills which made me blue (or rather red-faced from the extra peripheral blood flow), which was distinctly uncomfortable. Around then a friend several years younger had radical prostate surgery. His doc offered him penile injections for temporary tumescence. I asked if his doc would look at my limp lad.

I found Dr. Phil one of the most personable and congenial docs I'd ever met. We had what for me was a hilarious session in his office when he taught me to inject myself...ouch! Then we both monitored my growing manhood. He left the room instructing me to not touch myself or even think of anything remotely sexual. "Read Time magazine or something." I was to do the best I could to ignore my pulsing pecker...not easy. About 20 minutes later he politely knocked. I invited him in and exclaimed, "Doctor, it's a boy!" He then discreetly measured the angle of the dangle. We were both suitably impressed by my then massive member (hyperbole intended). He left again, reiterating his cautions about avoiding anything remotely stimulating: I was to think of *anything non-sexual.* About 20 minutes later, another scientific measurement; again we were happy with the results. After another absence and another measurement, my lad was lowering ever so slightly. Phil seemed satisfied he'd given me the right dose and showed me how to fill a syringe to that level. Then he gave me an Rx for the syringes and Prostaglandin and blessed me to go forth and dazzle my fellow men with my new-found perkiness.

I felt like a horny teenager again, tucking my semi-woodie into my pants and proudly walking down Davie Street in the "Gay Village" knowing my bulge was way visible. I went right to the baths to *carpe* the *diem*. Alas, it was mid-afternoon on a weekday, and the pickings were slim. After being rock hard for well over an hour I did give a good floor show in the shower as I shot a huge load. Wow! What fun!

Piercing my penis, however, was never fun. Still, it did extend my bath house career into the early 2000s, when I met a potential partner and finally set aside trying to act much younger than I was.

Around that same time, during my annual physical, my GP asked about my emotional life. I confessed to feeling a bit discouraged about my erotic life due to the inevitable effects of aging. He kindly asked if I'd like to work with a therapist and said he could refer me to a gay psychiatrist, which would be fully covered under our wonderful Canadian, single-payer system. Wow! I had not needed much health care so far and was astounded the government would pay for my mental health care as well. I worked with Dr. Don for a full year and found him very caring. He seemed to enjoy me as a client because my neuroses were pretty mild and easily managed. His approach to therapy was simple. He listened, asked questions, and urged me to tune in ever more to the emotions rather than the story. I was already pretty self-aware; his questions took me deeper. Invariably, he expressed acceptance of everything I was experiencing and feeling. Over several months of sessions, his acceptance of what I was experiencing in my aging allowed me to accept myself. We shared many laughs about my/our human foibles. I began to let go of my worries, realizing I have so much more to offer than merely a rigid willie. By the time I did step across that fateful threshold into my 50s, I felt much more confident about being lovable whether hard or soft.

Looking back, I see that "crisis" was a real turning point in my erotic and spiritual life. It is said that men are most turned on by the visual attractiveness they see in a potential sexual partner. The thrill of the hunt seems to be wired into most men's chromosomes. Indeed the queer male community seems largely driven by visual lust, both in our cruising and love of porn. I certainly was quite visually-oriented all the way through my 40s.

In general, it seems, women are less likely to be motivated to have a quick "hookup," and more likely to think long term. An old joke in the queer community:

Q - "What do lesbians do on a second date?"

A - "Hire a U-Haul!"

The maturing that Phil facilitated guided me to look deeper into potential intimate partners: beyond the skin-deep beauty of youth, which is of course totally fleeting. Now that the bloom was off my own outer rose, I became more aware of my own and others' inner beauty. James and Joel had been my first role models. And of course Harry Hay's "subject-subject consciousness," and Baba's dictum about seeing God in each other had also pointed out the same truth. Even though I had long longed for a deeply loving relationship, my persistent yearning for that quick visual lusty feeling had derailed my potential partnership with Kyle and several others. I thought I had to have my fix of hot sex with the ever-alluring Mister Right Now . The inner transformation that my mid-life crisis created was finally coming to treasure the more lasting warm satisfaction of love, without needing those quick hot fixes of my youth. It had still not occurred to me that I might actually be valued *because of my age*. That epiphany would come later... in my 70s!

———

IN VANCOUVER, *Men In Touch* began morphing. After Doug Fraser's passing in the mid-90s, 2 former participants began co-facilitating with me. But gradually in the next few years, their own lives went in other directions. The new management at Doe Bay on Orcas Island was less easy to work with, and I discontinued retreats there in 1997. By the end of the decade I no longer felt able to run retreats at Jemez Springs single-handedly and sadly let them go. I replaced all those with weekends in Vancouver, which were much simpler logistically. I called them ***MMMM! Men's Magical Mystical Massage*** and structured them so men could learn the basics of the type of massage I was offering in my private practice. It was an easy format to do by myself...at least for a while.

The Later Years ~ Ripening into Embodied Wisdom

By my second Saturn Return around 2000, the seeds that had been planted over the preceding 3 decades were truly blooming. My 60s and beyond have been about embodying what I learned and sharing that with others. It has been a time of less struggle and more sense of grace.

Chapter 12 - The New Millenium: Diving Still Deeper into Tantra

The 1990s drew to a close with dire predictions about the catastrophic events that would occur on "Y2K." I decided if the world was going to end, I wanted to be in my spiritual home in northern New Mexico.

I arrived in Santa Fe and stayed with a friend, who took me to an evening of "Sufi Dancing" on New Year's Eve. These *"Dances of Universal Peace"* are a beautiful ritual of meeting and greeting "The Beloved" in all forms. People of all genders gather in a circle around the musicians who are leading the movements. A leader guides the group to move while singing simple devotional songs, some in English and many in Arabic (as Sufism is the mystical aspect of Islam). People are guided to move in 2 circles in opposite directions with a moment of eye contact and shared singing with each person we pass. I had been enjoying similar Sufi Dances in Vancouver for 10 years, finding it a way to "make love" with many people completely non-sexually. At most, we would briefly touch hands. The powerful part was making eye contact with deliberately open hearts. It intentionally affirmed the presence of the divine in each of us. Having first encountered such intentional eye-contact in that Tantra weekend 25 years earlier, in 1975, then often in Body Electric events, I actually did experience the validity of the saying that "the eyes are the windows of the soul," and treasured the opportunity to practice my Baba's teaching to *"See God in Each Other."*

On New Years Day of 2000, I drove to Taos, which allowed me to connect with two parts of my soul.

The Taos Pueblo has been continuously occupied by Native People for around 1000 years. They live at the base of a mountain they consider sacred, in harmony with the land. When I first visited there in 1983, I had a soulfully emotional "memory" of how much these people had to struggle against aggression from the Spanish and then the American Cavalry to preserve and protect their simple way of life. I had the distinct feeling that I had lived there...like I was "home." So going back on the first day of 2000 reconnected me with that soulfulness.

Later I went to the Hanuman Temple in Taos, which held a beautiful kirtan (chant) to welcome the new millennium. The Temple was founded in the 70s by Ram Dass in honor of his guru, Neem Karoli Baba. While there, I felt a Shakti very much like what I had experienced over 2 decades earlier at Muktananda's ashrams in California and New York: an ineffably expanded state of mind and heart.

The next day I went to my beloved Bodhi Manda in Jemez Springs to continue welcoming the new millennium in a prayerful and peaceful way. I had been leading retreats there since 1991, and was welcomed back like family by Hosen and her twin sons, who were then in their teens. It was one of my spiritual homes, and a very sweet place to begin the new millennium.

Ever since reading **Be Here Now** almost 30 years earlier, I had an intense curiosity and even longing to visit the birthplace of Yoga in India. Yet hearing about the extreme crowding and grinding poverty had been intimidating. So I was excited, in the fall of 2000, to learn of a pilgrimage to India being led by Swami Rama's *Himalayan Institute*. They proposed to shepherd 500 people from North America to the *Kumbha Mela* in Allahabad in early 2001. It seemed like the perfect opportunity to be guided by experienced travelers to India in a context of devotion to Yoga and Tantra. Any ambivalence I had about taking such an extravagant journey were dispelled upon learning that several Body Electric friends were going and would be receiving additional instruction in the erotic aspects of Tantra by the renowned scholar, Dr. Rudolf ("Rudy") Ballentine[47]. I could no longer resist.

It was an astounding 2 month adventure, worthy of an entire book. The journey to get there was grueling, even though all went smoothly. I flew from Vancouver to San Francisco where I rendezvoused with several BE friends. There we boarded our chartered flights with Singapore, which did a superb job. The first leg from SFO to Hong Kong took 14 hours. The steerage section was packed, making sleep only a dream. After a few hour layover we continued 6 hours to Singapore, and a longer layover, but not enough to sleep or shower. Finally the last leg to Delhi was about 7 hours, arriving around midnight local time (about 12 hours different from Pacific Time). We were bussed to a hotel for a shower and cat nap and awakened at 0330 to catch a train to Allahabad.

The Delhi train station was a shock. At 4 AM the dozen or so platforms were covered with people sleeping on the concrete. I could not discern if they were waiting for trains or simply homeless. We needed to step carefully among them. Trains came and went. Announcements blared in brittle Hindi and garbled English. Our shepherds did their best to keep their flock intact amidst the cacophony. Finally a train arrived that we were told was ours. Then we had to find our reserved cars and berths. In Second Class AC, we were 4 to a compartment with seats that folded open into narrow beds. Finally, after nearly 40 hours of travel we had about 7 hours to be horizontal and possibly snooze.

I did not see much scenery: sleep was my priority on that train. We arrived in Allahabad (now called by the post-colonial name Prayagraj) around noon. Early January in northern India is very cold by their standards: 5C/40F at night and 10-15C/50-60F by day. No one has central heat: instead they huddle around bonfires made of anything combustible including old tires. There is usually an inversion which traps the air pollution, which is thick and acrid. Even at noon the sun is barely visible.

With remarkable coordination, all 500 of us were bused to our camp. We had 4-person tents, segregated by gender. I was delighted to be sharing a tent with Rudy B and 2 Body Electric guys. I later learned Rudy had arranged that; I was flattered. There were dining tents, a kitchen tent, and a lecture hall tent. We had an open-air latrine area, with wooden cabinets with flush toilets which are a rarity in most of India. There were outdoor sinks and showers in wooden cubicles. Water was heated in a large propane heater each afternoon so we could have hot, or at least tepid, showers. It seemed incredibly luxurious compared with how most Indians live. Yet some participants grumbled about being in "spiritual boot camp." They have no idea, I thought.

Over the 3 weeks, the daily routine was largely the same:

- 6 AM - wake up bell and chai

- 6:30-7:30 optional yoga in the lecture tent

- 7:30-9 breakfast and personal time

- 9-1130 lectures with staff teachers or visiting Swamis

- 12-1330 lunch and personal time

- 14-1730 time to walk the 1.5km (1 mile) along the river to the site of the Mela

- 18-1930 dinner and personal time

- 20-2130 entertainment (e.g. Indian musicians and/or dancers) in the lecture tent

- 2200 -bed time.

That schedule was varied by special events, like a 3-day *Yagna* (fire ceremony). We also had optional "field trips" to Varanasi (the most holy city in Hinduism) and Khajuraho (site of sacred erotic carvings).

The teachings offered by the Himalayan Institute and the custom teachings from Rudy gave me a truly authentic grounding in the ancient and esoteric Tantra tradition. There were optional lectures almost every day on some subject related to Tantra or Indian culture.

The biggest teaching was being immersed in Hindu culture. The *"mela"* is a 6-week long, spiritual festival and ritual that has been happening every 12 years since before written history began: at least 5,000 years. The atmosphere is charged with devotion. Pilgrims journey from all over India to bathe in the sacred rivers on certain auspicious dates. People often greet each other there speaking one of the many names of God, such as "Hari OM,"as a way to acknowledge one another's divinity. If you are curious to see this spectacle, there are many videos on YouTube. The mela is roughly similar to a Western conference, albeit outdoors. Many gurus set up camp with their disciples. They always welcome people dropping in to sample their teachings. It's a spiritual smorgasbord. One of the most charged events is the opening ceremony. Thousands of people wait for the signal of the official opening. By long tradition, the *naga babas* (naked sadhus) are at the head of the procession so they can be the first to take a bath in the sacred river. It's an incredibly joyous event (worth searching for on YouTube). I felt like I was on a completely different planet. There was so much love and devotion in the air; just being there was an incredible blessing.

Everywhere I went in India, public devotion is the norm. Small shrines are on many street corners, instead of the newspaper boxes that used to be ubiquitous in many western cities. They represent gods and goddesses: often Shiva Lingams[48]. People of all ages and genders stop to pray and to sprinkle flowers or coins.

One of the most amazing parts of the journey was a field trip we made to the ancient erotic temples of Khajuraho. These temples date back over a thousand years and depict a culture that clearly saw the erotic and spiritual as one. The single most powerful temple for me housed a huge *Shiva Lingam*. This massive representation of God's phallus stood over 9 feet (3 meters) high. It occupies the center of the temple. At the appointed hour for *puja* (worship), bells are rung, and people file in. I was astounded to see each person walk up to the *Shiva Lingam* and hug it and sometimes kiss it. This was practiced equally by women and men. I cannot imagine a much more graphic integration of the erotic and the spiritual!

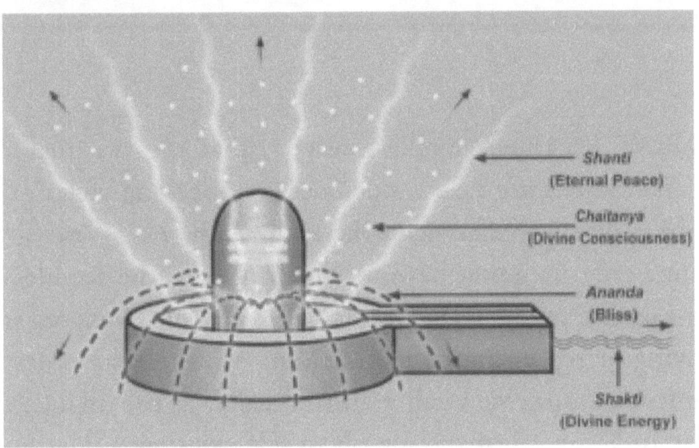

Even more amazing and the most powerful teaching during my entire 2 months in India was the light and openness in peoples' eyes. Despite the incredible crowding, I found people of all genders much more willing to make a moment of real eye contact when passing on the street, which felt like soul food. I found it strikingly different from most western cities. It's as though people really live the spirit of *Namaste*.

namasté
{nah-mas-tay}
My soul honors your soul.
I honor the place in you where
the entire universe resides.
I honor the light, love, truth,
beauty & peace within you,
because it is also within me.
In sharing these things
we are united, we are the same,
we are one.

THE GIST OF WHAT I learned (intellectually) is that the two major philosophies within Hindu culture take fundamentally opposing views on the ultimate nature of reality. Vedanta views the manifest world as "maya," an illusory distraction: only by going beyond all forms into the formless realm of meditation can one perceive the ultimate reality. Thus, Vedanta is ascetic: it urges denying or repressing or transcending sense pleasures, lest they become attachments. Tantra views all manifest reality as the divine *in myriad physical forms*. In Tantra, **desire is a path to self-awareness**. Desires are not shunned, but honored and followed as a means to deeper understanding. The seeker explores desires, and observes how it feels to fulfill them, then inquires what deeper desire might be more fulfilling. While Vedanta says *"not this; not that"*, Tantra says *"All This **Is** That"*: *there is nothing that is not divine.*

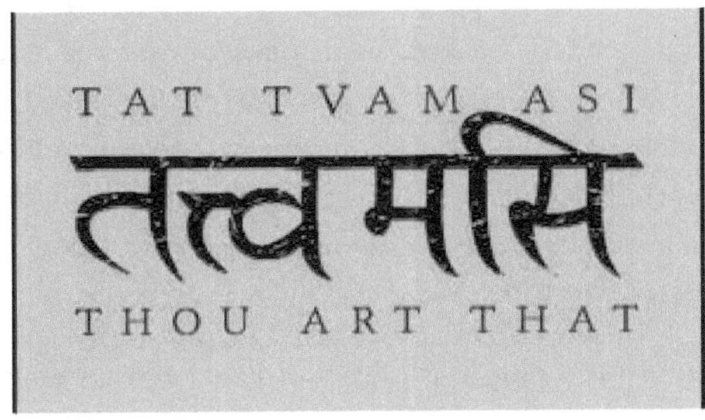

BABA MUKTANANDA USED many metaphors to convey the view that all physical forms are divine Pure Consciousness. He said Consciousness can be the most subtle, as well as the most dense (like rocks and dirt). He said that the potter sees the bowl, the pitcher, and the mug are all the same clay. The goldsmith knows that the earring, the necklace, and the chalice are all the same gold. In the same way, he said, our task on the spiritual journey is to not get fooled by appearances: to see all forms as God.

Baba's spiritual autobiography was entitled *"The Play of Consciousness."* This is all God's "lila", Baba said: it is all God's play (as in both drama and amusement). He said each person and each creature is hiding behind a mask of separateness. Most think they are indeed separate. The spiritual journey is to always be aware: "this too is God." In that way our entire lives become worship of the divinity we are.

LATER, AFTER RETURNING to Vancouver, I happily joined a group of fellow seekers in Seattle (most of whom I had already known through *Body Electric* events) to explore the Tantric mysteries with Rudy B, whom I had met at the *Kumbha Mela* encampment. Rudy had studied Tantra under Swami Rama, and was eager to teach and learn the erotic aspects of Tantra with a group of fellow-seekers. He flew west 3 times over 3 years to convene long weekends of sharing theory and hands-on practice. We were a wonderfully diverse group, spanning the spectrums of sexual and gender identity: gay/straight and cis-/trans-gender. We met in ways that both honored and transcended our usual identities. For example, one of the most powerful full-body orgasms I've ever had was sitting naked in the lap of a cis straight man. Because we were both open to fully embodied erotic flow, simply sitting together with open hearts and souls (without genital involvement) allowed us both to experience profoundly powerful orgasmic energy flowing from root to crown.

(Read more about my major learnings with Rudy and group in **Appendix: Resources**)

The most powerful experience I had with Rudy was his guided visualization/ meditation on Shiva. He spoke several times of Shiva being "the erotic ascetic" who was both pure stillness, pure consciousness, and utter erotic

potency.

He invited us to conjure an image of Shiva sitting in meditation. He then suggested we picture Shiva with a huge erection as he sits completely absorbed in stillness.

Finally he invited us to imagine going over and lowering ourselves onto Shiva's lingam. Allow it to penetrate from root to crown. "Be completely filled by Shiva's lingam. Sit in that stillness," Rudy suggested,

Baba Muktananda taught that Shiva is the formless Pure Consciousness that pervades and is the ground of all manifestation. I had never paid attention to the countless Hindu icons of him. Baba had never alluded to Shiva as erotic energy. He described Shiva's consort Shakti as the aliveness that creates all manifest reality out of Shiva's pure stillness. Baba taught that Shakti is the Kundalini: the cobra that is usually dormant at the base of the spine which can be awakened and move up through the subtle spine and light up all the chakras, opening the Heart and Third Eye, and eventually the Crown, giving the experience of utter Oneness.

Here Rudy gave me an image that felt both profoundly sexual and deeply spiritual: to be filled from root to crown with God's pure phallic potency in utter stillness.

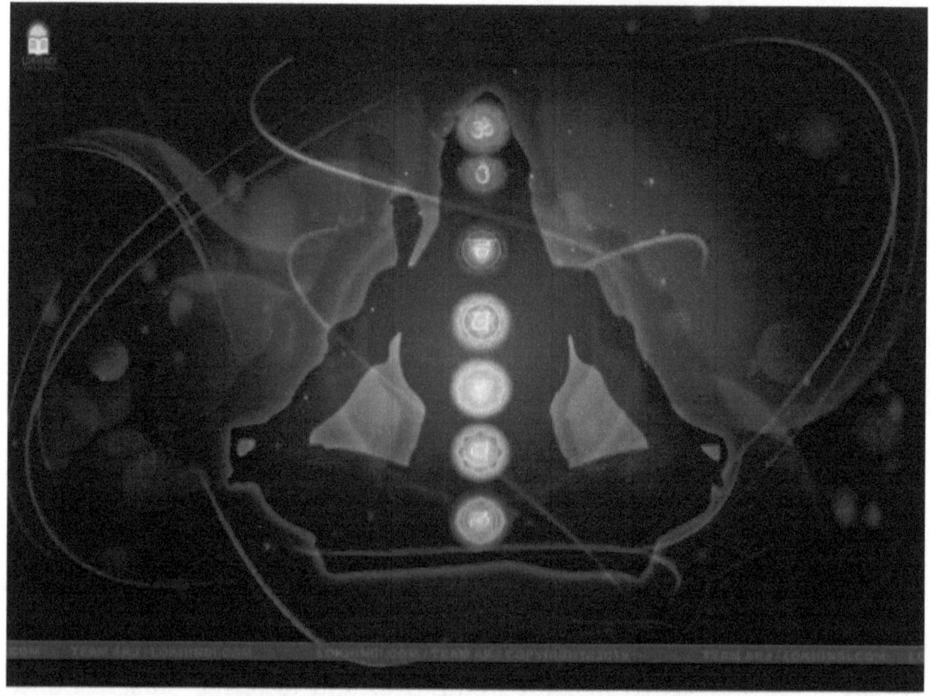

I USE THIS VISUALIZATION often, and find it a potent tool to take me far into the inner realms.

See **Experiential Practices**

My experiences with this group and with Rudy have greatly enlarged my sense of myself in terms of gender and sexuality. Gender used to be either male/female. Sexuality used to be either Gay or Straight. Being "bisexual" used to be suspect: a kind of (self-?) deception. "Bi now, gay later," was one common quip.

Now, seeing both gender and sexual orientation as a continuum rather than a binary, I am celebrating many shades of gray instead of merely rigid black/white. I am now open to all the keys on the gender keyboard, and am learning to hit more notes all the time. I increasingly approach each erotic encounter, with myself or with others, free of expectations and agendas: free to allow things to unfold. I am learning to surrender control, to be more in-the-moment, and invite or allow the *erotic energy itself* to be the guide into pure spontaneity, which in Tantra is called *Spanda*.

See **Resources for *your own* Healing Journey**

AROUND 2005, A DEAR yogini friend told me enthusiastically about a spiritual teacher in Vancouver who deeply touched her. Before Oprah made him a household name, Eckhart Tolle was quite accessible in Vancouver and offered small classes. I, too, was quite touched by his presence. About 40 of us showed up for one of his talks. The space was like a classic university classroom with a desk on a raised platform and rows of chairs facing the empty platform. While a few people spoke in hushed tones, most maintained a meditative quiet as we awaited the teacher's appearance. He came in quietly and sat behind the desk with a quiet smile. He gazed at us benignly and said nothing for an amazingly long while. The silence was thick. Finally he spoke with *very long pauses* between each of his phrases:

Don't listen to my words...

Listen to the spaces between my words...

Go into that space...

Be that spacious stillness...

He continued in that mesmerizing tone a long while. Indeed his actual words became almost irrelevant. The silence surrounding his words was palpable. Feeling guided into his interior state of spacious stillness, I could sense *this is where he lived*, not in the chatter that occupies most people's reality and sense of ourselves.

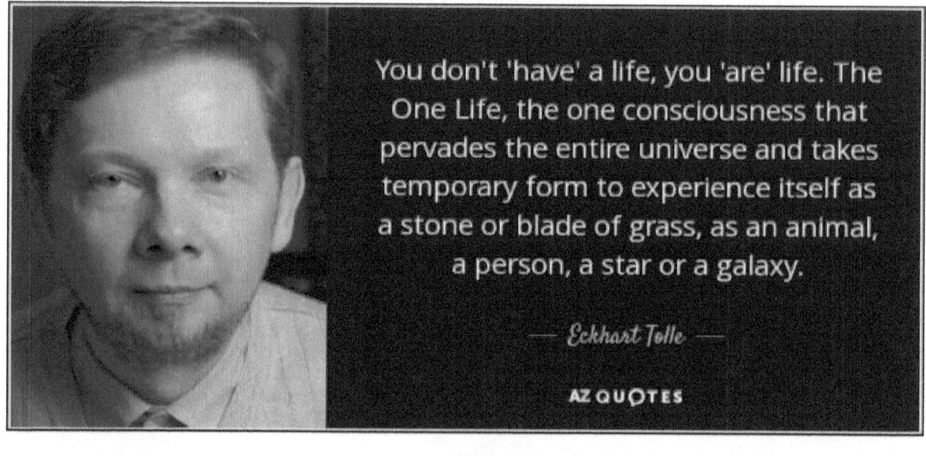

I READ A COUPLE OF his books. The one that most spoke to me was *A New Earth*. His most memorable teaching was that we all have *two purposes*: an **outer purpose**, to which we devote our outer awareness and energy (work, relationships) and an **inner purpose** which is the same for all of us: to be aware of our oneness with all that is.

Being in Eckhart's presence renewed and confirmed the inner stillness I had experienced decades earlier with Baba. I greatly appreciated that Eckhart used different, non-religious language to describe and point to the same ineffable inner state. He rebooted my meditation practice. I consider him one of the great teachers of our time, and appreciate that he comes from the West, and has absorbed and integrated the essential teachings of both East and West.

From my time with Baba, I developed a deep appreciation for *darshan*: the direct seeing of a very conscious being. While being in their physical presence is ideal, it is quite possible to have their darshan by looking deeply at their photograph, or contemplating their written or recorded words. Eckhart's image and words can convey his essence if you choose to contemplate them. All the great teachers each have their own unique path up the mountain. Those who have been to the top report that the paths are highly varied and they all lead to the same place: Oneness.

IN 2004 A CLIENT CAME to me who immediately touched my heart. Chuck was almost 52 (I was 59), and had been struggling to both suppress and express his gay feelings for decades. His internalized homophobia ran deep. About a year earlier, a friend his age suddenly died. That was a big wake-up call. He really wanted to begin expressing his gay self but was terrified. He told me of many times walking up and down the block outside the Pump Jack[49], too afraid to go in and in tears of conflict. My heart went

out to him.

I had been actively yearning for a partner for some time. Casual bathhouse cruising was getting old. I wanted to experience full intimacy. There was something about Chuck's almost child-like innocence and sincerity that deeply touched me. My own wounded boy felt safe with him. I was glad he had not become jaded by the too-often empty encounters that happen in gay club life. I felt like I could show him a healthier and more soul-satisfying way of being gay than he was likely to find at "PJ's".

I carefully contemplated and questioned the wisdom of reaching out to him for a personal rather than professional connection, aware of the power imbalance of having begun as client/healer and his total inexperience with gay life. Then I decided to do so. I sensed (or projected?) a purity in his heart that mirrored my own. I hoped that alone would guide us.

When I called him about a week later and expressed all the above, he burst into tears. I invited him to think about it. He called back the next day agreeing to my idea.

So began a 6-year journey together. Chuck was very monogamy-oriented for both emotional safety and to avoid HIV and STIs. I told him of my erotic massage practice, of which he had had a sample, and assured him that it never involved any sort of oral or anal penetration. I agreed not to be sexual with anyone beyond that client work. He seemed okay with that.

I was relieved to let go of my weekly bathhouse habit, which had become less and less satisfying as I got older and more "invisible." Yes, gay culture is quite youth-oriented. I confess to sharing that bias. Chuck was the oldest man I'd considered dating by far. From my studies of Behavioral Psychology, I was all too aware that the bath house scene was a perfect example of "Intermittent Reinforcement," which is the most addictive kind. I'd "get lucky" maybe 1 out of every 4 bath house visits. That had been enough to keep me going for decades.

Chuck worked a very demanding Monday to Friday job, so I arranged my own client work to be on the same schedule. We spent each weekend together, often going to an idyllic, island cabin I'd been time-sharing for many years.

It was sweetly satisfying in many ways. Yet there were a few major misalignments. Other than sharing caring touch and food, we had few common interests. He was passionate about intense, solo sports like wind-surfing and downhill skiing, which I did not share.

Nor did he share my interest in exploring the altered consciousness available in extended sessions of yoga and meditation.

Even though Chuck was sweet, gentle, kind, and nurturing most of the time, he had a quick and very hot temper. He could become furiously angry at me or others for what seemed to me like trifles. For me, these sudden eruptions were quite painful because I would be wide-open and vulnerable from his gentle TLC. He was aware of his short fuse, and always remorseful after his eruptions. So after suddenly feeling traumatized by his outbursts (even when they were directed toward others), I'd suddenly find myself soothing him and reassuring him.

Sometimes when his anger was directed at me, I, too, would get furious. I was amazed at my own fury. There was something about feeling attacked when at my most vulnerable that triggered my most intense self-protective mechanism. In an odd way, this was a growth experience for me. Seeing too much violent anger as a boy led me to repress my own rage. Somehow, here I felt both justified and safe letting my fury fly. To be clear, there was never any actual violence between us, either verbal or physical. Doors were slammed dramatically and voices were raised but no direct attacks ensued. Taking a walk to cool off would allow me to return to try to communicate from a calmer state. By then Chuck would typically be abjectly apologetic. I'd accept his apology and offer my own when it seemed warranted, and we'd slip back to our *status quo ante*: peaceful togetherness each weekend and little contact mid-week.

The other major imbalance was erotic. Chuck would have zero touch (except with himself) during his whole intense work week and bring his sexual charge to me on weekends. Meanwhile, I'd spent the week lovingly and erotically pleasuring many men. I needed to relax and *receive* nurturing touch. He was often horny for something more sexual. Even though I had been adhering to our monogamish agreement, it became clear over several years that much of my libido had been devoted to lovingly pleasuring my clients, which did not leave much left over for Chuck, my partner. I realized I was being unfaithful to the *spirit* of our agreement by not meeting his erotic energy fully with my own.

After about 4 years it was becoming clear to me that the situation was untenable for me; yet I could not see any way to improve it short of breaking up. I suggested he share erotic massage with some of the men he was meeting in ***Men In Touch*** events. He was too shy or insecure. I suggested some 2-on-1 massage with some of those same guys, and we did try that a couple of times. He felt intimidated seeing my expert massage techniques and seeing me get aroused in the process. I encouraged him to date others as well so I was not his only intimate other. He made a few tries at PJ's that did not feel good to him.

We tried seeing a therapist to iron out our issues. Sadly the therapist assigned by his employer quickly made Chuck feel like he was the problem who needed fixing. We were there as a couple, yet the therapist focused entirely on Chuck, probing him with questions without ever creating any trust or rapport, while totally ignoring me. Near the end of the session he told Chuck he had an emotional disorder. I was horrified how unprofessional and un-therapeutic this was. Chuck understandably wanted nothing more to do with him or with any other attempt at counseling.

In 2009 we took a holiday to my early roots in New York City and my ancestral roots in Ireland. This seemed to bring all our difficulties into sharp relief. By the end of the year, I knew I could not continue. In early 2010, after another tense and conflict-ridden trip to celebrate with my old friend, Eric, as he married the man of his dreams in Miami, I let Chuck know I could not continue. It was one of the hardest things I've ever done. As I fully expected, he was both furious and deeply hurt. I was deeply sad. We had shared a dream and both tried really hard to make the dream come true. I was doubly sad: for the loss of my own dream and knowing how terribly hurt Chuck was.

The winter Olympics were in full swing in Vancouver when we got back home. I vividly remember walking alone downtown to mingle with all the tourists from all over the world. The atmosphere was festive while I was in tears. Chuck and I did talk by phone several times. In one call, his hurt little boy said plaintively, *I thought you were my best friend!* All I could say was an achingly sincere, *"I'm so sorry."*

I made some important self-discoveries with Chuck. Even though I long for and feel capable of a devoted partnership, I do not feel well-suited to conventional monogamy. My dear mother said many times, "there is safety in numbers." I had learned that I want and need many intimates in my life of varying degrees of intimacy. I'd be fine to have only one partner for *sex* as long as I can have several *sensual friends* for massage exchanges, cuddles, and soulful conversations. I do not want to "put all my eggs in one basket," however beautiful that basket may be.

I learned that I **do** have a temper and can express fury when feeling attacked.

○ I am capable of doing so non-violently.

○ I view anger as an energy for initiating needed change.

○ I am now comfortable with my anger, even though I still do not enjoy the agitation involved.

Chapter 13 - The 2010s: New Models of Intimacy

I began the 2010s with an aching heart, feeling like it was time to let go of any idea of ever coupling again. A dear old friend, who knows me way too well, kindly and gently said, "Yes, I've been struggling with Codependency much of my life. I have a great book you might like to look at." He showed me his well-worn copy of *Codependent No More* by Melody Beattie and said I was welcome to borrow it. I devoured it. Even though I'd heard the term for decades and had a vague idea of its meaning, when I dove into Melody's writing, I was shocked how much she was describing me and my patterns in intimate relationships. Codependency was the only kind of relationship I saw growing up. All my relatives were in CD relationships, as were most of the people on TV. CD was THE template for how to be intimate back then. I had bought it without question and had lived it.

Just as my gaydar had been well-honed at a young age, so had my CD radar. I had an unconscious and uncanny knack for choosing partners to care-take or rescue: who needed me. *I needed to be needed,* and got way too caught up in the process of meeting their needs at the expense of honoring my own. Then of course I'd get frustrated and resentful, and, of course, I could not express that: to do so would be going against CD behavior.

As an empath, I easily tune into others' emotions. Sometimes it's hard to know which are mine and which are theirs. This skill has been very helpful in my professional work with clients: I'm often more aware of their feelings than they are and can gently guide them to greater self-awareness. In an intimate relationship, however, I finally learned that this same ability can be a liability: my partner's emotions become more important and take precedence over my own. Melody's writing and other readings I've done have made a huge difference in my awareness of this pattern. I am better able to make different choices.

Reflecting deeply and contemplating my life going forward, I realized I felt quite at peace living the rest of my life single. After several unsatisfying relationships, I was beginning to take the view that my path is to relate to the formless Beloved by loving *all the forms* who cross my path: to more fully live Baba's precept to "See God in *Each* Other."

It's a tall order. I formed the clear intention to let that mystery be a kind of *koan* to inform my life. I realized I'm blessed with many really amazing friends and clients, and probably have more quality intimacy in my life than 90% of people who are coupled or partnered. *"God is my lover,"* I told myself. *"I'll endeavor to love Her/Him in whatever forms show up."*

ON MY BALCONY ARE SEVERAL hummingbird feeders. It's an "open birdcage" with hummers and other beauties stopping by and flying off as they will. So that became a metaphor for my new love life: to enjoy each moment with each beloved and let them fly when they need to. Another metaphor is to savor the beauty of *every* flower in the garden and not need to pick *any* of them to take home.

Okay, so if I am going to "love everyone and serve everyone and remember God" as Neem Karoli Baba advises in Ram Dass' **Be Here Now**, how will that love and service express itself with so many different people?

I know I have different kinds of attraction or non-attraction to various people. I've found it helpful to use the chakra model as a way to understand that and to navigate the emotional complexities with each person.

I notice which chakras feel most resonant with each person I feel an attraction with. It's extremely rare to resonate on more than a few chakras. With some people, it's more of a heart or emotional connection. With some it's more intellectual. With some there's an erotic charge. With some it's more ethereal or spiritual. Of course the more chakras I feel in resonance with someone, the more I feel met, understood or loved.

When I feel some attraction to someone new, I usually am aware of some curiosity about them and/or some fantasies I'm having about them. I trust those impulses: letting my desires guide how I express myself with them. For example, do I notice something about their intellect that intrigues me? If so, it is easy to begin asking them questions about what topics seem to most interest them. Am I feeling some lusty desires? What clues are they giving about any such desires they may be feeling? I might say something like, "I'm feeling an interest in sharing some sort of touch with you. Might that be of interest?" If they show interest, then we can explore what kinds of touch we might each want. If they strike me as particularly spiritual, I might initiate conversations about our respective paths, then explore sharing one another's practices. In these examples, a single chakra can be an entry point for connecting on more and more chakra levels as we get to know each other better. I find with some people, there is a resonance with only 1 or 2 chakras, and with some there are delightfully many that light up. We are each always changing, so the chakras we share can keep changing over time. The trick is to be authentically in the moment with what feels right with each of us.

What about people I interact with only briefly, like passersby on the street or store clerks or bus drivers? As I go through my day I intend to be in-the-moment and available to acknowledge each of them with at least a moment of eye contact and a gentle smile that says "I see the divine in you." People often light up when being seen that way. It makes my whole day an ongoing love affair with The Beloved.

My most fulfilling experiences of intimacy are when I feel a resonance with another in all chakras. It is as though we are two mirrors, reflecting light back and forth, making the light brighter and brighter. Ram Dass has a beautiful description: "We enter into each other when we are in each other's presence. If you're not threatened, you can relax your separateness, let it fall, and enter into a kind of liquid merging with other beings."[50]

ANOTHER WONDERFUL TOOL for navigating intimacy came from my dear friend, Betty Martin, whom I met at the *Cosmic Orgasmic* week-long intensive in 1995. About 10 years later, over dinner at a restaurant in Seattle, she sketched on a napkin a schematic she'd been designing to help people better understand the various permutations of Giving and Receiving in any intimate encounter.

I was really excited by this way of parsing the pieces of human interactions, whether they be personal or professional, verbal or physical, sensual or sexual. I immediately agreed with her that if people understood what roles they were choosing, instead of the confused and confusing concoction most of us engage in, it would make for way more high-quality connections.

My very quick summary of Betty's schematic:

- In any intimate encounter, regardless of the degree of intimacy, it really helps both people to be clear in each moment whether they are choosing to be a Giver or a Receiver.

- We can be Giving by Doing, as in offering massage;

- We can be Giving by Allowing, by offering our body for our partner's pleasure;

- We can be Receiving by Accepting a Giver's offer, as in accepting massage;

- We can be Receiving by "Taking" our pleasure with an Allowing partner's full consent, as in using our own mouth, hands, and/or genitals on our partner's body for our own pleasure (again: ***only*** with their full consent).

- For a diagram and fuller description of the theory, see **Resources**

● In order to help learn these 4 roles, Betty has devised a **"Three-Minute Game"** which she had learned from Harry Faddis of *Body Electric*. See **Experiential Practices** or search online.

I have found this Three Minute Game highly instructive. I had known for decades that I much preferred massage to the usual erotic encounter. In a massage, it is fairly clear who is Giving and who is Receiving. In the passion of most of the sexual encounters I'd experienced, too much was happening at once in a busy blur. Both people were trying to please or excite one another and at the same time get the kind of pleasure or excitement we each really wanted. I've found it a formula for frustration. Equipped with Betty's wisdom, I now approach intimate encounters much more mindfully, and more important, much more *consensually*.

Just being clear what I actually want can be a challenge, and then saying it out loud can make me feel intensely vulnerable: the other person may say No, or, worse, they may reject me in some way or think worse of me. There is a real risk... **and** a real chance I will *get what I want*. As with any other skill, the more I've practiced, the easier it has gotten and the more rewarding my exchanges with friends and lovers. Wow. What a gift. Thank you, Betty.

I find the Game a wonderful way to get gradually acquainted with a new potentially intimate friend. We start with low-risk requests, like "Would you please caress my hands for x-minutes?" Something that simple can be hugely pleasurable, as well as instructive. As both people feel increasingly safe and comfortable, we can each explore more vulnerable requests, such as "Would you please tenderly kiss my (body part of choice) for x-minutes?" The gradual progression informs both of us how intimate we really want to get... today. Maybe that will change in a future meeting.

I also find the Game a wonderful way to be with long-term intimate others. Even after more than 10 years together, Ziji and I still find it a fun and useful way to be really in-the-moment with one another, letting go of assumptions from past experience, and discovering what our desires are now.

SO, AS THE 2010S PROGRESSED, I felt clearer than I ever had about my intimate life. I was quite content being "single." I was beginning to realize the truth of Sant Kirpal's beautiful aphorism, "Each embodied soul is a drop in the Ocean of Consciousness." Each drop has the same essence of Pure Consciousness; yet each drop is also a drop and not the Ocean. I was beginning to realize no one drop could fulfill me. I want to love the whole Ocean in the form of each drop.

From so many decades of meditation I was becoming increasingly aware that *love lives in me*. Most of my life I had been looking *outside myself* to find love. *"Where is that perfect person who will love me perfectly?"* That is the wrong question. Rather, "How can I cultivate more love in my own heart so that I can love everyone?"

Each drop I relate with may meet *part of* my needs for love and intimacy, and *no one person can meet them all*. So if I view God as my lover, and each person as a small sample of that vast Lover, then the totality of all my relationships fulfills me. What I'm also noticing is that the more I'm living my life with an open heart toward all, the more love is flowing *toward me*, even from strangers on the street and grocery store clerks. I'm glimpsing that it actually may be possible to love everyone. How amazing.

Many North American indigenous cultures share that outlook and express it with a kind of mantra in their ceremonies. In the Lakota language, *"Mitakuye Oyasin"* roughly translates as "All My Relations." Their entire world view seems oriented to the web of all life. It is the web that is paramount; individuality is not as highly valued.

Tantra teaches the same thing: everyone and everything is a manifestation of Pure Consciousness. That perspective is dramatically enlarging my view of love.

Leaving a Legacy

I also began to contemplate where my work life was heading and what legacy I could leave. Leading *Men In Touch* events solo had gradually become more arduous, even as I loved it. I had discussions with a few of the regulars who seemed most supportive of what I had been doing. I wanted to see if we could create some sort of team effort. Even though they each were supportive in theory, none was ready to step up to take on any of the work. Each had their own challenges about time, energy, and personal resources that made real collaboration impossible.

After 30 years of teaching yoga, offering holistic massage, and leading men's workshops, I was aware there was no visible record of my work. I could see and hear from men's feedback that they were positively transformed; yet the effects of my work seemed invisible to others, except perhaps to those closest to my clients and students.

I had taught or touched perhaps 1,000 people in those 30 years, and I wondered what I could do to "touch" many more. How could I give people far away an experience of being in one of our events or on my massage table? After brainstorming with several friends the idea emerged of making videos that offer instruction in simple, clothed, nurturing touch that can be exchanged between friends and family members of all ages and genders. I wanted to offer this kind of touch practice as a kind of active meditation, a sort of yoga, insofar as yoga means uniting a person's whole body/heart/soul in the present moment.

Once we hatched the idea, the universe moved with astounding speed. Jerry and Jeffery, a gay couple I knew, were hobby videographers: they loved making videos. They'd been to *Men In Touch* and also *Body Electric* and had a keen appreciation of the value of such conscious, intentional touch. So they were excited about the concept and offered to donate their time and talents.

In the spring of 2012, I reached out to a number of men and women I'd met in various workshops and thought would be particularly well-suited to displaying and discussing such touch. I explained the idea, which meant they'd potentially end up on YouTube, and asked if they were interested. The response was amazingly enthusiastic. We were able to do two shoots with two different groups, demonstrating different ways of exchanging this simple TLC: hands and feet, neck/shoulders, facial touch, chakra holding and "gourmet hugs." The sessions also included the groups discussing the effects they had experienced in that session. They went wonderfully! It felt like grace: like some mysterious force was saying, "Yes, this is important. Make it happen!"

Then began the painstaking process of editing the raw vids down into coherent and reasonably brief videos. Jeffery and I spent innumerable hours in our "spare time" (about once a week for a year). I created a simple website to present the videos to the world. I'm eternally grateful and indebted to Jerry and Jeffery for their selfless donation of their time and skills to this project. It's truly a labor of love.

You can go to **Sacred Touch Yoga** which will guide you to the videos on YouTube.

Chapter 14 - My Young Mentors

In the spring of 2013 I was surprised by the appearance of a truly remarkable young man in my life by the name of Ziji.

As I had for decades, I scheduled a *Men In Touch* workshop for Easter weekend. In my *MMMM! Men's Magical Mystical Massage*, I taught full-body relaxing massage including ways to integrate the genitals to create an all-chakra, calm aliveness based on the teachings of Tantra. I advertised through my own mailing list and on our **Facebook Page**.

A young fellow contacted me expressing interest. Two things caught my eye about him: his birthday is the same as mine: August 7, and his handsome face was turned looking over his right shoulder at a very young girl of 3 or so. I saw him beaming love at her. Who is this young man, I wondered. I was dimly aware of my inner, 3 year old Tommy whispering, *"I'm hungry for that kind of love from a man."*

As was my custom, I urged him to book an individual massage first, because much of the power of this type of massage is in the movement of subtle energy through the chakras, which is hard to fully experience in the workshop with men who are just learning. He liked the idea but said it may be a financial stretch to pay for both. So, I suggested instead of paying monetarily for his massage that, after he'd taken the workshop, he would repay me with a massage. He readily agreed, and we found a time for his session.

When he arrived I was again struck by his face and graceful energy. As usual before each massage, I invited him into my living room, offered my home-made chai (or other tea), and began a get-acquainted chat. I inquired why the workshop interested him, and what he hoped to learn. I discovered he's lived 2 years as a monk in a Buddhist monastery and was newly back in the world. He was eager to learn to integrate his deep spirituality with his strong libido. He had recently connected with some of the Radical Faeries who recommended me for his quest. "He's come to the right place," I thought.

As we were talking, he paused at one point to take a long breath. A look came over his face of both deep repose and great wisdom. Deep is the operative word: he seemed astoundingly deep for 27. I thought, "This very young man is a spiritual teacher for me."

Decades earlier I had seen the autobiographical film about Gurdjieff called *"Meetings With Remarkable Men,"* in which that young seeker was mysteriously guided from one spiritual teacher to another. (See YouTube.) Sitting chatting with this young seeker, I intuited we were both potentially having such an uncanny meeting.

Again, as I always do before a massage I asked if he had any particular wishes or boundaries to tell me about. To my great surprise he said, "Actually I'd like to massage you first. My grandmother taught me massage, and I think you'll enjoy it." Wow! He's already turned the tables on me...literally. I agreed, intrigued even more.

I showed him around my "Touch Temple" where I have my personal *puja* (or altar) with pictures of various gurus I revere. The table was already set up. He preferred a mat on the floor. Wow, again, "He's really taking charge" I thought. I folded the table away and put a mat on the floor. "How much shall I undress?" "Nude is fine with me." As I undressed he sweetly commented, "Look at your lovely body!" We were already way beyond my usual professional boundaries. My heart was melting.

I stretched out face-down on the mat, and he began his ministrations. "Hmm," I thought, "he has a lot to learn." His massage felt too pokey and proddy to my liking, and was way different from the long soothing Esalen strokes I'd learned 40 years earlier with Judith McKinnon in 1973..

When he had me turn face-up, I noticed he still had shorts on. He did not include my genitals. Despite the almost abrupt quality of his touch, I was utterly charmed by his presence. At the end, he sat next to me in silence for a few minutes. When I was ready to speak, I heard myself say, "It would be so nice to hold you." He smiled and did not move. So I slowly got up and said "Your turn."

I set up the table as I'd had it earlier. He removed his shorts and lay face-down. Now, I was even more eager to teach him *through my touch* what **Magical Mystical Massage** was all about. He purred wonderfully throughout, which I found a turn-on and very refreshing. In my decades of massaging men, I usually needed to coach them to breathe fully and allow sounds to express their experience. "Sounds are an eloquent language into themselves," I often urged. This young man was already fluent. He received beautifully, so it became a dance between us: the more fully he breathed and sounded the more inspired I felt to pour the love on. I sensed we were both tasting ecstasy. It has been observed in classical partner dancing that "a good follow makes a good lead." He was being that skillful "follow" or receiver, so I was in heaven as the lead.

I wound down as usual by leading him into deep quietness, the yogic Savasana, and silently left the room to allow him to commune with his soul free of any distractions from my presence.

While in the washroom, I had a stern inner discussion with myself, realizing I was feeling intensely attracted. "Don't go there! He's 40 years younger. He's your student! ***Don't go there!***"

I took a few full breaths to ground myself then quietly re-entered the Temple. He was still in a deep place. I guided him to take a few longer breaths as might be done after Savasana, and to wiggle fingers and toes and do some stretching to gradually return to outer awareness and ordinary consciousness. I invited him to roll onto one side and sit up.

"What are you experiencing?" He struggled to find words: clearly in a profound place. Then he again turned the tables: "It would be so nice to hold you!" My already feeble resistance completely crumbled. I suggested I sit on the table so we could be facing one another. We were way beyond what I usually do with new clients on a first session. Normally I'd be wearing gym shorts and a tank top and all the touch would be one-way. Now I was nude and he had already touched me all over.

We went into a spontaneous hug: no ordinary hug. Our arms and legs completely and fully embraced one another, heart to heart, belly to belly, groin to groin.

Both of us were fully charged erotically, not in a hot, horny way, but rather in a full-body radiant way. We both began to convulse in full body orgasms. I have no idea whether either of us was ever erect. Our torsos *were* the erections. The erotic energy surged vertically through us in waves from root to crown. We both let out spontaneous, orgasmic sounds for a long while. Our embrace was intensely passionate yet mysteriously calm. Gradually the convulsions subsided, the sounds quieted, and we settled into an utterly peaceful state that was timeless.

I forget how we got disengaged from that intense togetherness. I probably offered to get us some water. We probably slowly dressed in a daze. I'm sure we thanked each other and said we looked forward to being together at *MMMM* a few days hence.

Here I'd like to interject my own interpretation of that intense experience. I understood and experienced it as full-on kundalini mutual awakening accompanied by "kriyas," - a term I learned from kundalini master Baba Muktananda. When he awakened people's kundalini (the sexual-spiritual energy normally dormant at the base of the spine) people would have many spontaneous, involuntary (but controllable[51]) movements and sounds. People might laugh or cry, or chirp or bark. They might have spontaneous, rapid breathing, or go into yogic postures or *mudras*. Baba reassured us that all these "kriyas" (literally "actions") were a normal, if bizarre-appearing, cleansing activity being performed by "Goddess Kundalini." Trust her, he reassured us: these strange movements and sounds will pass after the cleansing is complete.

My own kundalini had been awakened by Baba decades earlier[52], and after so many years of meditation, the channels were pretty open. Ziji has been meditating intensively and conserving his sexual energy during 2 years at a Tibetan Buddhist monastery in Nova Scotia. We were both ripe for such an upward-flowing "ejaculation," which is what is classically taught in Tantra. We had been guided to move into *Yab Yum*, which in all the Tantric iconography depicts a female sitting in the lap of a male in full embrace.

(NOTE: THIS PHOTO OF us was taken almost 11 years later, in January, 2024)

As I learned with Rudy, this does not mean such practices are limited to a man and a woman. It represents the union of the Inner Masculine and Inner Feminine and can be practiced between two people of any gender. It can be a powerful practice.

In our case, I sometimes wonder how many lifetimes we had been preparing for that embrace. I feel safe in saying it was life-changing for both of us.

(from my journal):

He's such a gracious and loving Leo. Being with him really was a gift: he is so heartful and soulful. I told him I feel like I will be learning from him; he joked he can teach me physics. Near the end of our time, I said it feels like his deep Presence is teaching me to go deeper as well, e.g., I held still more and longer while massaging him, as his breath would simply stop. I sensed he could have stayed longer. In our YabYum we naturally took turns leading/following, and were by turns playful, feline, passionate, tender, and still...

(I reflected on) how many people look to someone else to fulfill what can only be fulfilled within. What struck me about Ziji is he, like me, is coming from a place of fullness overflowing, not an emptiness needing filling...two suns shining on one another, mirroring one another.

A few days later, Ziji was "just one of the guys" in my workshop. I did my best to treat him no differently than any of the others who were there to learn the mysteries of how to give and receive this full-body touch that connects the erotic and spiritual dimension in a full embodied way.

At the lunch break on Saturday, I told the participants about the various options in the neighborhood and what time they should return. I left last and went to Whole Foods to enjoy their hot food bar. No one else was there except Ziji. Fate seemed to insist we dine apart from the group. He suggested we take our food to the nearby park. So we had a quiet interlude over lunch...just the two of us. We both knew he was not "just one of the guys."

The Sunday session always has a different quality than the Saturday, in that I've shown most of the moves and can allow the guys to practice on one another with less guidance from me: just occasional reminders about their posture, breathing, and the various options. I keep time and guide them when to wind down. There is more time for me to be in observer mode. Once again, I was struck by the poise and confidence Ziji showed as he massaged his partners. He was the youngest man in the room and I was the oldest. I recall thinking, "this young guy is the most mature one here."

I believe I suggested after the weekend that we take a month's pause before seeing one another: a time to let the dust settle and get some perspective about the intensity with which we had connected. He readily agreed.

During that month I was by turns elated and fearful. I've learned that love brings up fears and insecurities: "Why would such an attractive lad want to get involved with an old dog like me?" "Will he stick around?" "Will he quickly find someone younger?" In any relationship there is the appropriate existential fear of losing the beloved. Of course we will lose them, either to betrayal or death. Or they'll lose us. Even as I basked in the beauty of what we'd shared, I pondered all the risks inherent in such an inter-generational love.

A month to the day, we met again at my place: our first "date." We chatted a bit to catch up, then dove into deeper waters. Despite my intense attraction, I raised some of my concerns:

I worried he might have put me on a pedestal. He's really only seen me in professional mode, not the ordinary me. He did not yet really know "me." Having met as student/teacher and having such a vast age difference can create a power imbalance, I cautioned. "I don't see a problem," he replied. I pointed out that I'm even older than his parents. We'll all be going through our decrepitude at the same time. Does he really want to deal with that? He seemed unconcerned.

We agreed that, even though neither of us was *looking for* a relationship, the intensity of our first meeting did seem to indicate we *were already in one.*

He also made it clear he was decidedly NOT monogamous. In fact, he was beginning a quest to experience sex with as many men as possible. Wow: how different from my previous partners! In a way, how refreshing. In another way, how anxiety-producing. I realized I really had to practice that "open bird cage" model I'd been telling myself was my new way.

Indeed, during the first year or two I got to be with my anxieties and uncertainties a lot. He was the perfect teacher to break my Codependent patterns. He does not have a Codependent bone in his body. He simply didn't play that game of "oh, whatever you want, dear!" I found him quite willful and unpredictable. Even after the most intensely intimate encounters, sometimes lasting several days, when we'd part he'd never offer plans for another meeting and would resist my attempts to do so. "Merge and separate," was his motto. If it's true that gurus burn up disciples' karmas, mine were quickly becoming toast.

Because I found Ziji so extraordinarily self-aware and conscious, I found it easy to view him as a manifestation of the formless Beloved. During our periods of separation, I was able to conjure him in meditation and feel an orgasmic surge of energy. That dance of being with him in form and then on the subtle plane inspired this poem after we spent several summer nights in a cabin on Gambier Island:

My cup is full...

and great-full.

The Beloved has come to me

in the most beguiling guise

looking like a mere mortal.

He has set my heart aflame

not for his mere bag of bones

but for the love that flows

from his pure heart

the light that shines

from his dark eyes.

May he bless many as he has blessed me.

May the whole world be ablaze with Love.

We both love summer, in part because we were both born on August 7. As "our birthday" approached, he said he had plans with his family most of the day and wanted to come over beforehand to do a "small birthday ritual." I could expect him at 9 AM. I was not prepared for what ensued.

We had already sat for meditation several times at my altar; he wanted us to do so now. Then he took out a liturgical text from his Buddhist background and slowly began to read.

"It's your birthday. Your life is one year shorter." He continued reading the suggestions about how to approach the coming year with greater intentionality about practicing meditation, aware that this human birth is a priceless opportunity not to be squandered. I was blown away. On this day when he was turning 28 and I 69, he was contemplating death as an existential reality at any age. I thought, "Wow, this young man really IS an old soul."

He told me of a week-long meditation retreat he planned to attend later that month about an 8-hour drive north in the interior of British Columbia. I asked if I could join him. I'd been regularly practicing meditation for 40 years, mostly in the Hindu tradition. Eric and a couple of other friends had introduced me to Buddhist practice, and I had studied Buddhist philosophy during my East-West Psychology MA program. I was eager to dive deeper into the practices that he followed. Being together for a whole week in that way sounded amazing, and it was. Like the two Leos we are, we sat right in the front row immediately facing the teacher. I loved doing the chants and meditations with him at my side. It felt like we'd done so in other lives.

One of the teachings of Baba Muktananda always stayed with me: "The Guru," he said, "is not this body. The Guru is the grace bestowing power of God. We can meet The Guru anywhere, any time, with anyone, or even a flower or bird or sunset. If we are open, The Guru is ever available to guide sincere seekers." As I chanted and meditated and hung out with Ziji over the 4 months since we met, I increasingly felt he was one embodiment of

The Guru for me. As we were preparing to leave the retreat on the last day, I invited him down to the creek where we had bathed. By the rushing water, I tearfully told him that I saw him as an embodiment of The Guru and asked if he would allow me to bow down and touch his feet. He demurred: "I suggest you bow down to the sun." I did. Then I told him of a powerful wish. *What?*, he asked. "My great wish is that you be with me when I am dying. I know that looking into your calm eyes would steady me if I am fearful." He nodded having heard me, and we shared a long, still hug. We silently went back to packing up the car and began the 8-hour drive back to Vancouver.

Much of our shared week had been in silence. So it seemed natural to be in silence as we took turns driving the beautiful rural road through the woodlands of northern BC. After hours of profound stillness between us, we stopped for dinner. After he parked, he put a hand on my thigh, turned to look at me directly, and said, "I'd be honored to be present when you are dying."

The full story of our now many years together would be way beyond the scope of this memoir. I'll try to summarize my major learnings with my wise young/old teacher.

He wanted to attend several successive workshops. Knowing he was already a high school teacher, I hoped to entice him to teach something at one of the workshops. The opportunity came when he described the Laughter Yoga he had taught his students. It sounded like a perfect addition to a ***Men In Touch*** event. He was brilliant: a total natural. Soon we were collaborating, with him taking on increasing amounts of the facilitation, as well as the administrative work I'd always found tedious. Doing them together was a total joy. Our team-teaching was immediately hand-in-glove. Decades earlier, co-facilitating the original editions of ***Men In Touch*** with Doug Fraser was a joy. Now, with Ziji, it was bliss.

For many years before we met, I had been time-sharing a waterfront cottage on a nearby island, going to once or twice a month for several nights. When Ziji was still teaching high school, he had long breaks around Christmas and the summer and was happy to join me there for us to have "retreats." It was there, away from our mainland lives, that we had some of our deepest intimacy.

Unlike me, Ziji has been quite adventuresome exploring medicinal ways to alter and expand consciousness. Before one of our summer retreats at the cottage, he suggested on this retreat that we share MDMA. I'd always been quite reticent to use substances, probably owing to all the detrimental effects I'd witness from excessive alcohol use in my family. Even though, when I left the Air Force behind in 1972 and began my new life in Berkeley, drugs were a happening thing, I barely dabbled. I know I was quite influenced by Ram Dass. After years of being deeply engaged with LSD experimentation, once he met his Guru and had his chakras opened, he realized all drugs were at best a temporary glimpse of the vast realms of consciousness beyond our usual egoic tunnel vision. With drugs, he observed, there is always a come-down. With yogic meditation practice, the process is more gradual and much more lasting. I liked that.

Yet, when Ziji suggested sharing "Ecstacy", my heart said Yes. Having studied altered states in my MA program, I was aware that "set and setting" make all the difference when ingesting psychoactive substances. I could not imagine a better set and setting than that island cabin with Ziji.

We had several days and nights to ourselves. He laid out a clear, methodical plan for when and what we ate before ingesting, giving ourselves a full day to savor the effects. It really was powerful for me. MDMA is known for its heart-opening effects, and, indeed, that was my experience. Forty years earlier, Baba's Shaktipat had profoundly opened my heart, allowing me to feel enormous love for myself, for many dear ones, and all beings. This experience with Ziji had the same effect. What was new this time was a palpable, undeniable awareness: "I AM love." That Ocean of Consciousness, I realized, is also an Ocean of Love. We are all immersed in It and made of It, and yet most of us are unaware of It and look for love outside ourselves. "Thou Art That," the Sanskrit mantra avers. I now knew that with every fiber of my being.

It felt like an incredible blessing to have a second opportunity in one lifetime to have such profound heart opening. It brought Ziji and me even closer. I could see even more clearly that the place to find real lasting and utterly dependable love is deep inside. Any outer beloved, however enlightened they may be, is an imperfect manifestation of that pure, inner, divine love. The only place to experience True Love is deep within. Then I hope to be an ever more pure channel to bring that love into the world.

That wondrous shared inner journey was matched by several magical outer adventures we shared in the American Southwest and in Cuba. They say traveling with someone can make or break a relationship. Even though we had a few rough spots sharing the hundreds of daily decisions while traveling, overall those trips continued to deepen us.

Because of our vast age difference and Ziji's obvious independent streak, I resisted labeling our relationship in any way. Yet I noticed over time that he became more proactive about scheduling regular together time. He also began referring to me as his partner when speaking with others. It was several years before he introduced me to his parents and other family. I knew at that point a threshold had been crossed. We were in a capital-R Relationship.

Even though our primary erotic connection was always more sensual than sexual, in the early years we did enjoy sometimes getting into full-on sex, with lots of slow sensual prelude and postlude. As the years are passing and my own libido is waning, we seem to be sweetly evolving into a less overtly sexual and more wonderfully sensual way of being together. *Yab Yum* is still our go-to position. I feel at one in that mutual sitting embrace. It feels like we are "home," as though we've shared that embrace for lifetimes. The sexual energy is more subtle. No longer do we have such intense orgasmic convulsions.

Instead, if he is sitting in my lap, I feel like I am deep inside him with energy, not my penis. When we reverse and I am in his lap, I feel utterly penetrated by him or by Shiva. It's as though the energy "penis" has filled me from root to crown. It's astoundingly intimate and satisfying: much more so than physical fucking has ever been for me.

I am experiencing that the very independence in our love life is its strength and keeps the spark alive. I am old enough to remember spark plugs in cars. They ignite the gas to create the motion. The "gap" was crucial. If the gap was too large the spark could not jump across. If it was too small the spark would be weak. I find Ziji and I are creating the perfect gap, so our spark keeps us firing quite well.

One of the lines from Gibran that always resonates: *"When you part from your friend you grieve not, for that which you love most in him is clearer in his absence, as the mountain to the climber is clearer from the plain."*

Despite our huge independence, I've come to trust that I can depend on Ziji when I really need him. As I am getting older and slowing down, I see that he is more than willing, actually eager, to offer support when I need it. When I first expressed the deep desire that he be with me on my deathbed, I was not envisioning a "till death do you part" commitment. Yet, I now know Ziji has signed up to be with me through my full "creeping decrepitude,"[53] as my beloved mentor James called the final phase of life. I am finding that profoundly comforting. I am learning that love can be both independent and dependable: not the Codependent model I was raised with.

So far, Ziji and I have hit only one major landmine in our mostly idyllic journey. We had learned we both love traveling together. In the spring of 2017, we planned a get-away to Cuba to catch some sun. There I painfully discovered we had different assumptions. In Vancouver, we had a tacit agreement that his vast appetite for cruising only happens in our "apart time." When we're together, usually for about 30 hours once a week, we are totally together. He saves his thrill-of-the-hunt to savor on his own time the rest of the week. I assumed our week in Cuba would be all "us time." Wrong! Cuban men kept eyeing him while I was invisible to them. He was enjoying the cruisy energy for sure; I was both enjoying seeing men's attraction to him and uncomfortable. I felt some odd tension. On our third or fourth evening, he invited me to go out to a club with him "to dance." Even though I love to dance, I'm still ill at ease in clubs: the combo of booze and cruising strikes me as a formula for unconscious connecting. Once there, even though we were sitting side by side, I felt suddenly alone: his whole attention was surveying the room. I invited him to dance and still sensed he was not with me. I felt more alone than if I'd arrived by myself. I felt abandoned. The music made conversation impossible, and dancing did not really connect us. Finally I told him I was not enjoying it and wanted to go. He preferred to stay. So I told him I'd see him back at the hotel.

It was already 11 and I was tired but could not sleep. I tried to meditate, but all I could feel was an aching heart. I was feeling abandoned and not wanted. When he arrived at 2, I was still sitting up. "How are you?" he asked cheerily. "Sad" I said. I asked how he was, and he said he had met a guy and that they had a nice time with each other. I tried to tell him what I experienced, but we were both tired, so the communication was not satisfying. We did not cuddle before sleep, which we usually do. All night and in the morning my heart was aching and contracted. We went for breakfast and continued our touring, yet I felt a disconnect. I sense he did too.

Over dinner I tried again to express my experience. I said I had not been expecting such a sudden shift in his energy and that I was blindsided by having him suddenly focusing on cruising and not really being with me any more. He made it clear he did not share my assumption about the whole week being "us time" and did not seem at all sympathetic to my hurting heart. I heard "this is how it is" from him. Things definitely felt out-of-sync between us. I didn't try to make him wrong. I simply said this is not my vision of how partners behave traveling on holiday together.

Still we have such fun traveling that we both rose above that emotional disconnect and had some fun adventures during our remaining days there. Back in Vancouver we settled back into our usual very comfortable rhythm, and my hurt heart gradually receded into the background.

Looking Death in the Face

In the mid-2000s, my spirit-brother, Eric, told me his men's group was doing a powerful practice. They had decided as a group to follow Stephen Levine's advice in *A Year To Live* and go through an entire year imagining their lives were going to end at the end of that year. I was intrigued. It sounded potentially profound.

Levine was inspired to write the book and recommend the practice after years of working with Ram Dass counseling people who had received a terminal diagnosis. What they both noticed is that almost all of them made radical changes in their lives after learning their lives were nearing its end. Their priorities changed. Some left work or started some project they'd put off for "someday." Some ended relationships or began new ones. All became much more focused on *what was truly important to them* in their final months of life. He had the idea of imagining having only "a year to live" as a spiritual practice: to see and choose to do *what was truly important.*

Decades earlier, when I read Carlos Castenada's *Sorcerer's Apprentice*, what had most stood out for me was his shaman's advice to "always walk with Death over your left shoulder." I realized at the time I had begun doing that as an Air Force pilot. I was aware as a student pilot, especially when I began flying solo, that literally my life was in my hands. An error on my part could be fatal. Mechanical failure could be as well. That awareness continued my whole flying career: death was always in my consciousness. That had made each day and each safe landing feel like a gift.

After I left flying behind at the end of 1979, that immediacy of death gradually receded from my consciousness. I all-too-briefly settled into a kind of comfortable complacency. That abruptly ended in the early 80s when gay brothers began withering and dying all around me. I knew I might very well be next. Again, each day of health seemed like a precious gift.

Then, after learning in 1991 that I was HIV Negative, life began again to seem more open-ended. I started taking each day more for granted. So hearing about *A Year to Live* sounded like a useful practice...someday. That day arrived in the spring of 2016, when my beloved friend, Kenyth, was diagnosed with Alzheimer's. He had been saying for years that, if he were diagnosed with a terminal disease, he would opt to "self-deliver," in other words to euthanize himself. He asked his doctor how long he thought he would have the mental ability to actually carry out that plan. "About a year," he learned...to his great shock and horror. So in his mind he had "about a year to live." I was reminded of the book and the practice, and decided to read the book and join Kenyth on his journey of only having one more year to live.

In my case, of course, it was just an exercise. I was in fine health. Death looked far off. Still, I have known for decades we can get hit by the proverbial bus at any moment with no warning. So my good health was only a mild distraction. I began living each day as if I knew that proverbial bus would hit me on April 30, 2017.

In some ways it felt pretty realistic. I updated my Will and other end-of-life papers, and even put in writing what I hoped my memorial service might include.

Then I began to have several "last" experiences. One of my great delights during summers in Vancouver is swimming at the beautiful outdoor pool in Stanley Park. I can walk there in about 15 minutes through the park, then swim under clear blue skies on the ocean's edge with gorgeous trees on one side and English Bay on the other. It's as close to heaven as I've ever been. Every Labor Day, when the pool closes for the season, I grieve summer's passing. In the summer of 2016, however, knowing that was my "last summer," I savored each swim all the more. On the final day, realizing it was my final swim ever, I was 110% present to every moment of the swim. It was cosmic. Of course, I felt sad getting out of the pool, yet also ecstatic, having been so fully at-one with the entire experience...totally in-the-moment.

So it continued as the year progressed. Offering my "final" *Men In Touch* workshop was poignant, as was my "last" Christmas with Ziji, family, and friends. As spring approached I realized it was important to begin saying good-bye to loved ones. I booked a train ride on Amtrak down to the Bay Area, with stops in Seattle and Eugene to bid farewell to loved ones there. When in Berkeley and San Francisco, I had some wonderful farewell visits. I of course explained to people what I was doing and why. A few made light of it with comments like, "Yeah, Cher has had several 'farewell tours' already." Most, however, genuinely met me in wanting to express heartfelt gratitude for our many years of deep friendship. There were long hugs and tearful expressions of love.

Then came the last month...the last week...the last day. Ziji and I planned to spend the whole day and evening together. We took a long walk in Stanley Park, sharing especially meaningful memories of our then-4 years together. Given that he marked our first shared birthday with that wonderful Buddhist liturgy about staying aware of death's inevitable arrival, we both readily embraced this exercise. We went for a special dinner, then to a kirtan. That for me was the absolutely most meaningful last activity I could imagine. Back in my home around 11 PM, I got ready for bed. As I lay in bed, Ziji read to me by candle light some passages from *The Tibetan Book of the Dead*, which are traditionally read to those on their deathbed. At one point, the text reads, "Now you are dying" and gives clear instructions about how to remain conscious during the journey through "the bardos" or layers of consciousness that precede and follow clinical death (cessation of heartbeat and breathing).

I went into a deeply meditative *Savasana*. Ziji came to the end of the reading and sat in silence with my "remains." Then he blew out the candles, kissed my forehead with the utmost lingering tenderness, and left.

It was well past midnight. I was both awake and in a deep state that is hard to describe. It was as though time had stopped. *I simply **was**.* Eventually I drifted off to sleep.

Next morning, and ever since, I've felt as though I really did complete my life then. Everything since feels like a bonus...and an amazing blessing.

I now view our mortality as a great gift. Being *really aware* of how fleeting life is makes each moment and each experience and indeed *each breath* so much more meaningful.

THAT SPRING OF 2017 was a very dynamic time on many levels. Flying home from Cuba, I remember telling Ziji enthusiastically that I really wanted to learn Spanish. I love the language and want to be much more skilled the next time I visit a Latin country.

Somehow all of the events of that trip set the stage for another amazing (even younger!) man to appear, named Angelito. A week after our return, I attended a *kirtan*, which is one of the major practices that opens my heart. Ziji and I often attend kirtan together, but that evening he was seeing a client. At the end of the 2-hour chant, I was feeling completely in my heart. Standing to leave, I saw Angelito sitting in the back, appearing to be in bliss. We had met briefly a year earlier at a Radical Faerie gathering near Vancouver. I had noticed him then: a tall, handsome, very young Mexican man. I found him gorgeous, yet did not even remotely consider any involvement between us. Now, seeing him unexpectedly a year later, with my heart wide open from the chant, I greeted him warmly and exclaimed, "Angelito, I really want to learn Spanish!" Without missing a beat he replied, "I really want to improve my English." He had just returned to Vancouver and would be around all summer. We began meeting once a week to share language. Because it was spring, we met in Stanley Park and took long walks in which we learned vocabulary. We'd each point to something to learn its word in the other's language. It was fun and sweet. He began asking more personal questions, clearly curious to know more about me. Then he totally surprised me by saying "I *really noticed you* last year but was too shy to reach out." I was charmed and flattered. I thought, "How gracious these Latin guys are," not even dreaming he was flirting with me. Yet over time, it seemed increasingly undeniable, and I began flirting back.

He's a naturally spiritual fellow, and we found we were interested in many of the same spiritual teachers, like Eckhart Tolle. We listened to some of his YouTube talks together and discussed them. Sometimes we put kirtan chants on Spotify and chanted along.

Ziji often shared stories with me about his intimate encounters, which I usually enjoyed hearing (when they weren't during our holiday). So I told him of this growing infatuation with this lovely lad who is actually 10 years younger than himself. He was as surprised as I was, and intrigued; he encouraged me to follow my heart and my desires. Sweet.

Angelito was more forward one day. He said that Gerald, a fellow faerie close to my age with whom he was staying, had told him how, years earlier, I had taught him Tantra massage. Then I was forward, saying I happen to know it was almost his birthday (22nd), and I'd be happy to give him a Tantra massage as a gift. He coyly agreed.

By now I was totally smitten by his Latin charms and classic "tall, dark, handsome" looks. I was developing a teen-age crush on him, and it was clearly mutual. So I was pleased and excited we were about to take our budding romance into actual touch, and not just touch, but my favorite kind of touch: Tantra massage.

When he arrived a few days later for his massage, I tried, as I had with Ziji, to maintain professional boundaries. Even though we were clearly in a personal (and budding romantic) relationship, I felt it was important for him to have the experience of "just receiving" and having his wishes and boundaries totally honored. I would keep shorts and a top on and only touch him with my hands, even though I was beginning to fantasize more than that. At first he kept his shorts on, which I honored by not touching the areas thus concealed. After about 20 minutes, however, as his body and heart began to trust my touch, he asked if he could slip them off. Of course! I had explained the option of my massage gently flowing over his genitals and asked if he would like that. "Maybe a little," was his shy reply. I again honored his wishes. So I was giving him my traditional Tantra massage. I wound down into stillness as usual and silently slipped away. When I returned he was radiantly glowing. He didn't have words for his experience. Instead, he said he wanted to touch me. Sure. He apologized that he'd made dinner plans with Gerald and could not stay very long. Fine. Then he stood up facing me and asked me to remove my clothes. Then he did some intuitive and subtle touch of my legs, torso, and genitals that astounded me. He was channeling some powerful subtle energy that was electrifying my whole body. We moved into a standing embrace that felt ecstatic. I was in heaven, and I sensed he was, too.

Thus began my "Summer of Love." There was something about Angelito's youthful innocence, his open heart and soul, and his sexy body that touched a place in me that was equally young and innocent and open. We became two teenagers exploring *first love*.

It really was an exploration. Neither of us had an agenda. Something beautifully integrated and whole was unfolding in and through us. The lad in me that had needed to totally hide my attractions and crushes when I was his age was able to live them now...at 72! It was profoundly healing for me. We gradually and gently explored a variety of sexual positions and practices in a wonderfully organic way.

In my gay lib days at the baths during the 70s, I refrained from anal sex because it felt just too vulnerable and intimate to share with strangers. The few times I tried it with guys I was dating, I felt awkward and uncomfortable. Then AIDS slammed that door shut!

When I felt Angelito humping me, a totally unfamiliar feeling came over me. My pelvic floor was opening in a way I'd never felt. My body welcomed his humping with my own spontaneous prone pelvic thrusts. Then, to both of our surprise, he was inside me. It felt so easy and natural and "right." My heart had already opened to him, so my body expressed that congruently and beautifully. I later told him of my history and how this was my first time being comfortably and joyously entered. He was surprised and honored.

My favorite moments were when he would put on some dance music and lead me around the living room in partner dancing, then literally pick me up and carry me into the bedroom for a romp. Wow: how astounding to have a strong young Latin lover having his way with me! I loved being swept off my feet in a romantic swoon!

I continued to keep Ziji abreast of all these surprising developments. This was new for both of us. He'd had lots of casual sex in the four years we were together; I had had none. He had not fallen in love with any of his hook-ups; I was falling deep. We both seemed somehow to trust this was fine in terms of "us." In fact maybe it was leveling the playing field a bit. I sensed that he was more astounded than I was that Angelito and I, a half-century apart in age, were in teenage puppy love. I also sensed he appreciated how healing it was for me. We continued our weekly visits, and, gradually, the pain I had felt in Cuba almost faded away... almost.

Ziji and I made plans for a summer retreat. But this time we needed to find a new venue, as the cottage I had been renting for nearly 20 years had been sold. We found an airbnb on the Sunshine Coast which would sort of do. That summer saw some of the worst forest fires ever in BC. Smoke was oppressive and pervasive. Was that what made our summer retreat subdued? My heart felt confused. I was in puppy love with Angelito, yet had a deep and mature love with Ziji, with a still-unresolved heartache from our Cuban misadventure. At some point I told him I was feeling confused about whether the term partner still felt authentic for me. He heard that without comment. To his credit and mine, we did not try to "work it out" in our heads. We continued coming together weekly as we had, cuddling, sharing yoga, meditation, and delicious food just as we had. We did not focus on the label.

In September I was saddened to learn Angelito would be returning home to Baja California. He invited me to visit, and I happily made plans to do so. I flew down in mid-November: in Scorpio season. That is significant for me: I usually go into a major funk in November as the days are getting short and wet and cold. I also always perk up in Sagittarius time, despite those conditions being even worse. I seem to be quite susceptible to astrological influences of the sun and moon. Sagittarius is fire, which always feels more enlivening than the watery Scorpio energy. When I arrived, Angelito was at first warmly welcoming. He was living with his mother, who was effusively welcoming as well. Yet quickly, his energy became diffident. He seemed ambivalent about being with me. I later realized he was struggling for clarity about what kind of involvement was right between us. His inner struggles manifested as moodiness and coolness. I was sad but also understood: this is how 50 years difference shows up: of course it's confusing, especially for one so young. I stayed grounded and open, and I suggested we meditate together. Sharing that practice gave us a more grounded way to connect.

One week into my planned two week stay the sun moved into Sag. Like night and day the energy between us shifted. He was brighter and friendlier. He had realized, "You're a teacher for me." That clarity seemed to lighten him up, and he was again more friendly and amorous. Still, something had shifted. We tried sharing massage, but he felt horny and needed to shift into jerking off. A couple of days later, he wanted me to teach him massage. So I put him on the massage table he'd borrowed and described what I was doing and why. He got impatient and wanted me on the table. Then instead of massaging me, he wanted to fuck. I tried to go along, yet it felt rushed and not nearly as loving as at the height of our puppy love summer. When it came time for me to leave, I sense we both knew the magic was gone. Our amazing summer of love had shifted with the seasons and winter was upon us. We kept in cursory touch on Whatsapp for a while, and his responses became fewer and farther between.

Afterwards, in meditation, I reflected that, in an amazing way, my Tantric love with Angelito truly had completed something very deep. I truly DO feel a "freedom from the other" that Osho writes about! I journaled,

> "This morning I am remembering our times together, including that last morning waking and sitting side by side in Baja, when his otherness first faced me then gazed, then merged with me. We truly met in Oneness. Now having so merged fully with an 'other', the illusion of otherness is gone. I now know in my heart and soul that all 'others' are truly my own dear Self."

"Part of the magic is that Angelito the man is on his own journey, and it's totally okay to be separate again, because now I know we, and all 'others,' truly are One. What a blessing!

"As I reflect on our dance, it seems the full-on sexual passion we shared was an essential ingredient in the opening of my kundalini. Ziji and I began that, which primed me. Yet I seem to have needed the physical penetration and unbridled mutual passion to complete the opening. We were wild animals, yet our eyes could meet in utter stillness. So there was the intense 'otherness' of our two bodies pounding and heaving and sweating and gasping, even as there was the serene stillness and timelessness.

"I am aware this morning of missing his physical presence: I do love him so. It's not painful. I smile just thinking of him. Truly it was the unbridled passion he and I shared that finally blew my chakras open. My Inner Woman finally felt [feels] deeply penetrated with love! I've been holding that door shut for 60 years!"

———

I CONTINUE TO REMEMBER him in my prayers and to give thanks for the healing he brought to my inner teenager. We had a sweet courtship, gradually opening our hearts and souls first, then expressing that through our bodies. That was so different from the shame-filled wanking in washrooms I had done at his age.

Fifteen years earlier, studying Tantra with Rudy Ballentine (see complete details here), I had learned the theory that we each have both masculine and feminine energies within us, and the Tantric ideal is to bring them together in an "inner marriage." Angelito had intuitively loved my Inner Woman. She loved him, and how he made her feel: *desired and wanted.* He helped me complete the "inner marriage" by fully engaging her sexually and inviting her passion to flow fully and freely. I honor Angelito as a major sexual healer for me. He guided me into full-bodied, full-hearted, soulful sex. I am forever grateful.

2017 WAS A BIG YEAR IN my love life. At the spring Radical Faerie gathering in May, I met another lovely young guy with whom I felt a mysterious connection. I had learned to trust those intuitions and attractions and to follow them. Andre and I had some sweet conversations during the weekend. At the closing circle, we "somehow" ended up sitting next to one another. I felt a wonderful subtle electricity between us. We agreed to stay in touch after the weekend.

A few weeks later we took a walk on the seawall in Vancouver's lovely Stanley Park.. We had such an easy, open, honest, and heartfelt conversation that I was reminded of my initial meeting with Eric over 40 years earlier. I told Andre of my lifelong "brotherhood" with Eric and said I sensed something similar with him.

That has proven to be true. Andre and I have a profoundly loving and fully embodied friendship that is not overtly sexual, yet wonderfully sensual in a Tantric way. He's been eager to learn the Tantric approach and readily resonates with it. We've done some delightful traveling together on Saltspring Island and New Mexico. When I tune into which chakras light up with Andre, I am delighted to say "all 7." It's rare to feel that, and I treasure our full body/heart/soul hugs. This love with Andre is another lesson in letting go of agendas and expectations. His life is quite nomadic, so I never know when or how often we'll connect in person. Yet I feel the subtle thread of energy connecting us no matter how great the physical distance is between us. He is an ardent advocate of "love networks," a term he learned at the Tamara intentional community in Portugal. I am delighted to be part of his love network, which includes Ziji and several other dear ones.

Deepening with Ziji

Before our next travel adventure after Cuba, we had a good talk about that experience and what we learned. We came to an agreement that he would forgo cruising when we're together. That has worked great ever since. It has often been a non-issue because much of our travels have been to rural BC or road trips in Arizona and New Mexico, where cruising is less of an option. But in 2023 and 2024, we traveled to Mexico, where cruising is easy. We spent about 10 days together in Mexico Ciy and Oaxaca before he went off on his own adventures. During our together-time, I felt him totally with me, and not on-the-prowl as he had been in Cuba in 2017. When he goes traveling on his own, I am happy he is expressing his abundant love and libido with others, while I enjoy leading a more solitary, contemplative life, including writing and editing this memoir.

Two years after our Cuban adventure, during the summer of 2019, Ziji went on his own inner journey using plant medicines. During that journey he had a major insight that he has not been the kind of partner to me that he wished to be. He formed a clear intention within himself to be more fully my partner.

That was the year I was turning 75, which felt like a milestone I wanted to mark with a modest party of 10-20 friends. Ziji somewhat reluctantly agreed to join me in celebrating "our 109th birthday" (34+75). He generally does not make a big deal of birthdays, even his own. I was glad he agreed. After 6 years together, it felt right to me for us to have some sort of visible affirmation of our love. He ended up really getting into it. We invited a number of mutual faerie friends, a few neighbors, and a few women friends, including our dear Francie from Bellingham.

Somehow the combination of his strong intention that spring to be a more committed partner and that celebration seem to have shifted us into a deeper place. I can really feel the shift: I'm feeling his presence and commitment much more fully. We truly do feel like partners. What a blessing!

Looking back on all the years since our first cosmic *Yab Yum* in the spring of 2013, I still marvel at how our love keeps deepening. The years add layers of richness. There is a mysterious quality to our strong connection that my intellect does not fully fathom. Still, I can see certain ingredients that we each bring and certain choices we make that continue to strengthen our bond:

- Regularity:

  ○ Communications: we've learned to maintain a daily dialog using app voice clips about what we are each doing during our times apart and how we are feeling, sometimes adding images to convey a fuller picture. This can include stories of our intimate encounters with others as well.

  ○ We choose to spend one overnight per week together, which is totally "us time." We love sharing talk of our lives, cuddles, yoga, meditation, food, and almost always some *Yab Yum*.

  ○ Travel: we continue to revel in shared travel adventures as well as intimate retreats in tranquil settings several times each year.

- Shared values and politics:

  ○ Our shared interest in the connection between the erotic and spiritual, which first brought us together, continues to richen our love. It was also our shared work for many years, and it continues to be a topic of conversation as I eagerly follow Ziji's leadership of **Men In Touch**.

  ○ We each avidly follow and share a progressive viewpoint about world and local politics.

● Independence: we were each happily single when we met and have brought that sense of inner fulfillment to our partnership. We are each quite comfortable with and indeed thrive on time apart. We each love solitude *and* quality time with others. All of that enriches our time together.

● Interdependence: when we are together we reach out to one another for help with practical things like home projects and for emotional support coping with the stresses in the rest of our lives. We practice active listening and Authentic Relating.

● Mutual respect: from our very first meeting, I've had a strong sense of Ziji's wisdom and have been open to learning from and with him. I continue to experience him as an embodiment of The Guru for me. He has expressed the same feelings about me. That depth of mutual respect forms a solidly enduring foundation that gets stronger with every passing year.

Witnessing gay men growing and evolving over three generations

My first images of gay men in the 1960s were confusing. When the media portrayed us at all, which was rare, it was invariably as effeminate and ditzy: "light in the loafers" was a typical disparaging term used to describe anyone suspected of being "that way." That confused me because the men I was having brief sex with in toilets and showers did not seem that way, and I did not feel that way.

Then, as I wrote earlier, when I first began coming out in SF in 1972, the older gays mostly seemed so wounded that their self-esteem was very low. There was a lot of self-loathing and mutual denigration (as in the film, *The Boys in the Band*). I was turned off by most of them.

As I began meeting and dating gay men my own age, we seemed much more comfortable with our gay selves than older "queens" did. Still, I've observed, even though my own generation is generally less wounded than the generation just before us, many of us carry scars from all the homophobia we grew up with. That makes it hard to form open-hearted connections. Most of my gay life, I've had one disappointing relationship after another with men of my generation. Happily, when I encountered the Radical Faeries, I met a few older faeries and some my age, who seemed emotionally healthy. They were all too rare.

As the 2010s came to a close, I was amazed at how much richer and fuller my love life had become than ever before. That was due to Ziji and these other lovely younger men who have magically come into my life. I am astounded at how conscious these younger guys are compared to how I and my contemporaries were at their age. The young ones I am meeting almost take it for granted that being gay is okay. They came of age in a period when, at least in much of the developed world, queerness is increasingly visible and respectable.

I never would have imagined I'd have to wait until my 70s to be meeting a whole new crop of queer men who are more ready to meet with open hearts and souls. I'm so grateful I have lived long enough to experience this further step in Gay Liberation. I'm also amazed that some of these open-hearted souls are genuinely attracted to me: not *despite* my advanced age, but *because of it*. It's clear that guys now in their 30s, who were born during the worst of the AIDS epidemic, are actually grateful to have older queer men as mentors and even as lovers. What a happy surprise!

My own evolution

Having spent my early queer years in utter shame about being sexual, especially being gay, I am in awe of how far I have evolved over the ensuing 60 years. My self-esteem is dramatically better. I am so grateful for all the gifts being queer has brought. It has forced me to question all the other cultural assumptions I was raised with and to chart my own unique course.

Seen through the perspective of the chakras and kundalini, I see that, in my teens and twenties, like many other men, I experienced sexuality residing solely in my pelvis. I felt separate from others and was ever on the lookout to bridge, through sex, that painful sense of separation. My penis had its own radar constantly scanning for another opportunity to have at least a fleeting feeling of connection. Of course that satisfaction was shallow and short-lived. Then I'd again be scanning for another fix. Buddhists refer to that state as *"Hungry Ghosts."*

I am so grateful to have been guided onto the path of Yoga and Tantra and learned practices that have gradually re-wired my energy pathways, allowing my sexual energy to move upward, instead of being locked in my pelvis. That erotic *chi* has gradually filled my heart chakra more and more fully to overflowing. Now, instead of looking for someone else to fill me up, I know that *the source of love lives in me*. So now I look for other awakened beings with whom to share this fullness in mutuality.

I cannot claim credit for this process. From a young age, I felt a longing to connect with God/Spirit. By some mysterious process I call Grace, I have felt guided. An unseen hand has consistently and dependably offered quiet direction to my life. My role has been regularity in the practices that give me access to that "still small voice within."

It is said in the Bhagavad Gita (Hinduism's "bible") that, when we take one step toward God, God takes two steps toward us. It is said in partner dancing (think waltz and tango) that a good follow makes for a good lead. God and I have been doing this two-step dance now for decades. I'm learning to be the "good follow" so God can be the masterful lead.

Chapter 15 - Subtle Eros

That progression of sexual energy up through my chakras has brought me to a profound knowingness of the inextricable oneness of Eros and Spirit. I now know that any separation between sex and spirit is completely artificial. All life on this physical plane comes out of sex. Spirit expresses itself through our sexual bodies. I joyously celebrate that unity.

I now see the truth of Osho's claim that sex can lead to love, love can lead to prayer, and prayer can lead to transcendence. Learn more about Osho's writing in **Resources**. He makes a distinction between 2 very different kinds of orgasm. He describes the ***Peak Orgasm*** as what most men and many women understand orgasm to be: it is centered around male ejaculation. It requires genital stimulation to build the penile charge. Once the peak is reached and ejaculation occurs, the male quickly loses erotic energy. This typically leaves a female frustrated.[54] By contrast, in ***Valley Orgasm,*** the sexual encounter begins the same way: with enough stimulation to feel some mutual arousal. Instead of continued stimulation to the peak, the partners relax into a quiet embrace. *"In ordinary sexual orgasm you meet as two excited beings—-tense, full of excitement, trying to unburden yourselves. Ordinary sexual orgasm looks mad. Tantric orgasm is a deep, relaxing meditation."*

In my decades of sharing sexual energy with men, I have noticed most males seem hard-wired to be goal-oriented toward the Peak Orgasm. In my teens, that seemed to satisfy me. By my 20s, after my cosmic encounter with Jim in Fairbanks, those quickies no longer resonated. My body, heart and soul yearned for a better balance of masculine and feminine energies. I wanted "a man with a slow hand," as the 80s pop song so sensuously described. I made my work and my personal erotic life about exploring and teaching the Valley. My Tantrassage integrates genitals without much stimulation: just enough to raise about a 50% charge, which I then spread out to the periphery and up through the chakras. If I sense my client tensing toward cumming, I encourage them to breathe more fully and relax and let the energy flow all over "so your whole body becomes one big erogenous zone." I guide them toward the Yogic Savasana: a state of being completely relaxed and profoundly aware.

In my own love life, that process and that state are also my ideal. I like it best if my lover and I take turns leading and following, being more active and more receptive, being Giver and Receiver. This can be by verbal agreement, as in Betty Martin's Wheel of Consent, (p.120) or more spontaneous. Two dance partners or two lovers, who are truly attuned, can non-verbally switch roles from lead to follow and back again seamlessly. Then the thinking minds have let go of control; the dance is being led by Spirit.

We Space

In the spring of 2018, my faerie friend, Bernard, brought a book he'd been reading about a new kind of meditation involving 2 people gazing into one another's eyes for extended periods, and speaking of what they were each "seeing" in a subtle level by looking into the "windows of the soul." He said I'd be the perfect person to practice with.

The book was *Mutual Awakening* by Patricia Albere. I was intrigued. *Body Electric* events almost always involve brief exchanges of eye contact as a way of connecting more deeply with new people in a group. Over the years, those moments were often the most profound and satisfying part of those weekends for me. There was something wondrous and mysterious about having permission to meet another in such an intensely intimate way: more intimate for me than sex.

I was intrigued in part because I already felt a soulful connection with Bernard, and I loved the opportunity to commune in this new way with him.

I was also excited to discover, at the front of the book, a quote from a teacher who had inspired me as an undergrad at the Jesuit Fordham University in the 1960s.

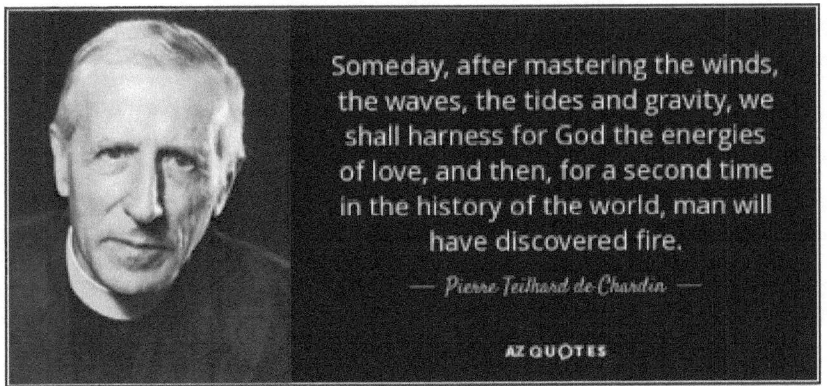

Teilhard was radical for a Catholic priest. He embraced evolution and saw the 7-days creation described in Genesis as taking place over billions of years through the process of evolution. He envisioned and was confident that we humans are evolving toward more and more love. For me, Teilhard's hopeful view of our human trajectory is far better than the standard Catholic doctrine that we are all besmirched by "original sin," and that we require the Church's intercession with God to achieve salvation. Teilhard saw humanity and the whole cosmos as evolving toward divine perfection. I felt a deep Yes. A decade later, I found the same perspective in the teachings of many of the eastern mystics. All these decades later, I continue to hold that hope.

Patricia Albere embraced this vision and also seemed to embrace my Baba's vision that Consciousness is the primordial essence out of which all created forms emerge. She promoted the simple practice of eye gazing as a bold act of participating actively in evolution by tuning into the creative impulse of the universe. As we gaze deeply, she observed, and simply allow ourselves to describe whatever images arise, we are glimpsing the divine creative impulse as it arises, giving it a voice and, thus, facilitating the world's evolution.

Her words, and her vision, lit my fire. Who IS this woman? I began to scour the internet for her other writings and interviews and talks. I could not get enough of her. I signed up for an online course (on Zoom, a whole new medium for me in 2018) that taught the fundamentals of this practice. I took to it readily.

Gazing deeply with total strangers (even on a computer screen) had amazing power. It often felt as though we were in intimate contact, even though we might have been located at great physical distances. Some were in Europe; some in Japan. Yet, we were together in - what? We were really meeting in the realm of spirit. Despite being total "strangers," when we opened to one another in this way, we seemed to be meeting beyond our individual differences in the place where we were *not different*: at that place of pure consciousness which is also pure love. Again that Ram Dass quote comes to mind: "We enter into each other when we are in each other's presence. If you're not threatened, you can relax your separateness, let it fall, and enter into a kind of liquid merging with other beings."[55]

The deeper I dove into We Space practice, the more it anchored my awareness of the underlying unity of all seemingly separate creatures. The Oneness out of which we all arise and to which we all dissolve became a much more constant part of my awareness.

Going back to Kirpal Singh's image of each of us being a drop in the ocean of consciousness, I began to become increasingly aware of the ocean as the foreground, with individual drops more in the background. I became like a fish realizing I'd been immersed in, (both surrounded and permeated) by water all along and had not been aware of it.

In the spring of 2019, I traveled to California 3 times to volunteer at some of Albere's seminars to gain a better grasp of this mysterious practice. By that fall, I felt confident to begin leading in-person practices in Vancouver.

This experience is quite mystical.

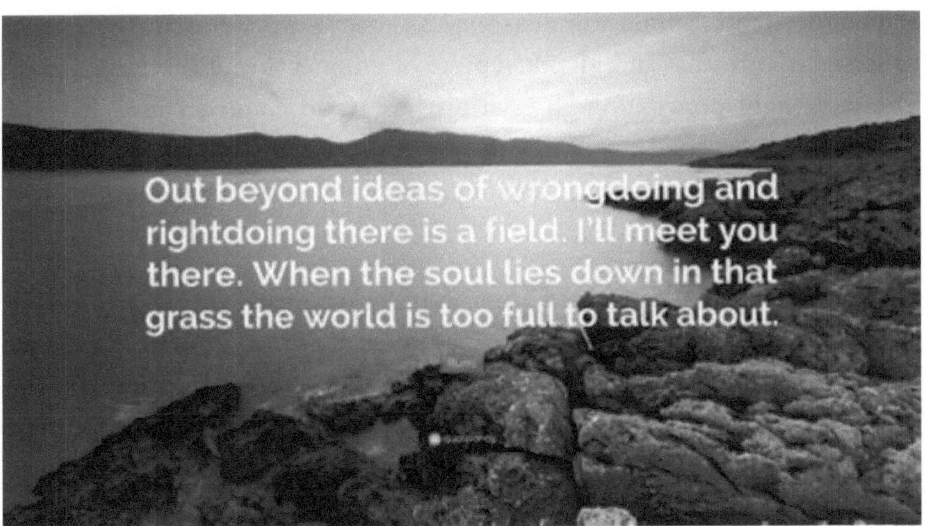

THICH NHAT HANH DESCRIBES this field as "inter-being." *"To be is to inter-be,"* he wrote. This practice is a powerful way to be ever more aware of *"all my relations*[56]*."* It was a way to practice Baba's teaching literally: to *"see God in each other."*

For me, practicing in this way has opened up a new dimension of relating with others. As we gaze deeply, I often experience their/my divine essence where we are not separate. We truly *are One*. Yet, I am also seeing and appreciating their uniqueness, their particularity, even their peculiarity. Both are present. We are One, and we are two. We are Ocean and drop. The drop of our individuality is very much in time/space. This body was born on a certain date. It has grown and developed and learned and experienced pain and pleasure. This body will decline, die, and decay at some point. On that individual journey, we each take on our unique ego and personality, as unique as our face or fingerprints. Yet the spirit out of which we took form and into which we will dissolve, simply IS...now and now and now...

The church I attended as a boy had beautiful stained glass windows. One way I can understand the multi-dimensional intimacy I experience in We Space is to see each "other" as an individual piece of uniquely beautiful stained glass. The same light pours through each of the myriad colored panes. It is the diversity that creates the stunning beauty of the whole window, the whole of life. In We Space, I love both the unique person and the universal One that we each also are.

Another insight I have gained from sharing We Space with many friends and strangers online is about the nature of spiritual growth. The term "enlightened" or "enlightenment" creates the impression that it's like throwing a switch. From my personal journey and witnessing others' journeys I see it as much more incremental. In the early stages, our ego is quite opaque: we believe our thoughts and feelings constitute who we are. While the ego is necessary to navigate life in a physical body, it also obscures the realm of spirit, like solid clouds obscure the vast blue sky above. The early stages of meditation begin to open small holes in the overcast revealing glimpses of that vast infinite space above. Over years of practice there are fewer clouds and mostly blue sky. The remaining clouds are the thoughts and feelings we need to navigate in the physical plane, and they are informed by the vast space of spirit. We realize our ego is simply a servant of that higher Self: a tool not unlike the computer I'm using to write this. "Not my will but Thy will," many traditions pray. The ego must bow down to that greater Self.

Even though I have been meditating for decades, this practice of We Space takes me deeper. I find myself having a greater ongoing awareness throughout each day that behind the different faces of those I interact with (strangers or loved ones) there is *a timeless realm of divine love*. My heart has opened more than ever. In some ways I find this practice more fulfilling than physical sex: truly profound. I think of it as "soul sex."

To meet your higher self

is to welcome the Christ.

To meet your higher self

is to hug the Buddha.

To meet your higher self

is to become the Guru.

This is liberation from God,

for the sake of God,

by the grace of God,

as when two mirrors face

one another, nothing between

but a gaze into the gazer,

igniting the formless radiance

of the sun in every cell

of your body, pouring

the milk of unborn stars

down your spine, setting

an amethyst of boundless sky

between your heartbeats.

Now shake off the illusion

of "higher" and "lower."

The Gaze you long for

is not above, but deeper

inside your chest

than you are,

where wonder precedes thought,

and "I" falls away in the wild

effortless clarity of Am.

What is your true name, friend?

This breath, gently given,

softly received

in silence.

~ Fred LaMotte

To learn more about **We Space** and **Interbeing**, see **Experiential Practices**

Time / Space / The Eternal Now

A perspective that has become increasingly clear to me from all the learning I've done with many amazing teachers over 50+ years is that we humans exist in at least two, distinct yet intersecting realms, which I'll call the Horizontal and Vertical or the Relative and Absolute. (Learn more about this in **Part II: Resources**)

Many indigenous people in North America hold a similar world view. In their "Medicine Wheel," picture the circle being horizontal. It is divided into 4 directions representing the 4 times of the day, 4 seasons of the year, and 4 major phases of human life. Our lives revolve in a circular way, just as earth revolves around the sun.

The vertical Earth/Sky axis is the center of the wheel, about which it revolves. It is the Timeless Now.

There are 7 Directions: 4 horizontal, and 2 vertical. Where those 6 intersect is the 7th Direction: the **Sacred Center of the Heart.** *Meditate on that.*

What I have loved about meditation all these decades is it gives me a chance to move into the center of the swirl of activity: to let go of Doing and to step into just Being. What I am loving now in We Space meditation is that I can do that with another person. Even though in the Relative realm, we are two different drops in the ocean of consciousness, as we practice, we become the Ocean. We are both drop and Ocean. Time and Space do exist, and we are utterly together in The Now where Time and Space cease to be the focus. It can feel like pure divine love.

If Time flows like a river, being in The Now is like standing on the shallow edge and feeling the water swirling past my feet: just standing with my feet rooted in Earth and my crown lifting toward the Sky/Cosmos. Time is flowing by; I am timeless.

Four Flavors of Eros: from densely physical to subtly metaphysical:

Over the decades of my erotic explorations, I've learned to enjoy many variations of sexual expression. Two involve the physical body, and two are more subtle.

- **Hard-ons:** My earliest experiences were all about getting hard, getting off, and the thrill of the hunt. My turn-ons were highly visual. I've read that males are hard-wired by evolution to seek sexual prey: to be turned on first by the *sight* of an attractive potential sexual conquest. The Yang Male energy[57] in all of us is goal-oriented: *I desire **that** (sexual object).* The desire leads to contact and stimulation geared toward genital climax, usually as quickly as possible. That was my only mode in my teens and early 20s, till I discovered...

- **Heart-ons:** I coined this term to describe what I experience as **the fullness of my heart *moving down* to fill my phallus**. It began with my first taste of real love-making with Jim in Alaska when I was 24. Over the next decade, that experience continued and deepened with delicious experiences of full-body, sensual massage with Judith, and then with Tantra and the Taoist Erotic Massages taught by *Body Electric*. My heart and my cock became much more connected. Still, those experiences were confined to those controlled settings. In more recent years, I've had the wonderful experience of developing intimate, loving connections with men **before** we engage our genitals. We share lots of sensual touch, hugs, and kisses. My body opens like a flower. They are not a sexual *object* but very much a *"subject*[58]*"*—a person my heart yearns to lavish with loving affection, and in whose affectionate embrace I can utterly relax while feeling vibrantly alive. This feels much more like my Yin Feminine expressing herself. My whole body wants to envelop their whole body. It does not matter what our genitals are doing or whether we're hard or soft. I have become one, whole erogenous zone meeting their whole erotic presence. In this kind of contact, it feels much less like the *doing* of "sex" and much more like the *being* of "love."

● **Inner Sex:** Ever since experiencing Rudy's guided visualization, which invited imagining sitting on Shiva's erect lingam (see Chapter 13), I regularly choose that image in meditation. As I am sitting, I breathe down to my pelvic floor and open to receive that powerful energy all the way up inside me: from root to crown. I find it profoundly satisfying. It connects the body/sex/heart/soul.

● **Soul Sex:** As I've experienced *We Space* with others, in person or on Zoom, I regularly have a palpable sense that our subtle bodies are meeting and mixing. Patricia Albere used the term *"inter-penetrate"* and the image of the smoke of 2 incense sticks mingling. There is an awareness that we are both *two* and *not-two*: in some ineffable way *we really are one.*

● *Yab Yum*: This exquisite practice from Tantra has the potential to bring together all 4 of these levels of erotic experience. Whether or not there is physical penetration of one partner by the other, there can be a palpable sense of a subtle penetration: an upward flow of energy through both. The physical bodies are entwined, yet are still two. The subtle bodies can completely merge. With Ziji, I regularly have the image in *Yab Yum* that we are two candle flames. I can see the flames surrounding each of us. We have separate wicks (our subtle spines). Gradually the flames grow

fuller and merge into one flame.

We are that one Light of Pure Divine Consciousness.

see **Experiential Practices**

AS THE 2010S DREW TO a close, I felt I had made huge leaps in love on many levels: at 75! Even though my mind and body were beginning to slow, I never felt so happy and fulfilled. What a gift to have reached such ripeness.

I joked with Eric:

"I'm now feeling tender and juicy.

Of course we know what happens after ripeness."

Chapter 16 - The 2020s: A Time of Change

It's not news to anyone that the 2020s are bringing huge changes to virtually everyone's life. The pandemic, the increasingly destructive effects of climate change, and the horrible, hot wars in Ukraine and in Gaza/Israel are causing huge stress and anxiety as well as death and destruction on a scale I've never witnessed in my lifetime. It makes me more aware of the horrors my parents' generation lived through: the Great Depression and then World War II.

For me, climate change and those criminal wars are creating a heightened general anxiety about the future of our planet. I'm doing what I can to reduce my own carbon footprint, and yet I realize I am a very small drop in a huge bucket. With regard to those wars, I pray fervently and hope sanity and compassion will prevail.

The pandemic has had a silver lining for me. **It forced me to stop working.** All my work had involved intimate contact: either with massage clients or in small classes involving yoga and conscious touch. After offering massage for 40 years, stopping felt surprisingly good. I had loved giving people loving touch. It affirmed and expressed my nurturing, feminine side[59]. Yet at 75, I realized it was time to stop. It felt right.

At *Men In Touch*, Ziji and I adapted well to touchless teaching. By the fall of 2020, we began offering Zoom classes in **We Space**, which were well received. It gave men a chance to learn a form of intimacy that does not involve physical touch, yet is profoundly intimate.

We had heard about, and began exploring **Authentic Relating**, which is primarily verbal and works very well on Zoom. AR evolved out of the human potential movement of the 60s and 70s. It is a set of "games" that teach and promote being more authentic. *"In our definition, authenticity is acting and speaking in alignment with your inner feelings, desires, and needs. This means that the way you feel, what you desire, and your needs match the things you're saying and doing."* (Sarah Ness, Founder of Authentic Revolution).

There are several groups around North America that offer online practice sessions and longer courses. Ziji and I immersed ourselves in many of these and took some intensive courses in the winter of 2021. We felt ready to begin offering our own that spring. As with We Space, AR gave our guys at ***Men In Touch*** new intimacy skills. Up until then, we'd been teaching slow, sensual, meditative touch based on Tantra, which was primarily non-verbal. Now we were offering speaking skills that encourage a different kind of vulnerable intimacy. The men loved it, and so did we.

To learn more about AR, see Resources

I found the combination of practicing and teaching ***Authentic Relating*** and ***We Space*** greatly expanded my own intimacy skills, and deepened Ziji's and my personal love relationship, as well. I am hugely grateful for such a growth spurt in my late 70s.

Passing the Torch

In the summer of 2021, I experienced an energy slump. Ziji and I had been planning for months to take a road trip to Saltspring and Vancouver Islands. I had been really excited about it. A few days before, I suddenly became so weak I worried it might be either a heart attack or a stroke and went to the ER. Hours of tests and observation were inconclusive. Still, I felt too low energy to join Ziji and sadly encouraged him to go on alone.

When he came home, I shared my worry that, at almost 77, I could no longer be confident I'd have the energy to show up fully in our *Men In Touch* events. We talked things over and tearfully agreed it was time to "pass the torch" to him to carry on without me. On the weekend of our birthday, we asked a few friends to witness and bless us in a small ceremony making that official.

I am delighted to report that Ziji has brought several, younger co-facilitators into *Men In Touch* and is carrying on brilliantly. I am not at all surprised and it greatly warms my heart. Had he not come into my life and become so involved in *Men In Touch*, as I began running out of steam, the work I've shepherded and loved for decades would have faded with me, which would have broken my heart. I'm so happy to know *Men In Touch* continues to expand, grow, and evolve under younger leadership.

Chapter 17 - Still "Growing Healthier"

———

When I had the inspiration at that first *Spiritual Gathering of Radical Faeries* to take the name Sequoia, I was only dimly aware of its symbolism. I knew I loved being around those beautiful, tall trees. Their quiet, powerful stillness comforted me. They resonated with my soul.

For me, trees have always been the most penetrating preachers...

In their highest boughs the world rustles, their roots rest in infinity;

but they do not lose themselves there, they struggle with all the force of their lives for one thing only: to fulfill themselves according to their own laws, to build up their own form, to represent themselves.

Nothing is holier, nothing is more exemplary than a beautiful, strong tree...

Trees are sanctuaries. Whoever knows how to speak to them, whoever knows how to listen to them, can learn the truth. They do not preach learning and precepts, they preach, undeterred by particulars, the ancient law of life.

A tree says: A kernel is hidden in me, a spark, a thought, I am life from eternal life. The attempt and the risk that the eternal mother took with me is unique, unique the form and veins of my skin, unique the smallest play of leaves in my branches and the smallest scar on my bark. I was made to form and reveal the eternal in my smallest special detail.

A tree says: My strength is trust... I live out the secret of my seed to the very end, and I care for nothing else. I trust that God is in me. I trust that my labor is holy. Out of this trust I live...

~ from Hermann Hesse's *"Wandering: Notes and Sketches"*

Later, I realized that, like all trees, Sequoias *keep growing* their whole lives. Each year they add a new ring of growth. They can withstand storms and fires and continue to grow for hundreds, sometimes thousands of years. What a role model for how to live a full life!

In Ottawa in the late 80s, "Babe" and I were brainstorming a name for my business. He brilliantly suggested ***"Growing Healthier,"*** and I loved it immediately. It includes trees' innate ability for life-long growth. It also suggests we humans can actually get healthier with age. "Health" comes from "heal" which in turn comes from the same root as "whole." To grow healthier is to become more whole. That is exactly the meaning and aim of yoga[60]: to unite the different parts of ourselves: body, heart and soul into one unified whole. That, of course, includes uniting sexuality and spirituality.

I am grateful to report that I am still adding more rings each year, now nearing 80. I truly feel and know that I am becoming more whole and more complete. I am still growing healthier, and trust that will continue till death's great wind topples this tree. Then may my decomposition continue to nourish new life.

Looking back on the many people I've had some degree of intimate contact with (including close friends, lovers, clients, and casual sex) over 65+ years of exploring intimacy, what strikes me is that *each one really IS unique*, much like the individual pieces of stained glass that make for a beautiful mosaic window transmitting the same divine light.

In my early years, I can see I was looking for a copy of myself. I was hungry for some sort of validation that I was not a total weirdo: that there was at least *one other like me*. Now, so many decades later, I realize I truly treasure my own and others' unique beauty. Each of us is a "perfectly imperfect" ray of light in the rainbow spectrum. I celebrate being weird, in myself and others. *Why be normal?*

Socrates' sage advice was *"Know thyself."* For me, every intimate moment with another person adds more to my self-knowing. With each intimate encounter I've had, whether fleeting or years long, I've learned more about who I am or *who I am not*. I've learned as much or more by observing ways I am *not like* another person. Of course, experiencing similarities is a wonderfully validating mirror as well.

The secret to finding "true love" is to *look within*: into the cave of the Heart... the connection with the formless, universal Beloved One. The Inner Beloved is the only One who *is always with us*, from before birth till after death. Then every "Drop" in the outer realm can be seen as an embodiment of that Beloved Ocean.

Seeing others as The Beloved makes them so, at least for ourselves, even if they do not yet see themselves as That One Beloved. I notice that many people respond lovingly when I am in a state of seeing them as The Beloved. It's as though they feel seen as who they really are: they open up in ways that mirror that divine love back to me. We both come away enriched. I am increasingly experiencing the power of Baba's seemingly simple teaching to *"See God in Each Other."*

Most people see us through the clouds of their own egoic "stuff" and we respond from our own clouded egos. The blessing of being in the presence of a true guru is that they look past our egoic clouds and see us as the same blue sky of Pure Consciousness that they are. Being seen at that divine depth is transformational.

What I now look for in Intimate Others is a resonance of our chakras, like being on a similar wavelength. We may have different tastes and interests as long as our deepest values align: especially living life with an open heart toward all.

When Spirit chooses to come into living forms, it does so through sex. Almost every living form has come out of some sort of sex. Thus, sex is a direct manifestation of Spirit. Sex can be seen as an expression of Spirit. Allurement is built into being in separate, unique forms. We are all inherently curious to experience, to see, hear, taste, and smell beings in other forms: to discover through our diversity the full splendor of our divine beauty.

I see clearly that, contrary to the teachings of the Catholic Church, we are born in *"Original Innocence."* Any "sin" comes later when the ego begins to experience the *illusion* of being separate by losing awareness of our original Oneness (the vertical dimension of the Eternal Now). It is possible to live in *both* the Horizontal plane of Time and Space, being aware of self and others as separate "drops" *AND* the Eternal Now in which self and others cease to be separate: we *are* the Ocean, the great "I AM" of Pure Consciousness and Pure Love. **Both are true.**

The more I have shifted into seeing the formless Beloved as my primary "partner," the more I have become aware of, and grateful for, that unseen Presence that has been subtly guiding my life from an early age. Some traditions, including my Baba, use the term Grace to describe that mysterious benign force of guidance that is ever available to anyone who opens to it through prayer. 12-step programs refer to surrendering to our Higher Power. Some Christians describe embracing Jesus as their "personal Savior." Many Buddhists and Hindus practice devotion to "The Guru," referring to their personal human teacher, whom they view as an embodiment of that Formless Guru, The One, God. For sure it is clear in my own life that, the more I have opened to Grace, the more Grace has guided my path. My head does not understand. My heart does. I am eternally and profoundly grateful.

In 2022 I decided to commission a bench in Stanley Park, and then had the daunting task of summarizing the essence of what I have learned into 3 brief lines. The result:

> MOODS COME AND GO. PASSIONS EBB AND FLOW. ONLY IN THE DEEPEST HEART IS THE LOVE I'LL ALWAYS KNOW: OUR ONE HEART! • SEQUOIA THOM

Chapter 18 - My Final Years

Since retiring, I have been moving into a more contemplative phase of life. In the yoga tradition, the fourth and final phase involves letting go of all worldly involvement and being more devoted to spirit. I am finding myself naturally drawn to do that. I am very grateful to have more free time for yoga, meditation, and spiritually inspiring reading.

I am also experiencing the inevitable and inexorable "creeping decrepitude" my beloved James quipped about so playfully[61]. I am finding walking increasingly challenging due to knee osteoarthritis, though happily I can still bike to my heart's content. On my bike, my inner 10 year old is alive and vibrant. Neck arthritis causes nighttime hand numbness, so sleep is getting more challenging. Now that I have few worldly responsibilities, daytime naps are a sweet alternative to a solid night's sleep.

I am being monitored for prostate and blood cancer, though neither is active. In the spring I was diagnosed with pancreatic cancer, which has a nasty reputation. I've been working actively with a naturopath in lieu of the medical torture of surgery and chemo. I am clear that my priority is quality-of-life over quantity. If you wish to stay abreast of my health news and major life events, please visit and subscribe to my blog: sequoia.wordpress.com

Until these last couple of years, I had vainly hoped that my yoga practices would miraculously shield me from the vicissitudes of old age. Alas, there is no escape. What they *are* doing is helping me be more attuned to the realm of soul and spirit. I trust that the mysterious grace that has guided me all these decades will continue to do so until it's time to leave this world. What more could anyone ask? I live in gratitude and take one day at a time.

As mortality looms large, and I have fewer worldly cares, I find it easier to tune into the realm of soul or spirit. Often now I can palpably feel the truth of Sant Kirpal's teaching that, "Each embodied soul is a drop in the ocean of consciousness." Like a fish becoming aware of being surrounded and permeated with water, I can experience being surrounded and permeated with pure consciousness... with God. This drop took form in 1944, and is kept somewhat separate from the ocean by the thinnest of membranes. When the time is right, it will be easy to let that membrane dissolve, reuniting "me" with the ocean once again. How wonderfully simple and natural!

Wishing you every blessing on your own journey of healing and self-discovery.

When Death Comes

by Mary Oliver

When death comes

like the hungry bear in autumn;

when death comes and takes all the bright coins from his purse

to buy me, and snaps the purse shut;

when death comes

like the measle-pox

when death comes

like an iceberg between the shoulder blades,

I want to step through the door full of curiosity, wondering:

what is it going to be like, that cottage of darkness?

And therefore I look upon everything

as a brotherhood and a sisterhood,

and I look upon time as no more than an idea,

and I consider eternity as another possibility,

and I think of each life as a flower, as common

as a field daisy, and as singular,

and each name a comfortable music in the mouth,

tending, as all music does, toward silence,

and each body a lion of courage, and something

precious to the earth.

When it's over, I want to say all my life

I was a bride married to amazement.

I was the bridegroom, taking the world into my arms...

I LOVE MARY OLIVER'S poetic embrace of living and dying. The last two lines especially resonate. The older I get the less I "know" and the more I live in wonder. My heart wants to keep expanding to love everyone and everything.

My own perspective on death is even simpler. I see death as the drop dissolving back into the ocean. Meditation has gradually attuned me more to Big Mind, or ocean, and less to my Little Mind drop. I see death as going home to where I and each of us was before birth: the eternal now of pure beingness, pure consciousness, pure love, which is also God. What is there to fear?

Epilogue

<hr>

Thank you for joining my healing journey that took me nearly seven decades to complete. Memoirs focus on a particular time period or a specific theme in the author's life. For me, the obvious theme was healing the sex/spirit split, and learning that love is the water I and all of us swim in. This review has given me a greater appreciation for all the gifts and grace life has showered upon me, that have enabled me to complete that epic journey.

My work with queer men offering yoga classes and holistic massage, and later the weekend workshops teaching those skills, began in 1980 and kept me thoroughly engaged until the pandemic forced me to suspend those offerings in 2020. I was 75.

That pause gave me a chance to step back and review my life. I appreciate even more all that I had learned. I am astounded at the transformation I have undergone since those early, guilt-ridden, teen-aged years. Teaching yoga and offering Tantra massage was a dream job. I was loving each of my students and clients quite directly, and being able to practice seeing God in each of them.

My hope in publishing my journey is to inspire you in some way.

- What insights have you had about your own life?

- What have you learned about sex, about spirit, and about the connection between them?

- What changes do you feel inspired to make?

My hope for future generations is that you come into this world knowing, or being shown that, the sexual energy that conceived you is also the very creative spark of the divine, which is creating and dissolving this world out of and back into itself *through us* in every moment. We are each a spark of that divine fire. Eros and spirit are inseparable. We are love itself.

I would be happy to hear from you about any/all of that. Feel free to email me: *sequoia (at) learnmassage.online*

How have you enjoyed *Divining Desire?* Of course, I'd love to hear your comments, and especially suggestions or requests for the revised edition [coming soon!]

Please help spread the word about DD by writing a brief review on Amazon. It need not be long. Apparently the number of reviews they get about a book has a big influence on how likely their algorithm is to suggest it when readers do a search by keywords. It's easy:

- If you purchased on Amazon, go back to your order. On the right hand side, you'll find a button "Review this product."

-

- If you bought from me or off-Amazon, go to their listing. Click on the Ratings, then on the left side, click Review This Product.

To stay abreast of my life and health, you can subscribe to **my blog**: *sequoia.wordpress.com*[1]

On the right sidebar, enter your email address, which will not be used or shared beyond the blog.

---

1. *http://sequoia.wordpress.com*

If you are curious to know what Ziji and his colleagues are currently offering, visit MenInTouch.org and subscribe at the bottom of the page. For background info about **Men In Touch**, go to MenInTouch.ca[2] then, on the right sidebar, scroll down to Categories and select Article, Poems, Prose, Photos, Videos, etc.

---

2. http://menintouch.ca

WAY BACK IN 1987, I recorded two 20-minute guided relaxations / meditations, which are now available for free on YouTube:

   • *Inner Space Meditation* is a journey through your body to become aware of the subtle energy and, even deeper, the pure consciousness that many mystical traditions say is who we are at the deepest level.

   ○ Go to **Sequoia Thom** on YouTube then select *Inner Space Meditation*

   • *Ocean of Consciousness* connects our breathing with ocean waves, which are audible. The ocean waves are a metaphor for the waves of thoughts in the mind. In this meditation we sink below the waves to the stillness deep beneath the surface.

   ○ Go to **Sequoia Thom** on YouTube then select *Ocean Of Consciousness*

Appendix: Resources for your own Healing Journey

This section is a bit like a cookbook. It will give you ideas and info about ways you can nourish yourself. But the pleasure of a cookbook is merely mental. The body is not nourished, nor is there sensory pleasure (other than the enticing photos).

For these latter benefits, please explore Experiential Practices.

What is meditation?

The fridge magnet summary:

Indeed, I've learned many forms and heard of many more. What they have in common is focusing the awareness on one thing (other than discursive thinking). Then, when the inevitable thoughts distract from that focus, choose to shift back to the chosen focus, thus retraining the awareness to not identify with thoughts as Who We Are.

The focus can be visual, auditory, and/or kinesthetic:

- **visual:** look steadily at any object that is pleasing, such as a flower, a candle flame, a crystal, an image of an inspiring person;

- **auditory:**

  - making sound to listen to, such as humming, chanting, or an interior sound like a mantra or prayer, or

  - listen to an outer sound, such as recorded music or something more neutral, like sounds in nature, and/or

- **kinesthetic:** any bodily sensation(s), such as breathing and posture, yoga asanas, martial arts, free-form dance. Many Buddhists practice a combination of sitting and walking meditation. In each, awareness of posture and breathing is emphasized.

Would you like to try it now? See **Experiential Practices**

My personal meditation practice:

My personal altar or "puja."

Every meditator finds their own way. It helps to experiment with many forms, as I have.

I share my practice with you, not to say my way is right: only that it is perfect for me. Take whatever parts resonate and leave the rest.

Where: While I have meditated on trains and planes and buses, I prefer a serene environment, either in nature or at home, where I've set up a special altar.

When: I choose a time when I'm reasonably awake and neither too hungry nor too full from a recent meal. Before breakfast, before dinner, and before bed are my preferred times (though I rarely do all 3 in one day).

How:

I sit in a comfortable cross-legged position on a cushion that raises my pelvis higher than my knees, so that my spine is easily erect.

I like to use a special shawl dedicated to meditation: it provides a little warmth and is a sort of cocoon providing psychic protection.

Once settled into position, I may use several focuses:

- I am naturally more auditory and kinesthetic, and less visual. So I usually close my eyes.

- I focus on my **posture**: staying comfortably upright with hands in my lap. I lightly touch the index finger and thumb of each hand in the classic *gyan mudra*, which is said to help contain the energy. If my mind is particularly chatty, I use a *mala*, which is a set of beads dedicated for use in meditation. The physicality of moving from bead to bead on each breath or repetition of a manta can help me get more grounded into my body, and out of my chattering head.

• I often begin with some simple *pranayama* to help steady the mind. Box Breathing is a favorite. Note: the length of the breaths should be *comfortable*; if the pauses at the top and bottom create any tension at all, reduce the length of them. Another simple *pranayama* is to **gently** lengthen the EXhale by drawing the tummy toward the spine. This deepens relaxation, expels toxins, and automatically creates fuller INhalations, as well. I keep my focus on the EXhales and let the INhales be spontaneous. I may do this for a few minutes until my mind begins to come more into the present.

• *Mantra*: Because I am primarily auditory, I find sounds an easy focus. Because the "monkey mind" is often talkative, giving the verbal part of the mind a simple word or phrase to repeat occupies it and reduces the likelihood of random chatter. One Western researcher found the word "One" quite effective. Both my Transcendental Meditation and Baba's meditation focus on the use of *mantra*. In India it is believed certain sounds were heard in meditation by the ancient enlightened ones, who have shared those sounds for future generations to use to reach those deep states of Pure Consciousness. The most famous is OM or, more precisely, A-U-M. It is the vibration of that Pure Consciousness. By itself, it is sometimes too subtle for my mind to stay with. At those times I use my Baba's full ***Om Namah Shivaya (ONS)***. Those 7 syllables give my verbal mind plenty to chew on. I play with synchronizing with my breaths: sometimes a full ONS on the INhale and another full ONS on the EXhale. Sometimes I'll focus on OM on the INhale, then *Namah Shivaya* on the EXhale. Sometimes I use ONS in the Box Breathing, with one repetition on each phase of INhale, Hold, EXhale, Hold. It's fine to improvise. It's only a tool.

• My understanding is that *Mantra* or any other focus is simply a way to quiet the mental fluctuations. Once the waves on the surface of the ocean have subsided, at least somewhat, then it's possible to see down into the depth of the Ocean of Consciousness.

• **How long to meditate**: the classic guidance is that it usually takes around 20 minutes for the chatter to get quiet. I find that varies. If possible, I like to sit for at least 30 minutes. If time is really tight, even a few minutes focusing inward and on the present moment is better than nothing.

• **Meditation in action**: I find many opportunities throughout the day to practice being "one-pointed" with whatever I am doing. Multi-tasking is the very antithesis of meditation. So, my overall intention is to do one thing at a time. If I am walking, I can make it a meditation by feeling my feet and body and breathing, and ignoring my thoughts. Being aware of surroundings is part of Being Here Now and adds to safety when walking. Washing dishes, brushing teeth, peeing and pooping, I focus just on those sensations and the breath, and let go of chatter as much as I can. Throughout the day, even when using my mind (as I am now writing this), I periodically pause and look up (thus giving my eyes a relaxing shift of focal length), and become aware of my body, breathing, and surroundings. Then I return to my task. That can be a true pause that refreshes. Of course, the best meditation is when I can do nothing and just Be Here Now.

• **The Goal:** *There is no goal!* It's all about the journey. Even after 50+ years as a dedicated meditator, I am not "there" (wherever "there" is). What I can say is that I am more Here and Now (thank you, Ram Dass). What I have observed:

○ Over the years, the view on my journey has changed from thickets of thoughts to vaster vistas.

○ My chattering mind is less chatty. The waves are generally calmer than in my early years of meditation, and they calm down more quickly when I meditate.

○ Buddhists talk about Little Mind and Big Mind: Little Mind is the Chatter Box we all *have*. It's our internal binary computer that helps us navigate this material world. Big Mind is the field of Pure Consciousness we all *share*. For new meditators, Little Mind is in the foreground, and Big Mind is dimly perceived, if at all. Over the decades, I've noticed a Figure-Ground Shift. Just as we can view this drawing as a vase or two faces in profile, now I am more continuously aware of the field of Pure Consciousness between, around, and behind all my thoughts. My inner sky is much less filled with clouds (thoughts can be understood as condensations of that Pure Consciousness) and much more with Blue Sky: the limitless field of Pure Consciousness itself. I also notice I am less often anxious. Anxiety most often comes from thoughts about the future. When I come into this moment, anxieties evaporate. Finally, I have noticed I am much more often in my heart than in my head. My heart feels simple gratitude and love.

THE HINDU / YOGIC UNDERSTANDING of the flow of subtle energy through the chakras:

The American artist Alex Grey has an astounding gift for being able to see the Subtle Body and render it onto canvas. Some of his images depict clearly how the energy body looks when energy is flowing freely from root to crown. To me it looks like a fountain or an erect phallus erupting. See https://www.alexgrey.com/art/collections/sacred-mirrors/ then find the blue images.

At *Men In Touch* we've used this image to create a template for offering a coherent massage that connects all the chakras together. We call it the *"Fountain Flow."*

see **Part III Experiential Practices**

HERE ARE THE HIGHLIGHTS of what I learned from Rudy Ballentine about Tantra[62]:

- Tantra is an alchemy that transforms seeming opposites, like Matter/Spirit or Sex/Spirit. Instead of viewing them as binary opposites, Tantra sees them as the 2 poles on a continuum. They are seen as different frequencies of one energy, like the various notes on a keyboard or the infinite gradations of colors in the rainbow spectrum.

● Tantra is completely empirical. There are no moralistic *shoulds* or *should-nots*. Everything is an experiment: trying things out and "gathering data" to inform future experiments.

● *Tapas* and *Spanda*:

○ *Tapas* is defined as restraint;

○ *Spanda*: is the root of our word *spontaneous*.

○ Some experiments can involve applying a *Tapas*: some deliberate *restraint*, which can create a shift in consciousness and awareness by stepping outside of expectations and ingrained habits.

▪ An example of a tapas in a non-erotic context would be writing with one's non-dominant hand, which leads to a very different experience and outcome.

▪ Some unusual sensual touch: use only 1 finger to explore any/all areas of your partner's body they are comfortable having explored. Notice the effect for each of you. If you are both ready for more intimate non-sexual touch, try the same exploration using only your nose. Of course, take in all the aromas you encounter along the way. Again share verbally with one another what you each experienced.

▪ In the erotic arena, an example might be focusing one's attention on an area of the body not usually considered highly erogenous and simply noticing the effect.

● Consider making love to your partner's inner elbows or knees, using only your hands and/or mouth.

● Men may choose to delay and abstain from ejaculation during love-making and observe where Spanda takes the energy flow.

○ In Tantra, Spanda is viewed as a Goddess. Practitioners of Tantra cultivate surrendering to "Her" to guide the flow and interaction, getting the usual ego agendas out of the way.

● We **all are both** Feminine and Masculine, regardless of our plumbing. Hormones and social conditioning lead each person to manifest their own unique presentation of the qualities of each. These are not fixed and can change many times throughout life.

● The Tantric ideal is to create an "inner marriage" of our Feminine and Masculine aspects: to be *both/and* rather than *either/or*. The aim is not to create a bland homogenized blend but, rather, to be able to play all the keys on the keyboard. No key is out of reach.

○ Rudy taught us a practice of "feminine and masculine breathing," which is done with another person. It can help each person develop a stronger connection with each of those energies. The details of the practice are in the Appendix.

● Going further on gender, Rudy offered a wonderful presentation based on Genia Pauli Haddon's *Uniting Sex, Self and Spirit*. She divides the primal energies of Masculine and Feminine into four quadrants, each of which can be further divided into Healthy, Deficient, and Excessive manifestations.

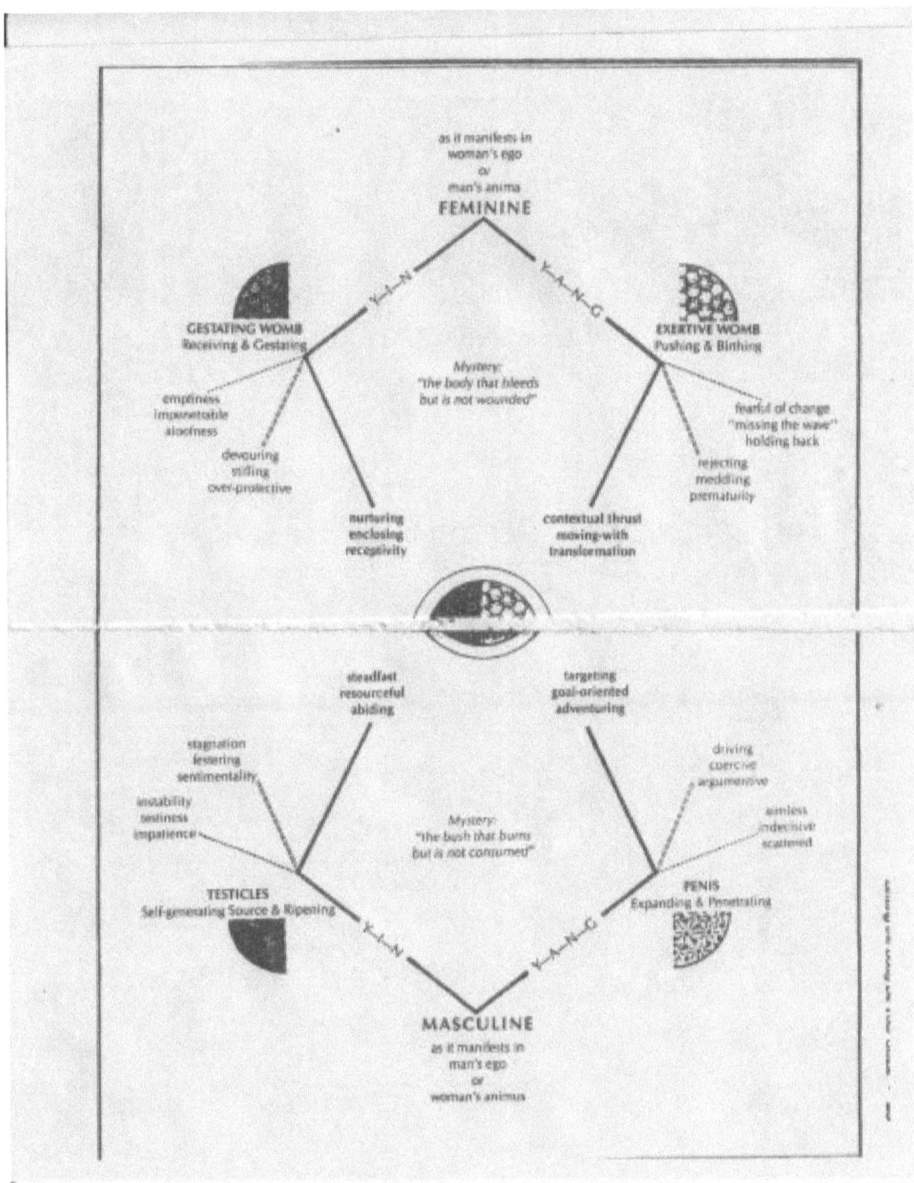

● Kinsey's pioneering study, first published in 1948, enumerated 7 categories of sexual orientation. He emphasized that it is much more nuanced and fluid, and can change over time.

EXCLUSIVELY HETEROSEXUAL
MOSTLY HETEROSEXUAL
EQUALLY HETEROSEXUAL AND HOMOSEXUAL
MOSTLY HOMOSEXUAL
EXCLUSIVELY HOMOSEXUAL
NO SEXUAL CONTACTS OR REACTIONS
THE KINSEY SCALE

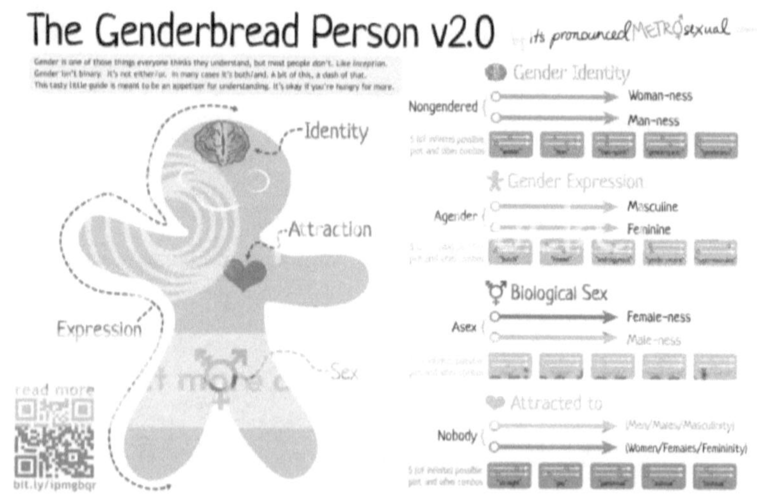
The Genderbread Person v2.0
its pronounced METROsexual
Gender Identity
Nongendered
Woman-ness
Man-ness
Gender Expression
Agender
Masculine
Feminine
Biological Sex
Asex
Female-ness
Male-ness
Attracted to
Nobody
(Men/Males/Masculinity)
(Women/Females/Femininity)
Identity
Attraction
Expression
Sex
read more
bit.ly/ipmgbqr

TIME / SPACE / THE Eternal Now

An image that has become increasingly clear to me from all the learning I've done with many amazing teachers over 50+ years is that we humans exist in at least two distinct yet intersecting realms, which I'll call the Relative and Absolute.

- I experience the **Relative** realm as a Horizontal plane of Time and Space. Time flows through it like a river. There is a sense of constant outer Doing. Our minds are constantly dwelling in either the past or future.

- **The Absolute**: There is a Vertical line through that horizontal plane that is **The Eternal Now**. It simply IS. There is no Doing, only Being.

- Seen together they resemble a gyroscope, with the vertical axis the still point about which the Relative Realm swirls. Images of galaxies also show that quality.

The Taoists in China have given the world the now-ubiquitous Yin-Yang symbol. It shows a dynamic flow between one pole (Yang/white) to the other (Yin/black). Each has a dot of the other color within it, indicating neither is purely Yin or Yang. They are ever revolving and transforming into one another, just as day and night flow seamlessly into one another with no sharp demarcation.

It is usually depicted (on paper or screens) in 2 dimensions making it appear to be a vertical wheel. However, I prefer to imagine it on the horizontal plane: the relative dimension of time/space. This image shows the solid vertical earth/sky axis about which it revolves: the still center. I like to see it being a variation of the gyroscope.

At the still point of the turning world.

Neither flesh nor fleshless;

Neither from nor towards; at the still point, there the dance is,

But neither arrest nor movement. And do not call it fixity,

Where past and future are gathered. Neither movement from nor towards,

Neither ascent nor decline. Except for the point, the still point,

There would be no dance, and there is only the dance.

~ T. S. Eliot ~

(excerpt from The Four Quartets, Burnt Norton, II..)

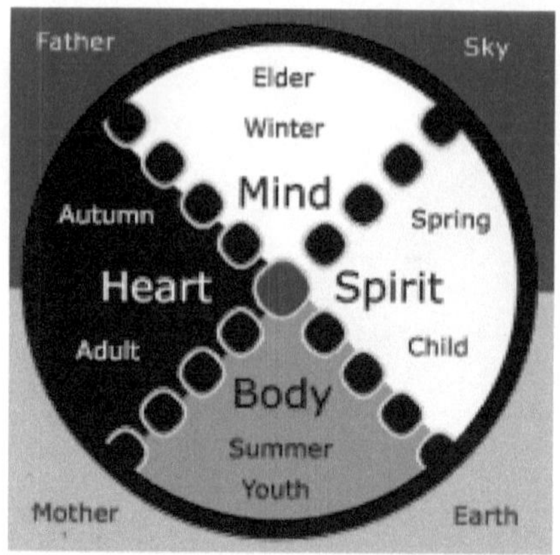

THE INDIGENOUS MEDICINE Wheel and the 7-Directions:

Because indigenous traditions were largely oral, there is great variation among different tribes about the meanings of the different parts of the Medicine Wheel.

In 2009, I had the opportunity to *absorb into my whole body* what had been merely appealing philosophical concepts. I had the great good fortune to participate in a Naraya Dance for All Peoples at Wolf Creek, OR, led by Clyde Hall. See danceforallpeople.com Over 3 days and nights, he led dozens of us, mostly non-Native faerie folks, in a transformative ceremony.

During daylight hours, we offered prayers to the directions and learned some traditional chants. Then, after dark (quite late, nearing summer solstice), we spent hours around a tree which had been chosen as the sacred Earth/Sky axis. Holding hands, we circled around that tree in a simple, slow side-step, singing these ancient, sacred songs. As we revolved, it felt as though we were part of the revolving earth, constantly shifting through each of the 4 cardinal directions, each with its own symbolic significance. The stillness of the tree steadied us as we revolved. I experienced being in deep trance: both in time and outside it. Each rotation felt like living one day through its 4 phases or living one full year through its 4 seasons.

Ever since then, I have felt like replicating a small version of that every morning. See Resources

BETTY MARTIN'S WHEEL of Consent:

This is a powerful tool for dissecting and deepening awareness of the different components present in any form of intimate relating. It applies equally to sharing touch, talking/listening, or any other form of interaction.

Note: If you learn better by doing, skip this theoretical part for now and go directly to Betty's Three-Minute Game in Part III Her short video on YouTube gives clear instructions on how to play.

THERE IS A HUGE AMOUNT of information contained in this seemingly simple schematic. To dive deeper, I recommend Betty's website, bettymartin.org, and her many videos on YouTube. Her newly released book is a gem of straight-forward clarity.

THE Body Electric's [1] *Sacred Intimate Training*[2]

In this training:

- We learned or reviewed a number of tools to be with our clients *for their pleasure.* The pleasure of intentional erotic touch was viewed as inherently healing.

- We had many scheduled "SI sessions," in which men were randomly paired up for fixed periods, where one was the "client," who was coming to the Sacred Intimate for some sort of healing experience (healing here meaning "making more whole").

- In each session, the client's desires and boundaries are deliberately expressed and very intentionally honored.

---

1. https://bodyelectric.org/all-workshops/

2. *https://bodyelectric.org/all-workshops/*

○ When a person can ask for exactly the kind of touch they most desire, and have that request honored and celebrated, it can be a healing experience for both people.

○ There is so much sexual wounding in our world when people take sexual liberties without getting clear consent. So the foundation of Sacred Intimate work is that both people's boundaries are essential. If a client's request would cross the SI's boundaries, he first thanks the client for their request, then offers an alternative that is as close as possible to fulfilling the client's request without violating the SI's boundaries

● We also had supervisory groups where we could debrief our experiences in each role with one of the facilitators, and offer peer support as well.

EXPERIENTIAL PRACTICES

If the cognitive wisdom above is like reading a cookbook, these *practices* promote embodiment: like cooking the food and savoring its delicious nourishment.

Would you like to try different kinds of meditation now?

Here is a brief (under 5 minute) sampling:

- **Visual:**

  ○ Look around your present environment.

  ○ Choose any object that is pleasing.

  ○ Then, steadily look at it with soft eyes for 1 minute.

  ○ When thoughts intrude, simply return to the present moment of you and your chosen object.

  ○ Then, after 1 minute, notice how you feel different.

- **Auditory:**

  ○ Close your eyes, and take in all the sounds in your present environment for 1 minute.

  ○ Some sounds may be more prominent and others more distant or in the background. Listen for the most distant ones to allow your field of consciousness to grow huge.

  ○ When thoughts intrude, simply return to the present moment of you and sounds.

  ○ After 1 minute notice how you feel different.

- **Kinesthetic:**

○ For 1 minute, close your eyes and focus on any bodily sensation(s), such as breathing and posture. An easy choice is feeling where you are "grounded," the parts of your body touching the supporting surfaces, such as your butt or feet. Adding awareness of the breathing is optional.

○ When thoughts intrude, simply return to the present moment of your bodily sensations.

○ After 1 minute notice how you feel different.

● If you notice one (or maybe two) of those focuses was/were easier, then, in the future, you can go deeper into that/them. Most people naturally prefer one.

● Then, at each practice, make the time a bit longer: maybe 3 or 5 minutes for a few days or even weeks. Many traditions agree that around 20 minutes a shift occurs toward a quieter mind.

● The metaphor is of waves (of thoughts) on a body of water (consciousness itself). By focusing awareness on one object, the waves of thoughts gradually subside.

● Eventually we are able to be aware of awareness itself. ***That is Who We Are.***

More on Breathing: It is said that "the breath is the bridge between the body and the mind." It goes on 24/7 and is usually outside of our awareness. Yet, we can become aware of it and exert some control over it. So, breathing is a great focus for meditation, either by itself or in combination with any of the above focuses. Learning to control the breathing through *Pranayama* can greatly assist in calming the "monkey mind."

● **Here is a simple practice:** observe the INhales and EXhales, and allow them to be whatever length is most comfortable. Then, begin to notice the ***point of stillness*** between those two phases. It may be only a fraction of a second between when one breath phase ends and the next begins, yet there is a ***point of stillness.*** In that moment, the mind is also still! So it is a glimpse, however fleeting, of Pure Awareness. **Be aware of being aware:** that Pure Awareness or Pure Consciousness is Who You and I are.

LOVING KINDNESS MEDITATION (Metta): There are many variations of the phrases I've been using. As I understand the practice there is a progress of levels of challenge:

● It is always recommended to begin with ourselves. If we cannot love ourselves, we cannot love anyone. If this is a challenge, spend weeks or months just focussing on yourself:

▪ May I be happy.

▪ May I be free from suffering.

▪ May I dwell in the heart.

▪ May I be healed into wholeness.

▪ May I be at peace.

● Only after that self-directed practice feels totally authentic is it recommended to begin to add others, starting with people we feel close to and safe with, truly wishing them those same blessings. Note: these phrases are in addition to the above; always begin with yourself.

▪ May ___ be happy.

▪ May ___ be free from suffering.

▪ May ___ dwell in the heart.

▪ May ___ be healed into wholeness.

▪ May ___ be at peace.

● Only after this level of practice feels totally authentic is it recommended to begin to add people we feel neutral towards, such as the clerk at the store or bank, or a neighbor, truly wishing them those same blessings. Note: these phrases are in addition to the above; always doing the "easier" ones first. If you do not know their name, simply picture them and substitute "you."

- May ___ be happy.

- May ___ be free from suffering.

- May ___ dwell in the heart.

- May ___ be healed into wholeness.

- May ___ be at peace.

● Only after that neutral-person practice feels totally authentic is it recommended to begin to add others with whom you feel some mild negativity or animosity, truly wishing them those same blessings. Note: start with people with whom the degree of negativity is mild, and gradually progress to people with whom you feel stronger negativity, animosity or anger. If it begins to feel inauthentic, scale back for a while. Remember: *this is a practice.* We can gradually learn to bring more people into our growing heart, but only as the heart truly feels ready.

- May ___ be happy.

- May ___ be free from suffering.

- May ___ dwell in the heart.

- May ___ be healed into wholeness.

- May ___ be at peace.

Eventually, if and when it feels authentic, include *all humans* or even *all sentient beings*.

I have come to experience that the practice nourishes or "waters" my own heart. In addition, I believe we can psychically touch others with our love.

VISUALIZING AN EROTIC Embrace with Shiva or another God/dess:

1. Create a quiet, meditative space and time for yourself.
2. Use conscious breathing or any other practice that you know can guide you out of your ordinary, egoic mind, and into a more expansive state.
3. When you sense yourself in that more spacious place, visualize any human form that represents *for you* the embodiment of erotically integrated spirit: some God/dess who really lights you up. The image of Shiva with a full erection may work for some. For some, it may be a "sexy Jesus." For others, it may be a version of the Divine Feminine into whose warm loving embrace you can melt in child-like safely (a Divine Mother) or feel turned on by her erotic power (the hot Goddess consort).
4. Really let yourself *feel the bodily sensations* of being in such intimate contact with the body of this divine being. Breathe and move in whatever ways are spontaneous and authentic. Consider touching any parts of your body that add to your feeling of being fully alive. Allow yourself to **make sounds** as you exhale... sounds that express and amplify whatever you are experiencing.
5. The energy (Spanda) may take on a life of its own. Go with it.
6. When you sense the energy subsiding, gently and slowly let yourself become aware again of your immediate surroundings. Notice the colors, and sounds, or even smells around you. Come fully into the present moment of your outer life.
7. When it feels right, get up and resume your day.

"FOUNTAIN FLOW"

1. Create a quiet, meditative space so you can tune into subtle energy.
2. Stand with feet about hip width apart, without shoes, so you can feel the floor/ground underneath.
3. Take a few full breaths letting yourself sink roots down from the soles of your feet into the earth.
4. Let your arms rise up like tree branches reaching for the sky on each INhalation. Then, let them relax down on each EXhalation.
5. Imagine that the earth beneath you is the Yoni and that your body is the Lingam.
6. Bend over to touch or reach toward the Earth/Yoni, and use your hands to draw that earthy energy slowly and sensuously up your inner legs like a caress.
7. Bring the energy to touch and connect with your Root (pelvic floor)
8. Then continue slowly inviting the energy up along your centerline, touching each chakra in turn: the Sexual, Belly/Solar Plexus, Heart, Throat, Third Eye, and Crown.
9. Then let your hands continue to rise higher imagining the energy erupting out your Crown to unite with Cosmic Oneness.
10. Then slowly flow your hands down along the outside of your torso and legs till you are again touching or reaching toward the Earth/ Yoni.
11. Repeat as many times as feels satisfying
12. Come to standing again with feet rooted in Earth/Yoni and feeling your erect body as Shiva Lingam, full to overflowing with eros-spirit vitality.
13. Stay as long as you like; then continue your day, noticing how you can carry that awareness into activity.

Once you've experienced the inner connectedness and pleasure this practice provides when done on oneself, you'll be ready to offer it to a friend or lover. It works best if they are on a massage table, or they can be standing. I sometimes use it as part of an Undressing Ritual before massage or love-making.

THE INDIGENOUS MEDICINE Wheel and the 7-Directions:

- **Practice:** Ever since being taught the Naraya dances by indigenous elders in 2009, I have felt like honoring that tradition by replicating a small version of that practice every morning.

  ○ I face each direction in turn and offer prayers, beginning with:

  ○ **East:** *air, eagle, yellow, sunrise, morning, spring, birth, childhood, rapid growth, new beginnings, eagerness to learn, curiosity, exuberance, delight, play, and gratitude ~ welcome!*

  ○ **South:** *fire, red, coyote, afternoon, summer, heat, young adult passion and path-finding, sexuality, anger, and co-creation ~ welcome!*

  ○ **West:** *water, black, bear, introspection, evening, autumn, mature adulthood, completion, harvest, fulfillment, grieving, letting go, waning, winding down, and generosity ~ welcome!*

  ○ **North:** *white, earth, buffalo, white hair of elder (wisdom and simplicity), white snow of mountain (groundedness, purity, mutability: changing forms into liquid, ice, vapor, and remaining ever water), nighttime (stillness, sleep, dreams, meditation), winter (cold, death, peace) ~ welcome!*

  ○ **Earth** (I squat down placing both hands on the ground/floor): *Sacred Mother, I give thanks for all the blessings I receive from you* (pausing to remember them). *I pray for every one of your children* (naming a few who need blessings at this time). *I pray that they and every one of your children, Mother, be happy and free from suffering, that they dwell in the heart and are at peace.*

  ○ **Sky** (standing with arms reaching upward): *Father Sky, let me be guided by you and shine your light in the world this day.*

Betty Martin's Three-Minute Game:

Betty's version involves 2 people taking turns asking one another either or both of these key questions: "For the next ____ minutes,

1. How would you like me to touch* you *for your pleasure*? (the Serve-Accept quadrants); OR
2. How would you like to touch* me *for your pleasure*? (the Take-Allow quadrants)

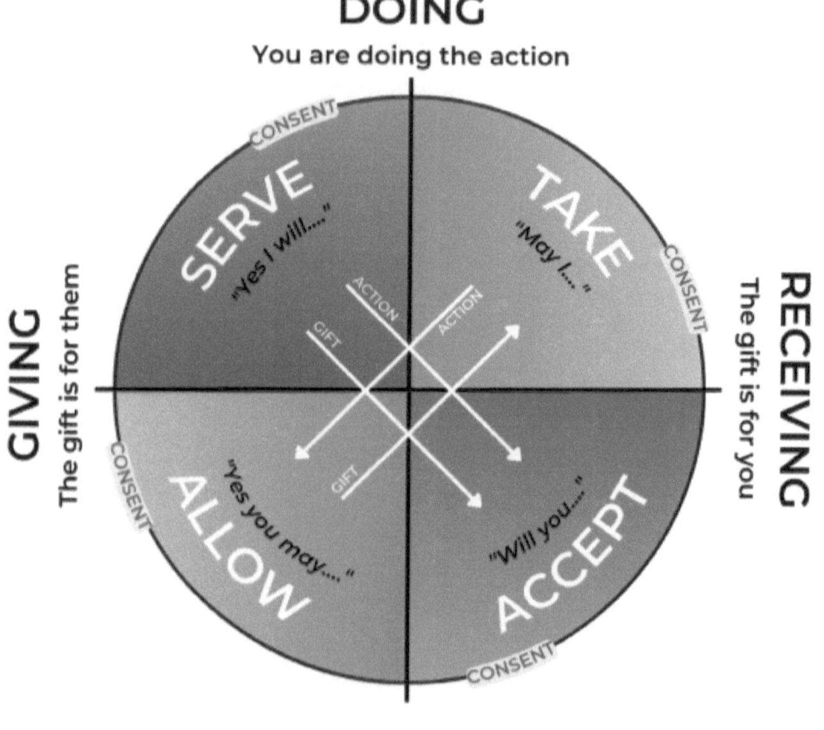

*NOTE: This exercise does not need to involve touch. For example, by changing "touch" to "connect with you" or "be with you," many kinds of contact are possible. For example,

For Question 1:

- Please tell me about (some specific topic)

- Please tell me how beautiful/handsome I am, using as many extravagant compliments as you can

- Please sing my favorite song to me

- Please gaze into my eyes

For Question 2:

- Please listen to me talk about something that is bothering me

- Please watch me practice a new dance step I've been practicing

- Please allow me to gaze at your (face, body, eyes, genitals, etc.)

A crucial part of this game is **boundaries**:

- Clear **time boundaries** are agreed to and honored. They can be renegotiated by mutual consent.

- The person who is Giving (Serving or Allowing) is free to decline the asker's request or offer a modified option that is both comfortable for them and aims in the direction of the asker's request.

FEMININE/MASCULINE Breathing:

Both the Yoga and Tantra traditions use the breath to move subtle energy in order to alter states of consciousness. The intention of the following practice is to develop the skill to circulate *chi* or *prana* with a partner (of any gender) to take turns emphasizing either feminine or masculine energy. This can have the effect of connecting the sexual energy in the pelvis with the loving energy in the heart. We can learn to give and receive love through our sexual organs as well as directly through our hearts.

• This is a somewhat advanced form of breathing practice. If you are new to *pranayama*, I suggest you find a good teacher to learn the basics first.

• It may be easier to learn this standing. Once both partners are comfortable with the practice it can be done sitting opposite one another or in *Yab Yum*.

• In the beginning, even 1 or 2 minutes may be challenging, so stop and relax whenever either of you feels tension or fatigue. Once comfortable you may naturally extend the time as desired.

• The feminine breath is INhaling while imagining energy entering the genitals, then breathing the energy up into the heart, and EXhaling while imagining energy pouring out from the heart into your partner's heart.

• The masculine breath is the opposite: INhaling while imagining energy entering into the heart and breathing the energy down into the pelvis, and EXhaling while imagining energy pouring out from the genitals to your partner's pelvis/genitals.

• The 2 partners are breathing out-of-sync: one is INhaling while the other is EXhaling. This can be challenging at first: be patient. Stop and rest if it causes mental or physical tension.

• Partners can decide how to divide the time:

○ equally between each role, or

○ if one partner feels they need to develop greater comfort with one polarity, they may ask to emphasize that.

○ It is important to practice each role for at least a short while.

● Options:

○ Since it can be difficult to do the breathing and visualizing at the same time, it can help to give the energy flow a physical dimension. Join hands, then the partner who is EXhaling gives the other partner's hand a gentle squeeze as they begin their EXhale. Squeezing your partner's hands represents "giving energy" to your partner, and thus helps to keep the directionality of the flow of energy clear. This makes it easier to keep aware of which partner is doing which phase.

○ A more intimate option is to place your hands on one another's heart and genitals:

▪ The partner doing the feminine breath places their right (giving) hand on their partner's heart chakra, and their left (receiving) hand on their partner's genitals.

▪ The partner doing the masculine breath places their right (giving) hand on their partner's genitals, and their left (receiving) hand on their partner's heart chakra. (Note: this configuration may feel slightly awkward. Feel free to experiment with variations.)

▪ The giving hand can signal the start of the EXhale with a gentle squeeze.

○ This practice could be a prelude to others, like We Space, or meditating in *Yab Yum*, or other forms of intentional intimate touch.

Annotated Table of Contents

———

These Annotated Contents summarize and contain links to each section. You can get the overview there, then:

- **Follow me through time:** begin at the beginning and follow my meandering path, one step at a time, *or*

- **Follow your curiosity:** Pick and choose to dive directly into whatever sections draw you, and jump around to your own delight.

Looking back on my many decades, I am seeing my life in three major phases. I'm intrigued to notice how my eros-spiritual development correlates with the astrological understanding of the influence of Saturn return on all our lives. The planet Saturn orbits the sun about every 29 years. When it nears the position of our birth, around age 28-30, 56-60, and 84-90, people often experience exceptionally significant shifts.

Foreword

Preface

Introduction:

- **Synopsis of my transformational journey**

- **What do I mean by "God?"**

The Early Years - Lost and Alone

Before 28, I lived a painfully inauthentic life in which my sexual activities and desires were hidden from friends and family. Those early years were full of confusion, uncertainty, shame, guilt, and low self-worth. The split between my erotic and spiritual sides was intensely painful. It created a deep yearning to connect them and feel whole, with no idea how. I longed to live an open, honest, and authentic life.

Chapter 1 ~ **Early Stirrings:** pre-puberty (1944-1956)

- Early disconnect from my own body and feelings

- Yearning to heal that split and glimpsing a genital-heart connection

- Loving, longing, and letting go: my heart broken open - first of many

Chapter 2 ~ **A Tortured Teen** (1956-1962)

- Cycle of Catholic guilt/confess/repeat

- The utter secrecy and shame about my sexuality in my teens: no one I could speak to at all utterly alone and feeling torn apart

- Complex connection with the Feminine...in myself and in girls, women, and effeminate men

Chapter 3 ~ **Graduating from Guilt** (1962-1966)

- Fordham University: thinking for myself, leaving the Church;

- Inspired by Fromm's *Art of Loving*, Frankl, Dag Hammarskjold (his mystical side and disconnect from sex), Zorba The Greek, Kahlil Gibran's comforting wisdom;

- Special friends: Paul G and his sister, Andrea

Chapter 4 ~ **Trying to Fly in the Closet:** (1966-1972)

- Piloting was a boost to my self-esteem

- Air Force showers

- Jim: my first love and first heartbreak; he led me to embrace being gay

- breaking up with Andrea

o Mike aka "Michelle" in Sydney

The Middle Years

A Sexual / Spiritual Growth Spurt:

Finding New Ways of Living and Loving Authentically

Chapter 5 ~ **Flying Free** (1972-79)

o **My first Saturn Return was a dramatic 180 degree course change**

o **Exploring meditation**

o **My first taste of Tantra**

o *Institute for Yoga Teacher Education* and a Masters in East/West Psychology

o **The baths: mostly visual - a living porn and teen mutual masturbation**

o **I yearned to find and share more whole-hearted kinds of intimacy**

o **Exploring love without lust with Nancy**

Chapter 6 ~ **Soaring Higher with Baba**

● **My initial skepticism, then**

● **A life-changing experience with a mysterious man I'd barely met**

Chapter 7 ~ **Unhinged by Michael then major epiphany**

● **Instead of quick sex, Michael re-awakened my connection with my Inner Child**

● **In tandem with Baba, he helped me glimpse Universal Love.**

Chapter 8 ~ **Trying on the "Married" Model with Kyle**

● **Feeling the cultural pull to "settle down" at 32**

● **Then feeling like a caged animal**

- Learning I need a lot of space in my intimate relationships

Chapter 9 ~ **Finding "the Faeries"** and my Playfully Erotic Self (1979)

- Men frolicking like playful boys: making eros fun

- Connecting as a tribe outside mainstream gay culture: creating a new model

- Meeting James, my Eros-Spirit Healer

- Learning about love from a much older man: he had no agenda

- Discovering the "beauty that hides in all flesh," to use his phrase. Love and beauty are ageless

Chapter 10 ~ **The 1980s: Continuing Healing the Eros-Spirit Split**

- Beginning to integrate sex and spirit: chanting kirtan then offering Tantric massage at the baths

- Tantra's teaching: the theory resonates (reading Osho's *Neo-Tantra*)

- AIDS; Irene Smith; Ward 5B

- Exploring Sacred Intimacy: *The Body Electric & Intimate Explorations for Men*

- Doug Fraser: inspired to begin *Light Touch Retreats* that later became *Men In Touch*[1]

- Exploring Canada and a Whirlwind Romance

Chapter 11 ~ **The 90s: Tantra with All Genders**

- Vancouver: finally finding home

- Deepening the healing through *Sacred Intimate Training, The Cosmic Orgasm,* and assisting at many weekends of *Celebrating the Body Erotic* (men's and all-genders)

---

1. *http://menintouch.org*

- Mid-life Crisis at 50: fears of being old and unattractive

- My erotic life was my clients & baths: intermittent reinforcement

- Erectile Dysfunction: blue pills and injections

- Kenyth: confidant and dear straight friend

The Later Years: Ripening into Embodied Wisdom

By my second Saturn Return around 2000, age 56, the seeds that had been planted over the preceding three decades were truly blooming. My 60s and beyond have been about embodying what I learned and sharing with others. It is being a time of less struggle and more sense of grace... and deep gratitude.

Chapter 12 ~ The New Millenium: Diving Deeper into Tantra

- India: The *Kumbha Mela*

- Rudy's teachings on Tantra

- A last try at conventional coupling with Chuck

Chapter 13 ~ The 2010s: New Models of Intimacy

○ Resigned and content to be living single

○ Moving beyond codependency: my "open birdcage" model

○ Betty Martin's *Wheel of Consent* and *Three-Minute Game*

○ Eckhart Tolle

○ Delighting in seeing each "other" as an embodiment of the One Self delighting in itself in many forms—a huge shift for me

○ Leaving a legacy; *Sacred Touch Yoga*

○ Loving without agenda or attachment: "I am love"

Chapter 14 - My Young Mentors

○ Ziji helps me to go beyond codependency: "merge and separate"

○ Becoming grounded in my Self[63]

○ Ziji and others are not the source of love: Love lives in me. I am That. *Aham Prema*

● The Beloved in flesh appears: Angelito

● Andre: 7-chakra loving friendship in a "love network"

Chapter 15 ~ **Subtle Eros**

● Osho: Peak vs Valley Orgasms

● Patricia Albere and We Space: "Soul Sex"

● Time/Change/The Eternal Now

● 4 Flavors of Arousal

Chapter 16 ~ **The 2020s: A Time of Change**

● Authentic Relating

● Passing The Torch

Chapter 17 ~ **Still "Growing Healthier"**

○ My rings of growth

○ The Beloved within

○ Original Innocence

Chapter 18 ~ **My Final Years**

Epilogue

Appendix: Resources for *Your Own* Healing Journey

Cognitive Resources

● What is meditation?

- Betty Martin's *Wheel of Consent*

- The Body Electric's *Sacred Intimate Training*: the format

- Seeing and moving subtle energy: the chakras

- *"Fountain Flow"* as a template for Tantra Massage

- Time / Space / The Eternal Now: like a gyroscope

- The Indigenous *Medicine Wheel / the Seven Directions / the Naraya Dances*

Experiential Practices

Reading a cookbook can be fun and pleasurable, yet provides little actual sensory pleasure, such as taste or smell, and zero bodily nourishment. For that, of course, we need to prepare the dishes and consume them, hopefully slowly and mindfully to fully savor all of their delights.

In this section you'll find many practices I have found greatly beneficial to my body-heart-soul over these many decades. Follow your own intuition about which ones call to you, and then actually practice them. Take them for a test drive, maybe several times to get a real feel for their effects on you. Then save the ones that resonate and leave the rest for another time. Enjoy!

- Simple sample meditations using visual, auditory, and/or kinesthetic focuses

- My guided meditation on YouTube

- *Metta* ~ Loving Kindness Meditation: a sample set of phrases to explore the practice

- A visual eros-spirit meditation

- "Fountain Flow" as a template for Tantra Massage

- We Space - Interbeing Meditation

- Indigenous Medicine Wheel & the 7-Directions

- Betty Martin's "Three-Minute Game": how to play

- Feminine/Masculine Breathing

Annotated Table of Contents

Acknowledgments

Acknowledgments

―――

"It *takes a village to raise a child,"* says the traditional African proverb. Indeed, it takes a village to bring a book from conception through gestation and into the world. What a joy it has been for me to collaborate with so many friends and colleagues in this birthing!

You've already read about many of my friends, lovers and teachers. I have huge gratitude to each for their many gifts and teachings. This retrospective has greatly deepened my appreciation of the truth of "all my relations," as indigenous North Americans teach.

Specifically, in birthing this baby, I want to thank my professional editor, Hunter Flournoy. After I had written what I thought was a pretty complete story of my healing journey, he surprised me by saying "Write more!" He thought my 200 pages were too concise, and encouraged me to put more meat on the bones I had written. "This story deserves 300 or 350 pages," he exclaimed. I know I tend to write concisely because, as a reader, I find it laborious to plough through what too often feels like excess verbiage. With Hunter's encouragement and support, I really enjoyed fleshing out my stories.

I offer a deep bow of gratitude to Parker Green McLean for generously offering his artistic input on the design of the cover.

My beloved partner Ziji devoted a good part of a holiday we spent on Pender Island, BC, last May to go through the draft in great detail suggesting both large conceptual changes and minute grammatical corrections. He continues to cheer me on.

Similarly my dear friend, Andy Martin, went through a printed version of my draft and brought his editing skills from working as an editor for PhD candidates to give me very detailed corrections and thoughtful suggestions.

Next I have several friends who are themselves published authors, and each gave me wonderful support and insights. Alphabetically they are Alfred DePew, Andrew Lawler, Don Shewey, Eli Ramer, and Stephen Silha.

Other dear friends offered suggestions large and small to make the layout simpler and clearer: David Greenshields, David Hoe, Eric Lichtman, Francie Allen, Gordon Matchett, Jason Brien, and Mark Fleming.

Several of the wonderful guys in my Berkeley Men's group (Larry Mandella, Stu Lord, Tom Horton, and Tom Rucker), with whom I'm still deeply connected more than 50 years after we began meeting, were eager to read my rough draft, and gave me many encouraging comments. In particular I want to thank Stu for service "above and beyond." He is a self-described comma-fanatic, and combed through my draft in fine detail to correct my haphazard punctuation.

I'm so grateful that Joseph Kramer and Rudy Ballentine (Swami Ravi Rudra Bharati) both gave me a thumbs-up about the details I wrote about them and their wonderful work.

Finally, I was and am deeply moved by the loving testimonial offered by my dear friend David Mielke in his eloquent, and very personal Foreword.

Each of you has enriched my experience of chronicling my healing journey. I hope our shared effort brings healing to untold others in generations to come. With great love and gratitude. Namaste.

sequoia

March, 2024

---

[1] Part 3, page 1.

[2] Gay Liberation is often considered to have begun with the "Stonewall Rebellion," in June, 1969. The Stonewall Inn was a Greenwich Village bar frequented by drag queens, and had been routinely raided by police for many years. On a hot summer night, the drag queens fought back, igniting a groundswell of "coming out (of the closet)" in major cities in North America, Europe, and eventually beyond. The Inn was designated a National Monument in 2016 by President Barack Obama

[3] Right Relationship is part of the Buddhist Eightfold Path. It is understood that following that path leads to equanimity.

[4] Back then, I was still thinking of a patriarchal creator God separate from "His" creation.

[5] For years I wondered if it was a virgin birth, as I could not imagine my parents actually doing that yucky deed. It turns out (I learned from an old aunt long after my parents had passed) they were careless about condoms during his brief visit home from the war in Germany to attend his own father's funeral. This was shocking news, as they were devout Catholics, and "artificial birth control" is considered punishable by eternal damnation.

[6] The fateful first glimpse led to a life-long appreciation of the intact penis. When I first learned in high school about circumcision, I felt, and still feel, intense anger that my penis was mutilated without my consent. I have campaigned to ban the practice of genital mutilation in people of all genders. Whether for religious or health reasons, I passionately feel circumcision should only be performed on those who are mature enough to give informed consent.

[7] I kept those dark emotions bottled up until I found a safe container to release them over 30 years later. Stay tuned, or skip ahead to read about my powerful catharsis in Chapter 10, in the section about Irene Smith.

[8] What are little boys made of

What are little boys made of

Snips & snails & puppy dogs tails

And such are little boys made of.

What are little girls made of

What are little girls made of

Sugar & spice & all things nice

And such are little girls made of.

[9] "Intact" is my preferred term for the natural penis complete with foreskin. In much of North America, circumcision is so widespread that some refer to the intact penis as "uncircumcised," or "uncut," which is a double-negative. It seems to imply a deviation from the norm. I hope the natural penis again becomes the norm. The decision to cut or not to cut a newborn boy's penis often stirs deep feelings, even among religious groups who have long held it as a sacred ritual. American Jews are actively debating the practice.

[10] *cum* is slang for come, which refers to orgasms in any gender. In men, it can refer to ejaculation as well as to the semen.

[11] another slang term for ejaculate or ejaculation.

[12] Actually those were the more polite terms. The really derogatory term was "cock sucker," which was invariably sneered with utter contempt.

[13] I was trained in good posture by my military Dad, who had me marching around our apartment at a young age. "Attention!" he'd command, which meant stand tall and straight. Perhaps my poised demeanor came from Mom. She was deliberately "lady-like." She enrolled me in a former all-girls' grammar school where the nuns brought in a woman to teach us all ballroom dancing. The "young ladies" wore white gloves and the "young gentlemen" wore gray gloves. We were all quite proper.

[14] In recent years I've discovered I'm not alone. There's a veritable cottage industry of artists portraying Jesus as a sex symbol. Search for "image sexy Jesus."

[15] The American side was less than pristine, since all the summer cottages and St. Lawrence Seaway freighters dumped their raw sewage straight into the river.

[16] in the very act of wrongdoing, especially in an act of sexual misconduct.

[17] Dag Hammarskjöld was a Swedish economist and diplomat who served as the second Secretary-General of the United Nations from April 1953 until his death in a plane crash in September 1961.

[18] Many years later I would learn first-hand with my clients that there are many men leading conventional married lives who also have a hidden pink streak they express covertly. That was especially true in my generation and earlier. Too often they succumbed to the tragic trap of marrying a woman and raising a family only to discover that their duplicity was too torturous to endure. Younger queer guys are more likely to accept and proclaim their queerness at an early age.

[19] *The Boys in the Band* was first a New York off-Broadway stage play then a 1970 film remade in 2020. It depicts a birthday party among a group of gay men in Manhattan in the late 1960s.

[20] Back then we did not have the current distinction between sexual orientation and gender identity; they were conflated. Visibly effeminate men were publicly shamed for their feminine presentation. It was a form of misogyny. Drag queens were and still are rebelling against that oppression by being exaggerated versions of the feminine. In the now-iconic Stonewall Rebellion in 1969, it was the drag queens who fought the cops. Gay men who were/are more masculine could more easily hide from public shaming. But for those of us from repressive religious backgrounds, the internal shame ran deep.

I am heartened by the current Trans movement. Boys/men who feel mis-gendered can actually explore transitioning to their "real" gender, and not have to rebel the way the bitchy drag queens did.

Then there is the whole label and culture thing. Since the 90s, in public health, there is a new label of MSM: Men who have Sex with Men. There are many guys who do not embrace the gay culture, and live otherwise straight lives and find (often covert) ways of satisfying their homo desires.

[21] Maharishi Mahesh Yogi had brought TM to the West and was revered as the guru.

[22] Stanley E. Russell ran events called the Joy of Sex. His organization was The Cosmic Joy Fellowship, in Sausalito, CA, See classified ad in Yoga Journal, Nov, 1975, p. 15.

[23] The philosophy of Tantra is vast and goes way beyond sexuality.

[24] IYTE soon morphed into The Iyengar Institute, which I found dismaying. When I enrolled it had an eclectic and inclusive or even ecumenical orientation to many forms of Hatha Yoga. Once the Iyengar devotees took over it became much more dogmatic. Only their teacher, BKS Iyengar, was considered to offer the orthodox methods. While I continued to value the technical precision and academic rigor, I grieved the narrow focus the school took on. When I graduated in 1981, I declined to apply to be a "Certified Iyengar Teacher" preferring a more eclectic approach.

[25] GI" is an abbreviation of Government Issue. It is American slang for military personnel. The GI Bill enumerates a set of fringe benefits, such as education, home loans, etc., that is available to all who are "Honorably Discharged."

[26] *Baba* (Sanskrit for "father") is a ubiquitous title for male monks and renunciates in India.

[27] Years later when I first saw images of laser-beams they reminded me of the ruby-red light emanating from Baba.

[28] In the Hindu tradition, a mantra is one or more words that have been channeled thousands of years ago by the enlightened sages of ancient India and have been passed down from guru to disciple over countless generations. They are considered sacred because they carry great power to transform the mind and purify the heart. In addition to Om Namah Shivaya, Baba also taught Om Guru Om and Aham Sah. The latter is done with the breath and means "I am That," referring to That Pure Consciousness, or God.

[29] There is a 15-minute video on YouTube of Baba giving Shaktipat: Muktananda - The Guru's Touch 1/2

[30] *Shakti* means spiritual energy. Baba had done such intense spiritual practices over decades, and been initiated by an enlightened Master, that he was able to transmit his *Shakti* to thousands of us. The process is called *Shaktipat*, or spiritual initiation. It can be done through a look, a touch, a word, or simply through intention.

[31] In Baba's tradition, there is power in receiving a mantra directly from one who has fully experienced its power. He welcomed people to come forward and ask for the mantra (even though it was written in large letters above him and we had all been chanting it.) When a person asks, they are opening themselves to receiving a gift, which is very much what this is: an inestimably precious gift. Whenever anyone asked, he'd nod and bless them by brushing them with peacock feathers, then direct his assistant to hand them a "mantra card" which contains a succinct and powerful description of the mantra's full meaning. A couple of years after first receiving my own mantra card, I had the courage to go up and ask Baba if I could teach the mantra in my own yoga classes. In the same way he nodded, blessed me with those beautiful feathers, and had his assistant hand me a large stack of them. I still have some. If you write and ask, I'll send you a pdf of that original card. Consider it coming from Baba through me. Write *sequoia(at) t-l-c.ca*

[32] In the Hindu tradition, the capitalized Self refers to our divine, universal nature, which is Pure Consciousness and Pure Love. The lower-case "self" refers to our limited ego, which suffers the delusion of being separate..

[33] Baba Hari Das was a disciple of Ram Dass' guru, Neem Karoli Baba. Ram Dass studied yoga with him in India and latter helped him come to the US in the early 1970s.

[34] After that Gathering, a tradition developed among the Faeries of taking a "faerie name" in a ritual way. I like to think I was the first one to do so.

[35] The trees were named after a Cherokee man, who became famous for creating an alphabet for their language. In Cherokee, the name means "peacemaker."

[36] This is It / This is really It / This is all there is / And it's perfect as it is.

There is nowhere to go but Here / There is nothing Here but Now / There is nothing Now but This.

And This is It / This is really It / This is all there is / And it's perfect as it is.

[37] Rajneesh, Bhagawan Shree, Neo-Tantra, Harper & Row, New York, 1980, 26

[38] Ibid., 44

[39] Actually the *very first time* I heard Kirtan was in Sydney at the musical, *Hair*. Even then it awakened an ancient memory.

[40] Kirtan has caught on among yoga practitioners. You can find kirtan sessions in most major cities. It's best practiced in real time with a group. There is great power in being surrounded by others who are singing in unison in that spirit of saying "Yea God!" in Sanskrit. You can get a good taste online. Go to Spotify or your favorite music streaming app, and search for kirtan. One of my favorite kirtan leaders is Krishna Das, who, like Ram Dass, was initiated by Neem Karoli Baba. He is really channeling powerful *Shakti* in the chants he leads. Either alone or with a special other, create a meditative atmosphere, and then **chant along** in the "call and response" pattern of the chants. Just as you would not get much benefit by watching a yoga class, similarly only listening to kirtan is of limited value. The juice is in the active participation of actually chanting. The words are repeated each time and easily learned. Twenty minutes or more will begin to induce an altered state. See where it takes you. Enjoy the journey into the heart of Pure Love.

[41] His name for the school was inspired by Walt Whitman's wonderful poem, "I sing the body electric!"

[42] On YouTube, there is a 3-minute trailer for a feature length film entitled ***"Ward 5B"***. It powerfully conveys how revolutionary Irene's vision was.

[43] In the ensuing 35 years, Doe Bay has morphed into a rather upscale "Resort and Retreat," which is still quite beautiful for those who can afford it.

[44] All of us had been required to take several preliminary weekend workshops, one of which was devoted to this incredibly healing practice.

[45] To learn more about The Three-Minute Game, go to Wheel of Consent in Chapter 13.

[46] *Daddy Love God: A Sacred Intimate Journey*, Don Shewey, p.2, quoted with permission.

[47] (now Swami Ravi Rudra Bharati).

[48] Shiva Lingam is the Sanskrit name of a Hindu devotional icon, usually sculpted or cast, that symbolizes the masculine and feminine aspects of the universal creative life force.

[49] "PJ's" is a long-time watering hole for mainly manly queer guys in Vancouver's gay village.

[50] Ram Dass, *Be Love Now*, 2011, p. 200.

[51] Baba's use of the term *kriya* refers to actions that arise *spontaneously* as a result of kundalini awakening. These actions can be suppressed if not wanted. The Kundalini Yoga tradition of Yogi Bhajan uses kriya to refer to *deliberate* sets of practices intended to awaken kundalini. In the latter, the person is the initiator of the "action." In the former, the Kundalini Shakti is behaving spontaneously (as Spanda).

[52] There is a YouTube full-length documentary about Baba and his rare gift of awakening people's kundalini.

[53] ***"My creeping decrepitude has crept all the way to my crypt."*** ~ James Broughton

[54] Osho seems to have had a completely binary and hetero-normative view of gender: people with penises are goal-oriented towards ejaculation, while people with vulvas require much slower, more full-body contact to reach their own orgasm(s) which are much more global and less genital in focus. I am more in agreement with Rudy's view, which echoes Haddon (see Chapter 11) that each person contains and can express a full-spectrum of sexual energies from the *Yang Masculine* to the *Yin Feminine*. What Osho calls the *Valley Orgasm* is an expression of the latter.

[55] Ram Dass, *Be Love Now*, 2011, p. 200

[56] Many North American indigenous people have a simple phrase, *"**All my relations,**"* they use in ceremonies to convey their understanding that all life is one intricately woven tapestry: that each of us is deeply connected with every other living being in the vast web of life.

[57] see Haddon's description of our 4 primary gender expressions in Chapter 13.

[58] I first encountered the idea of "Subject/Subject Consciousness" articulated by Harry Hay with the Radical Faeries. I had been experiencing a great deal of sexual objectification among gay men: "He's hot; he's not!" While I greatly appreciate Harry's strong encouragement to see one another as subjects, I disagree that all same-sex relationships are subject-subject, while all hetero relationships are inherently objectifying. Harry was over-compensating for growing up feeling inferior and marginalized by trying to make us queer folks superior to straight people. I see us all as needing to outgrown objectification and see one another as subjects.

[59] See Haddon's quadrants (Chapter 13) as either Yin Masculine or Yin Feminine.

[60] "Yoga" in Sanskrit comes from the same root as our English word "to yoke" or to unite together.

[61] "My creeping decrepitude has crept all the way to my crypt."

[62] To dive deeper into Rudy's teachings, I highly recommend his book, ***Kali Rising.***

[63] I am using the convention in Indian/Hindu writing, where the small-s self refers to our ephemeral ego, and the large-S Self refers to our shared infinite Oneness of Pure Consciousness.